Democracy Delayed

CHARLES W. EAGLES

Democracy Delayed
Congressional Reapportionment
and Urban-Rural Conflict in the 1920s

The University of Georgia Press
ATHENS AND LONDON

Paperback edition, 2010
© 1990 by the University of Georgia Press
Athens, Georgia 30602
www.ugapress.org
All rights reserved
Designed by Mary Margaret Wade
Set in Linotron 10 on 13 Melior
Printed digitally in the United States of America

The Library of Congress has cataloged the
hardcover edition of this book as follows:
Library of Congress Cataloging-in-Publication Data
LCCN Permalink: http://lccn.loc.gov/89005044

Eagles, Charles W.
Democracy delayed : congressional reapportionment
and urban-rural conflict in the 1920s / Charles W. Eagles.
xiv, 173 p. ; 24 cm.
ISBN 0-8203-1185-5 (alk. paper)

Includes bibliographical references (p. [151]–166) and index.
1. United States. Congress. House—Election districts—History—20th
century. 2. Apportionment (Election law)—United States—History—
20th century. 3. United States—Politics and government—1919–1933.
4. Rural-urban migration—Political aspects—United States—
History—20th century. I. Title.
JK1341 .E24   1990
328.73'07345'09042 20   89-5044

Paperback ISBN-13: 978-0-8203-3622-0
ISBN-10: 0-8203-3622-X

British Library Cataloging-in-Publication Data available

The author is grateful for permission to use portions of Chapter 1
that first appeared in *The Historian* (November 1986).

To Daniel and Benjamin

Contents

Preface
ix

Acknowledgments
xiii

1
The Historiographical Importance
of Urban-Rural Conflict in the 1920s
1

2
Reapportionment before 1920
21

3
The Controversy in the 1920s
32

4
Voting on Reapportionment:
A Test of Urban-Rural Conflict
85

Conclusion
116

Appendixes
125

Notes
133

Bibliography
151

Index
167

Preface

AFTER THE 1920 CENSUS, the United States Congress failed to reapportion the House of Representatives. In fact, no reapportionment occurred between 1911 and the 1930 census. The unprecedented delay meant that some Americans continued throughout the 1920s to be overrepresented while others remained underrepresented in the House of Representatives. Historians have paid little attention to this situation; indeed, only a few are even aware of the anomalous failure of reapportionment in the 1920s. Several scholarly accounts in the 1930s assessed the problems involving reapportionment in the previous decade, but no systematic study has appeared. Since then, political scientists, especially experts on reapportionment, have frequently commented on this failure of the 1920s but usually only as part of larger, more general studies of reapportionment or the Congress. They have not attempted to understand the problem in its specific historical context. Political historians, who would have been more likely to put the controversy into its proper historical context, have only rarely referred to the issue. In 1948 Frederick L. Paxson's *Post War Years* did so but neglected to explore the topic and its possible significance. A recent study of the decennial national census devotes only about fifteen pages to the reapportionment controversy of the 1920s in a chapter entitled "The Tribal Twenties Revisited."[1] The struggle over reapportionment in the 1920s certainly warrants closer historical investigation.

The subject of congressional reapportionment first came to my attention in reading David Burner's *The Politics of Provincialism: The Democratic Party in Transition, 1918–1932*, and later Andrew Sinclair's *Prohibition: The Era of Excess*. Like other scholars, each made only passing references to reapportionment. In his impressive study of Democratic politics, Burner merely pointed out that the changes wrought by the 1922 congressional elections "occurred within an outmoded congressional map that the House had refused to revise according to the census of 1920.... Throughout the twenties, in fact, the 1911 distribution remained." He attributed the lack of reapportionment to both partisan and urban-rural conflicts. More directly, Sinclair said, "The refusal of Congress after the Census of 1920 to give the cities more seats in the House of Representatives was a frank confession by the country members that they wished to continue ruling the cities."[2] Neither scholar wrote more than a few words on the matter, but both suggested its significance and its relationship to an important urban-rural division in the nation in the 1920s.

Alerted to the topic by Burner and Sinclair, I searched in vain for an extensive discussion and analysis of reapportionment in the 1920s. Textbooks, monographs, articles, and essays by recognized authorities on twentieth-century United States history, and particularly its politics, had not explained what had happened to reapportionment in the 1920s and even seemed unaware of it. Frustrated by the lack of a thorough explanation, I decided to look for myself and see if the topic might be worthy of serious study.

An initial cursory examination of the *New York Times* for the period confirmed the importance of the urban-rural theme in the controversy over reapportionment. The larger issues gradually began to come into focus. Further research in the *Congressional Record*, congressional hearings, and contemporary newspapers and periodicals reinforced the impression that urban and rural forces collided over reapportionment.[3] Eventually this modest study of congressional reapportionment in the 1920s resulted from the research. In addition to telling the unique story of Congress's failure to reapportion the House of Representatives in that decade, it seeks to use the controversy to test the urban-rural thesis.

The first chapter establishes the historiographical importance of the fight over reapportionment, which contained innumerable examples of urban-rural rhetoric.[4] It analyzes and reviews the scholarly literature on the 1920s and proves the prominence of an urban-rural interpretation for many events of the time. In the 1920s and again beginning in the 1950s, an urban-rural interpretation was popular, especially for explaining Prohibition, immigration restriction, the Ku Klux Klan, religious fundamentalism, and other phenomena of the colorful decade. Borrowing from the social sciences, historians have usually imposed an abstract urban-rural model to explain events of the 1920s and have lacked concrete evidence from the time to confirm the existence of such conflict. The fight over congressional reapportionment provides extensive contemporary evidence of urban-rural conflict.

The second chapter sets the stage by briefly reviewing the pre-1920 course of congressional efforts to reapportion the House. Primarily on the basis of published works, it demonstrates that apportionment of the House of Representatives from the writing of the Constitution down through the nineteenth century had frequently been controversial but that Congress had always resolved its disagreements and passed reapportionment legislation within a couple of years of the decennial census. Even the sectional conflicts in the Civil War era had not blocked reapportionment. Only after the 1920 census was the pattern of prompt action broken.

The more extended narrative in Chapter 3 describes in detail four stages in the struggle over reapportionment during the 1920s. The controversy finally ended in 1929, when Congress passed a law for reapportioning the House of Representatives based on the forthcoming 1930 census. Drawn almost exclusively from primary sources, the chapter reveals for the first time the repeated use of explicit urban-rural arguments by the participants in the battle and by commentators watching the controversy. It grounds the urban-rural theme in the life of the 1920s and thereby makes it more than a sociological model imposed on the decade by later scholars to explain events. The chapter also discusses the myriad other issues involved in reapportionment such as the appropriate size for the House, the merits of including aliens in the enumerated population, and the best statistical procedure to use for allotting seats.

Chapter 4 asks whether the voting in the House of Representatives on reapportionment reflected the rhetoric of urban-rural conflict and actually followed urban-rural lines. Quantitative analysis of eight roll-call votes on reapportionment provides the means to test for urban-rural divisions in the House. The results are important because new quantitative evidence is employed to check what has usually been an impressionistic historical interpretation. At the start of the research, I assumed that the analysis of voting in the House of Representatives would either contradict the urban-rural thesis with new quantitative evidence or provide quantitative support for the urban-rural thesis. If the research worked to disprove the long-held interpretation, it would help correct long-held interpretations of the decade. If the study reinforced the urban-rural thesis, I planned to take heart from J. Morgan Kousser's recent lament over historians' common fascination with provocative new theses. Kousser has observed with regret that historians, unlike other social scientists, "are attracted by interpretations which claim to overturn or replace older ones entirely, rather than those which stress their continuity with previous structures of understanding."[5] The conclusion explains the relationships between the urban-rural rhetoric and the voting and between the reapportionment fight and the larger urban-rural interpretive framework.

Democracy Delayed employs an unusual combination of historiography, narrative history, and quantitative analysis to explore an important subject too long neglected by historians of recent America. It furnishes both compelling new evidence of the reality for people at the time of urban-rural conflict in the 1920s and an appropriate test for the urban-rural interpretation that historians have applied to the decade.

Acknowledgments

OVER THE YEARS a number of people have encouraged and advised me about my work on reapportionment, but they bear no responsibility for the final product. Samuel T. McSeveney, Howard W. Allen, Ballard Campbell, David Burner, and Robert Himmelberg shared their own expertise in quantitative political history; each read all or part of the manuscript and offered valuable criticisms. Anonymous readers for the University of Georgia Press, the *Historian*, and the *Journal of American History* offered significant suggestions for revising the manuscript or related work. Gaines M. Foster and Robert M. Collins read the entire manuscript, and their comments saved me from many errors and improved the work. Howard Allen and Sue Patrick commented perceptively at the 1987 meeting of the American Historical Association on a paper based on the manuscript. At different times, Daniel J. Singal and James C. Cobb suggested that I pursue the topic toward a book.

Much of the research could not have been accomplished without the assistance of Sherrie Sam and her excellent interlibrary loan department in the University of Mississippi library. The staff of the government documents collections also provided efficient and friendly access to many vital sources.

Special thanks go to two people who assisted with the quantitative aspects of the research. To a letter asking for advice, Ballard Campbell responded with uncommon kindness and thoughtfulness. He later took time at a professional convention to discuss my project at length and to give indispensable advice, and subsequently he answered several letters with a similar thoroughness and specificity. Douglas Bell provided indispensable help in processing the roll-call data.

I am pleased and happy to have worked on this manuscript with Malcolm Call and the University of Georgia Press. I appreciate his continuing interest in my work, and I admire his accomplishments with the Press. I was fortunate to have Gertrude Calvert copyedit the manuscript for the Press; her expert eye caught many errors and generally cleaned up my writing.

I depend on my wife more than anyone else. Brenda read the entire manuscript with her usual care, interest, and discernment; her comments and suggestions, especially regarding the historiography, greatly improved the work. More important, she had confidence in the project from the beginning. Although our little boys rightly remain unaware of reapportionment and contributed nothing substantial to the completion of this book, the dedication suggests their real importance.

1

The Historiographical Importance of Urban-Rural Conflict in the 1920s

BATHTUB GIN, rumble seats, and flappers have long entertained and amused students of the 1920s, but other aspects of the decade have usually offended historians. They have found Prohibition, fundamentalism, the Ku Klux Klan (KKK), and nativism reactionary, unattractive, and antagonistic to basic American values. Efforts to restrict immigration, for example, have been criticized because they derived from prejudice against foreigners, especially those from southern and eastern Europe, and hence violated American principles symbolized by the Statue of Liberty. Similarly, the KKK's violent suppression of minorities had no place in a nation that claimed to believe in equality. To explain such movements, many historians have employed an urban-rural interpretation, claiming that the offensive features of the decade generally emerged from a reactionary rural and small-town America. In their view, the strongholds of the Klan, prohibitionism, fundamentalism, and nativism lay in the nation's countryside and not in its urban areas. The cities, by contrast, represented tolerance, progress, and aspects of American life attractive to many historians.

Historiographical studies of the decade by Henry F. May, Richard L. Lowitt, Burl Noggle, and Gerald N. Grob and George A. Billias failed to recognize the importance of the theme and to discuss the fluctuations in its appeal.[1] A review of the literature on the 1920s reveals that contemporary analysts first used an urban-rural framework to explain incidents of their own time but that the urban-rural interpretation came to dominate historical writing only after 1950.

Basic conceptions of urban and rural, as used both in the 1920s and in the later historical literature, originated in sociological theories developed in the late nineteenth century. In 1887 Ferdinand Tonnies first proposed the typology of *Gemeinschaft* and *Gesellschaft*, which have been translated most easily as community and society and which resemble the later categories of mechanical and organic solidarity of Emile Durkheim and the traditional and rational authority of Max Weber. In discussing *Gemeinschaft* and *Gesellschaft*, Tonnies remained neutral and showed no preference for either one.[2] Sociological laymen of the 1920s and since have thought of the scholarly distinctions between *Gemeinschaft* and *Gesellschaft* as being similar to the differences between rural and urban societies. More important, they have usually favored the rise of *Gesellschaft*, or urban society, and resented the persistence of *Gemeinschaft*, or rural community. The theoretical source of the rural-urban interpretation was, therefore, the work of Tonnies, but many proponents of the rural-urban theme have remained unaware of his contribution and have apparently rejected his neutral assessment of community and society.

Writers employing the rural-urban concept during the 1920s included John Dewey, H. L. Mencken, Lewis Mumford, H. Richard Niebuhr, and Walter Lippmann. Though they may have independently observed the significance of urban-rural conflict, they probably also had some familiarity with the sociological theory, had been influenced by the growth of rural sociology, and had known about the results of the 1920 census. Rural sociology developed dramatically in the 1920s and reached a high mark in 1929 with the publication of *Principles of Rural-Urban Sociology* by Pitirim Sorokin and Carle C. Zimmerman.[3] In addition, the 1920 census showed that the United States had become an urban nation because for the first time a majority of Americans lived in urban areas of twenty-five hundred or more inhabitants. The population shift from rural areas to towns and cities received considerable attention and appeared to mark a watershed in the nation's development. Commentators in the 1920s undoubtedly knew about the demographic change, but they employed the terms *urban* and *rural* in imprecise, impressionistic ways without regard to the specific standard applied by the Census Bureau.

As early as 1922 John Dewey argued in the *New Republic* that William Jennings Bryan and his campaign for Christianity and against science did not speak for the people as Andrew Jackson had represented the frontiersmen. Instead Bryan represented an "intellectual frontier" of "fairly prosperous villages and towns that have inherited the fear of whatever threatens the security and order of a precariously attained civilization, along with the pioneer impulses of neighborliness and decency." Without explicitly pointing to urban-rural conflict, Dewey explained that for rural, small-town America an "attachment to stability and homogeneity of thought and belief seem essential in the midst of practical heterogeneity, rush and unsettlement," all of which characterized the booming cities of the decade.[4]

Several essays in the 1922 assessment titled *Civilization in the United States* also suggested that urban-rural conflict had great significance. Lewis Mumford claimed that "those who do not wish to remain barbarians must become metropolitans" and "participate in some measure in the benefits of city life." He saw developing in the United States a "breach . . . between metropolis and the countryside" caused in part by the "envy and resentment of the farming population." More specifically, Mencken mentioned Prohibition as pitting "the civilized minorities collected in the great cities" against "predatory bands of rural politicians," and Louis Raymond Reid's essay "The Small Town" agreed and added the Ku Klux Klan as a further example.[5]

A Dartmouth College sociologist analyzed the "psychology" of the revived Klan in a 1924 book. John Moffat Mecklin found that "the Klan draws its members chiefly from the descendants of the old American stock living in the villages and small towns of those sections of the country where the old stock has been least disturbed by immigration, on the one hand, and the disruptive effect of industrialism, on the other." In the South and the Midwest, according to the Mississippi-born Mecklin, a "psychological need for escape from the drabness of village and small town life plays no small part in the appeal of the modern Klan to the average American." Though he acknowledged that the Klan's enemies included Catholics, Jews, and immigrants, Mecklin concluded that the KKK was "essentially a defense mechanism against evils which are often more imaginary than real," yet Mecklin failed to connect the "evils" to urban-industrial centers.[6] Nonetheless, his analysis of the Klan shared some characteristics of the works by Dewey, Mumford, Mencken, and Reid.

A 1927 book by Andre Siegfried, a French economist and sociologist, expanded the use of the implicit urban-rural model. In *America Comes of Age* he observed that the "difference in attitude between the old-fashioned small towns on the one hand and the industrialized city districts on the other hand is of first importance, and explains much in post-war American politics." He thought that the Ku Klux Klan set native-born, Protestant, rural America against Catholic, immigrant, urban America and declared that the "essential characteristic of the post-war period in the United States is the nervous reaction of the original American stock against the insidious subjugation by foreign blood."[7]

At the end of the decade, H. Richard Niebuhr offered a similarly explicit explanation of fundamentalism in *The Social Sources of Denominationalism*. He argued that "the conflict between urban and rural religion took on dramatic form in the theological battles of Modernism and Fundamentalism" in which Bryan championed the rural religion. Niebuhr expanded his discussion of fundamentalism two years later for the *Encyclopedia of Social Sciences*. "In the social sources from which it drew strength," he concluded, "fundamentalism was closely related to the conflict between rural and urban cultures in America." Fundamentalism was strongest in the isolated communities of rural states, where change was resisted, while the opposing modernism was most powerful in the dynamic industrialized urban states. In the 1920s fundamentalism was "a powerful symbolism representative of the antagonism of political and economic minorities against the eastern or northern urban industrial majority."[8]

By far the most complete early use of the urban-rural thesis appeared in an essay by Walter Lippmann in the *Atlantic Monthly*. The divisive political issues in the nation in 1927, according to the journalist, arose "out of the great migration of the last fifty years, out of the growth of cities, and out of the spread of that rationalism and of the deepening of that breach with tradition which invariably accompany the development of metropolitan culture." Identifying the issues as Prohibition, the Ku Klux Klan, xenophobia, and fundamentalism, Lippmann said that they were authentic expressions of the politics, the social outlook, and

> the religion of the older American village civilization making its last stand against what to it looks like an alien invasion. The alien invasion is in fact the new American produced by the growth and prosperity of America.
>
> The evil which the old-fashioned preachers ascribe to the Pope, the Babylon, the atheists, and to the devil, is simply the new urban

civilization with its irresistible economic and scientific and mass power. The Pope, the devil jazz, the bootleggers, are a mythology which expresses symbolically the impact of a vast and dreaded social change. The change is real enough. The language in which it is discussed is preposterous only as all mythology is preposterous if you accept it literally.[9]

Lippmann explained the significant issues of the decade as examples of a deeper conflict between urban America and the countryside, and clearly the Jewish and New York–born commentator sided with the city.

The social, economic, and demographic forces stressed by Lippmann, Mencken, Dewey, and other observers in the 1920s received scant attention in Frederick Lewis Allen's pathbreaking *Only Yesterday: An Informal History of the Nineteen-Twenties*. Writing after the onset of the Depression, the *Harper's* editor saw the 1920s as a distinct period bracketed by World War I and the Depression. From the gloom of the Depression, Allen looked back at the 1920s and saw among the prosperity and frivolity the great effects of the war. He detected a pervasive postwar "sense of disillusionment" that made the nation feel "it ought to be enjoying itself more than it was, and that life was futile and nothing much mattered." "America Convalescent" experienced a "revolution in manners and morals" and turned its "emotional interest upon a series of tremendous trifles" in the "ballyhoo years." According to Allen, people found excitement and fulfillment in Mah Jong, sensational trials, jazz, crossword puzzles, boxing, and other fads and frivolities. For him, therefore, the trial of John Scopes for teaching evolution was just another postwar "spectacle," Prohibition resulted from "war-time psychology," and the KKK was another form of postwar intolerance growing out of the Red Scare.[10]

The original edition of *Only Yesterday*, a Book-of-the-Month Club selection, sold more than sixty-seven thousand copies. By 1970 various editions had sold more than 1 million copies.[11] Hastily written by a journalist, the popular work lacked the scholarly apparatus of footnotes and an extensive bibliography, yet Allen's interpretation in *Only Yesterday* dominated scholarly study of the 1920s for the next two decades. His emphasis on the effects of World War I displaced the incipient urban-rural interpretation while retaining some of its antirural perspective. Though sometimes modifying or extending Allen's view, succeeding writers basically agreed with it. More important, they accepted Allen's demarcation of the 1920s as a special historical epoch.

During the next twenty years a host of prominent historians pointed to World War I as the key to explaining the 1920s. A concern for the impact of the war preoccupied many historians during the isolationist 1930s, and later they hoped the nation could avoid the errors of that decade after World War II. In addition, historians writing from a Progressive perspective saw in the decade a conservative reaction to the crusades for reform at home during the Progressive Era and for democracy in the world during World War I. Whether concerned with isolationism or reaction, historians continued to portray the 1920s as infected with illiberalism and hence as unattractive. In *The Great Crusade and After, 1914–1928*, a volume in the History of American Life series, William Preston Slosson emphasized "the absurdities and extravagances of American nationalism," which was largely "a product of the war," that he found in the Klan and the move to limit immigration. The title clearly suggested that either Slosson or the series editors, Arthur M. Schlesinger and Dixon Ryan Fox, assumed that the war and the 1920s formed a distinct period in American history because of the great crusade's effects on the postwar decade. Six years later two new textbooks also stressed the war's impact. Frederick Logan Paxson's work claimed the war "did much to alter the environment of life and deflect the currents of thought" and helped to produce an "unstable state of mind" in the 1920s. In the first edition of *The Growth of the American Republic*, Samuel Eliot Morison and Henry Steele Commager compared the 1920s to the post–Civil War period and concluded that both were characterized by "an ardent nationalism that took repressive and intolerant form." The 1920s were "an era of materialism and reaction" in which people were "weary of reform and disillusioned by the crusade of democracy." Nationalism and disillusionment, according to Morison and Commager, bred nativism, religious fundamentalism, the KKK, and other examples of intolerance in the postwar era. George E. Mowry, writing on the eve of World War II, suggested in a brief essay that World War I had greatly affected American democracy. The sources of the post–World War I "instinct for herding and the desire for conformity" as exemplified by the Klan were to be found, Mowry argued in 1941, in the "mental solidarity" and "mental conscription" of wartime. In a 1947 textbook, Harold U. Faulkner continued the emphasis on the war by ascribing to it the "spiritual reaction," the "nationalism," and the "nostalgic desire" of the 1920s. In 1950 in a volume in The Chronicles of America series, Faulkner declared that "to explain the America of the twenties the historian inevitably goes back to the world war. The inanition and disillusionment which followed this costly struggle account for much."[12] The interpretations presented by Slosson, Paxson, Mowry, and other scholars in the 1930s and 1940s exceeded Frederick Lewis Allen's in sophistication and complexity, but basically they agreed with *Only Yesterday*. World War I largely explained the central themes of the unpleasant 1920s.

Though the idea of postwar disillusionment remained strong, writers in the 1940s began to revive the urban-rural theme earlier advanced by Lippmann, Dewey, Niebuhr, and others. As early as 1940, Arthur M. Schlesinger, Sr., in "The City in American History," hinted at the importance of conflict between cities and rural areas in American history. Attempting to promote urban history, he claimed that the greatest urban-rural conflict occurred in the late nineteenth century with the rise of the city. Though not examining the 1920s specifically, the urban-oriented Schlesinger helped to keep alive and promote the urban-rural theme. Seven years later the historian Kenneth C. McKay's study *The Progressive Movement of 1924* once more applied the theme to the 1920s. The Democratic party in 1924, he contended, split into "two antagonistic elements" along urban-rural lines, with "one, the old, established, propertied agrarian elements from the South and West; the other, the newer, more alien and urban Democratic vote of the cities." The two forces "broke sharply" over Prohibition and the Klan. Without citing the earlier proponents of the urban-rural thesis, McKay perceived the same forces at work in the Democratic party in 1924, but he did not extend his analysis to embrace other aspects of the decade. By 1948 F. L. Paxson had dropped his earlier stress on the impact of World War I and had adopted the explicit idea of "urban-rural cleavage" to explain Prohibition and other issues. Also in 1948 the eminent English political scientist Harold Laski similarly discovered Protestant rural America of the 1920s to be "hostile . . . to innovation, uninterested in most social experiments, and inclined to think that anyone who lives in one of the great cities is almost around the corner from sin." Prohibition, the KKK, and fundamentalist religion appealed to rural America, according to Laski, and not to the melting pot of urban America.[13]

In the early 1950s, scholars revitalized the urban-rural thesis in several important studies that restored it to a dominant position. Samuel Lubell's *Future of American Politics* interpreted Alfred E. Smith and William Jennings Bryan at the 1924 Democratic convention as symbols of "the habits and prejudices, hopes and frustrations, prides and hatreds of two different cultures and historical eras." "The brown derby and rasping East Side accent, which stamped Smith as 'one of our boys' to the sidewalk masses," Lubell explained, "sent shivers down the spine of Protestant respectability. In turn, the traits which made Bryan seem like the voice of pious morality to his Prohibitionist, rural Protestant following—the liberal use of biblical phrases, the resonant Chautauqua tones, the heaven-stomping energy—made him sound like the voice of bigotry to the urban masses." Lubell was primarily concerned with the effects of Franklin Roosevelt on American politics and did not explore the urban-rural conflicts of the 1920s in detail—but he clearly liked Al Smith.[14]

More specialized works by John Higham and Norman Furniss applied the urban-rural framework to social and cultural aspects of the 1920s. In his study of American nativism, *Strangers in the Land*, Higham devoted two chapters to "the tribal twenties" and efforts aimed at "closing the gates" of immigration. Higham concluded that the KKK and nativism were powerful in the small-town and rural areas, while the urban areas were the immigrants' strongholds. Though his interpretation omitted any explicit reference to urban-rural conflict, Higham's findings clearly supported the reemerging thesis. Furniss's study of fundamentalism relied on Niebuhr's earlier analysis, though he did not completely accept it, and argued that fundamentalism was strongest in rural areas.[15]

The most important work on the 1920s in the early and middle 1950s came from Richard Hofstadter. His analysis of the 1920s derived from his immersion in the social sciences and from his concern with McCarthyism. In the late 1940s and early 1950s, Hofstadter had studied the work of Karl Mannheim, Theodore Adorno, Bruno Bettleheim, and other social scientists and had come to support greater interdisciplinary work by historians. In 1954 he joined some of his Columbia University colleagues from the social sciences in a seminar on political behavior that focused on McCarthyism. Hofstadter's essay "The Pseudo-Conservative Revolt," which resulted from the seminar, proposed that conflicts over status or prestige, as well as struggles over economic matters, characterized American politics. The former, according to Hofstadter, occurred more frequently in prosperous times and tended to be irrational, whereas the latter usually predominated in periods of economic difficulty when people rationally pursued their own economic interests. In a number of works during the 1950s, Hofstadter applied his concept of "status politics" to McCarthyism, Populism, Progressivism, the New Deal, and the 1920s. In his Pulitzer Prize–winning *Age of Reform*, he dealt with the 1920s only in passing as an "Entr'acte" between Progressivism and the New Deal. His main concern with the 1920s was to explain the demise of Progressivism. He argued that the reform spirit slackened most in the small towns and rural areas of the South and West (the old "Bryan country") because Americans there felt a decline in their status and therefore suffered anxiety. Among urbanites Hofstadter detected a "widespread revolt among liberals and intellectuals against the village mind and the country mind"; in the countryside he saw "a growing sense that the code by which rural and small-town Anglo-Saxon America had lived was being ignored and even flouted in the wicked cities and especially by the 'aliens,' and that old religion and morality were being snickered at by the intellectuals." To protect their challenged prestige, rural Americans struck out at the urban sources of their declining status through their support of fundamentalism, the Ku Klux Klan, and Prohibition. Hofstadter found, therefore, many "rural-urban conflicts" in the 1920s, and he attributed them to status anxiety among rural folk.[16]

The *Age of Reform* followed the customs of treating the 1920s as a distinct era and of lamenting the reactionary influence of rural America, yet it constituted a breakthrough in understanding the decade. Reflecting the growing consensus view of American history, it focused on noneconomic forces and deemphasized class conflict. Derived from his study of social psychology, Hofstadter's status anxiety concept provided a theoretical underpinning for the rural-urban conflict thesis. Even though many have since criticized the idea of status anxiety, it influenced many later studies, especially by Hofstadter's graduate students. Reviewers of *The Age of Reform*, however, ignored Hofstadter's analysis of the 1920s and concentrated instead on his bold interpretations of populism and Progressivism; later historiographical reviews by Burl Noggle, Richard Lowitt, Arthur Schlesinger, Jr., and others still failed to recognize Hofstadter's contribution to the return of the urban-rural thesis.[17]

In the next two years Hofstadter's brief analysis of the 1920s received support from Edmund A. Moore and Arthur M. Schlesinger, Jr. Examining Smith's 1928 presidential campaign, Moore found major "sociocultural" divisions along urban-rural lines in the Democratic party and the nation. The first volume of Schlesinger's *Age of Roosevelt* grandly surveyed the 1920s. In discussing Al Smith's earlier bid for the Democratic nomination in 1924, the liberal Schlesinger revealed his prejudices in his succinct summary of the decade's tensions:

> Rural America was digging in for its rear-guard stand in the twenties. In the Eighteenth Amendment, it made one last effort to impose its mores on the cities. Through the Ku Klux Klan, it sought to maintain racial purity against the city immigrants. In a series of smaller actions, of which the Scopes case in Dayton, Tennessee, was the most spectacular, it tried to protect the dogmas of traditional faith against urban heresy. When Democrats gathered for the convention of 1924, McAdoo and Smith were more than rival candidates. They were antagonistic symbols for the emotions of agrarianism, prohibitionism, fundamentalism, and xenophobia.[18]

Temporarily forsaking his usual emphasis on struggles between the haves and the have-nots, Schlesinger in *The Crisis of the Old Order* adopted the concept of urban-rural tension to explain briefly the fights of the 1920s.

The short, suggestive analyses of Schlesinger, Hofstadter, and others combined with the growing monographic literature on the 1920s to prepare the way for a fuller explication of the theme of urban-rural conflict. William E. Leuchtenburg provided it. A colleague of Hofstadter at Columbia University and a native of New York City, he had already written on the ideological and economic conflicts over flood control and public power development in the Connecticut River Valley during the 1920s. In 1958 he turned his attention to the spectrum of issues in the 1920s for a volume in the Chicago History of American Civilization, and, as Don S. Kirschner has noted, he "quickly picked up" the "thread" of Hofstadter's argument and "stitched it into his study of the postwar years."[19]

From its opening pages, Leuchtenburg's *Perils of Prosperity, 1914–32*, stressed that in the 1920s the city "challenged," "threatened," and "imperilled" the rural way of life, but "most of all, the older America was alarmed by the mores of the metropolis." Older America feared the new ideas and values of the city especially because the war experience had shaken its confidence in the nation's power of assimilation. Leuchtenburg's examination of the 1920s revealed, therefore, considerable conflict between urban and rural values. His eleventh chapter, entitled "Political Fundamentalism," discussed the anxieties of many citizens that resulted from the nation's large number of foreign-born, the growth of cities, "the new intellectual currents of moral relativism and cosmopolitanism," and "the disturbing knowledge that Americans themselves no longer had their former confidence in democracy and religion." Rural and small-town Americans associated the threats with cities and revealed their fears in attempts "to deny real divisions in American society by imposing a patriotic cult and coercing a sense of oneness." As examples of political fundamentalism, Leuchtenburg offered immigration restriction, the Ku Klux Klan, Prohibition, and fundamentalist religion.[20]

The move to restrict immigration resulted from rural America's worry that, as Leuchtenburg put it, "America might be transformed ethnically by an invasion of alien elements from without" that would only increase the urban challenge. Also concerned about the growing power of cities, the new Ku Klux Klan "preyed on the fear that the country was already in peril from elements within." The Klan appealed, said Leuchtenburg, to native-born Protestants in small towns and rural areas, who "felt themselves eclipsed by the rise of the city." Similarly, the "prohibition movement [was] centered in the rural areas of the country, especially in the villages where the Baptist and Methodist preachers could speak with authority on matters of politics and morals." According to *The Perils of Prosperity*, prohibitionists "regarded the city as their chief enemy, and prohibitionism and pervasive anti-urbanism went hand in hand." For Leuchtenburg, "The campaign to preserve America as it was, to resist the forces of change, came to a head in the movement of Protestant fundamentalism climaxed by the Scopes Trial." More than just a contest over academic freedom or a battle between faith and science, the 1925 trial, and fundamentalism generally, was "a war of country and small town against the city." Leuchtenburg thought that fundamentalism, immigration restriction, the KKK, and Prohibition "all had in common a hostility to the city and a desire to arrest change through coercion by statute."[21]

The politics of the 1920s also revealed urban-rural animosity. Leuchtenburg, for instance, attributed the Progressives' lack of power in the decade to a shift from "the old-style evangelical reformism, under leaders like LaFollette and Bryan, to a new style of urban progressivism, which could call itself liberalism." A "breach between the two traditions" weakened Progressivism. More specifically, he saw dramatic urban-rural conflict in Al Smith's 1928 presidential campaign in which "all the tensions between rural and urban America came to a head." According to The Perils of Prosperity, "The rural voter or the city voter loyal to traditional values . . . responded to Smith as a symbol of a great many attitudes and beliefs which were alien to his own. Once this tension developed, every episode in the campaign tended to exacerbate the sense of alienation which non-urban and non-eastern voters felt toward Smith."[22]

Leuchtenburg recognized that the "war between the country and the city had been fought for decades," as the nation passed through "a painful transition" from rural to urban dominance. By the 1920s, however, the nation had begun consciously to reject rural values as the city openly displayed contempt for rural America. "Rural leaders," he argued, "in turn attacked the city as the modern Gomorrah, raising the ancient cry of the debauchery of the metropolis," and they "viewed the city as a great incubus sucking the life's blood of the countryside." While urban-rural hostility increased, each side became tense because of its ambivalence about its way of life. Rural people knew that cities were in some way appealing, and urbanites were "among the most reluctant to see the death of the old order." To Leuchtenburg, the outcome was clear: "It was [not] an age merely of a war between urban and rural values but also a coming together of the city and the country" in a new "single-standard society" based on urban values. The theme of urban-rural conflict explained much of what happened in the decade as the nation completed the transition to an urban nation.[23] Though rather evenhanded in his treatment of rural and urban America, Leuchtenburg obviously preferred the latter.

Initially most reviewers responded positively to The Perils of Prosperity, though some missed the urban-rural theme. Clarke Chambers praised Leuchtenburg's "clarity of analysis" in portraying the period as "an era of transition, tension, and paradox" during which the United States moved from a rural to an urban society. A positive evaluation by James H. Shideler, an agricultural historian, noted that the "consistent theme is the rural-urban conflict of attitudes." A reviewer in the *Annals of the American Academy of Political and Social Science* lauded Leuchtenburg's success in developing the urban-rural concept, and an editorial writer for the *St. Louis Post-Dispatch* commented that the book "makes brilliantly obvious" the significance of the shift from rural to urban America in the 1920s. In the *New York Times*, however, Harvey Wish saw nothing to distinguish Leuchtenburg's work from that of Frederick Lewis Allen, Preston Slosson, and other students of the 1920s. John D. Hicks, later author of *The Republican Ascendancy, 1921–1933*, considered it "a sophisticated book, full of subtleties, and designed for the wary reader," but he failed to recognize the urban-rural theme and also said the work merely "reflects accurately current interpretation on almost every aspect of the period covered." Hicks further charged that the index to *The Perils of Prosperity* was "not analytical," when it was in fact the first historical work to contain entries for "urban-rural conflict."[24]

Later assessments were considerably more mixed. Referring to the urban-rural interpretation, Richard Lowitt called *The Perils of Prosperity* a "brief but brilliant account." Burl Noggle, on the other hand, has given Leuchtenburg's book little favorable comment. His 1966 historiographical essay on the 1920s relegated Leuchtenburg to a footnote, and a similar essay seven years later again mentioned him only in the last footnote with the judgment that his book "is a fast-paced narrative incorporating much post-1929 research, though still sounding like *Only Yesterday*." Noggle caught the tone and the style but missed the substance. In a similar vein, Roderick Nash in *The Nervous Generation* mentions Leuchtenburg as "an exciting writer," whose book "is reminiscent of *Only Yesterday*." In their historiographical analysis of the 1920s, Gerald Grob and George A. Billias omitted any mention of *The Perils of Prosperity*, though they do discuss urban-rural conflict. In spite of the neglect of Leuchtenburg's work by some historiographers, *The Perils of Prosperity* has sold nearly four hundred thousand copies,[25] and its urban-rural interpretation has become ubiquitous in discussions of the 1920s.

Since 1958 American history survey texts, twentieth-century texts, collections of essays and documents, and monographs have usually employed an urban-rural theme in treating the 1920s. John M.

Blum in *The National Experience* in 1963 discussed "one nation divisible" in terms of "rural hostility to urban culture," and John Garraty's *American Nation* depicted the 1920s as "the aftermath of the great war" yet related the "tensions and hostilities" of the time to the "conflict between the city and the farm." Among textbooks on twentieth-century America, David Shannon in 1963 analyzed the "tensions" that resulted from an "urban-rural division," and Gerald Nash in 1971 focused on the "social tensions" he found "between rural and urban America" in a "decade of contrasts." A recent text by David W. Noble, David Horowitz, and Peter N. Carroll also discussed nativism, the Ku Klux Klan, Prohibition, and fundamentalism as examples of the "conflict of cultures in the twenties." In 1984 Robert Divine described a "rural counterattack" against the "dominance of urban centers." Among document editors, George E. Mowry, E. David Cronon, and Loren Baritz also employed the urban-rural theme, as did Joan Hoff Wilson in a collection of essays on the decade. More specialized texts have also adopted the urban-rural interpretation. In *The Urban Nation*, Mowry, who had many years earlier stressed the impact of World War I on the 1920s, enthusiastically embraced an urban-rural interpretation for the decade. Donald McCoy's *Coming of Age* accepted the theme but warned that historians "frequently exaggerated" its importance.[26]

Articles and monographs on the 1920s have often tested, adapted, and modified the urban-rural argument. In 1964, for instance, Paul L. Murphy reverted directly to Tonnies's model of *Gemeinschaft* and *Gesellschaft* to try to explain examples of intolerance in the 1920s that had been seen as characteristics of urban-rural conflict. More specifically on the Ku Klux Klan, Robert Moats Miller said that the revived KKK was "a rural, village, and small-town phenomenon," though probably "less in a statistical than a psychological sense." Similarly, David Chalmers in *Hooded Americanism* found that the KKK protected "traditional American values . . . found in the bosoms and communities of white, Anglo-Saxon, Protestants, whether in the small towns or *transplanted* into the newly minted urban America," and Charles C. Alexander argued that growing southwestern cities contained Klan members who sought "to preserve the values of their rural upbringing" even though they no longer lived in rural areas. Students of Prohibition continued to follow an urban-rural theme. British writer Andrew Sinclair in 1962 agreed that "the old America of the villages and farms mistrusted the new America of the urban masses. Prohibition was the final victory of the defenders of the American past." Repeal of Prohibition meant, according to Sinclair, that the "old order of the country gave way to the new order of the cities. Rural morality was replaced by urban morality." *Symbolic Crusade* by sociologist Joseph Gusfield proposed that urban-rural "cultural dichotomies became increasingly sharpened in the Prohibition issues" of the 1920s. And Robert A. Hohner acknowledged that the urban-rural thesis "obviously explains a great deal about the prohibition movement," but in his study of Virginia he also found substantial urban support for Prohibition.[27]

An urban-rural view of fundamentalism also persisted. In a study of the Social Gospel, written under Hofstadter, Paul Carter in 1956 stressed that fundamentalism was a rural phenomenon and part of a larger clash between rural and urban folkways. Lawrence Levine, another student of Richard Hofstadter, portrayed William Jennings Bryan as the defender of a rural, Protestant faith that was under strong challenge in the 1920s. "To speak of the 1920's as an era marked by those severe tensions and contradictions of a time of transition may seem trite," Levine admitted, but he did just that. He discussed the decade as a period of transition from rural to urban dominance. Bryan's advocacy of Prohibition and his defense of fundamentalism revealed his commitment to rural values and morality and "symbolized the cultural schism between rural and urban America," according to Levine.[28]

One of the more thorough applications of the urban-rural approach appeared in the work of yet another student of Richard Hofstadter. David Burner's *Politics of Provincialism* (1967) analyzed the transition of the Democratic party from a rural-based to an urban-dominated party and seemed to see its difficulties as representative of the society at large. "More than ever before the city and country stood at odds during the 1920's," declared Burner. Within the Democratic party the conflicts appeared as battles between urban and rural Democrats over Prohibition, the Klan, and Roman Catholicism. Out of the struggles emerged a strengthened party that found its greatest support in cities.[29]

An increasing number of scholars have questioned or directly challenged the urban-rural thesis after employing the techniques of the new social history, particularly quantification, to examine specific elements of the thesis or its applicability to an individual locality. Most, however, have continued to be critical of the ideas, values, and movements usually associated with rural and small-town life. In 1967 Kenneth Jackson disputed the "neat rural-urban dichotomy" in explaining the Klan. Intolerance, Jackson suggested, may have been even greater in the cultural diversity of the city than in the homogeneous rural areas. His study of the urban Klan contended that a majority of all Klan members lived in cities with more than fifty thousand population, that the Klan's leadership and press were urban, and that urban Klaverns exerted disproportionate power in the state and national Klans. Even Jackson, however, admitted the importance of the "urban migration of rural, old-stock Americans" and suggested that the urban Klan grew most in rapidly expanding cities where the members were usually Protestant, native-born Americans. Though he claimed to reject the urban-rural analysis, Jackson in fact accepted the idea of cultural conflict in the 1920s; he emphasized that some people who lived in cities and belonged to the Klan actually subscribed to and defended "rural" or traditional values. A more effective challenge to the urban-rural interpretation of the KKK came from Robert Alan Goldberg's *Hooded Empire*. His close analysis of the Klan in Colorado revealed the significance of local problems and concluded that "at least in Colorado, the urban-rural dichotomy proved useless as a guide to understanding the secret society." In his study of the Utah KKK, Larry R. Gerlach concluded that "the urban-rural dichotomy is an essentially specious division."[30]

Scholars have also denied the importance of urban-rural conflict in explaining Prohibition and fundamentalism. In 1963 James Timberlake's *Prohibition and the Progressive Movement, 1900–1920*, proposed that Prohibition was not an urban-rural struggle but a middle-class, Progressive reform that had supporters among native-born Protestants both in cities and in the countryside. He did not deny a cultural conflict but said it did not correspond to urban-rural lines. Norman H. Clark's study of Prohibition in Washington also disproved an urban-rural split. As a result, Joseph Gusfield retreated from his earlier emphasis and in 1968 pointed to the significant support for Prohibition among the urban middle class, as well as among rural Americans. With regard to fundamentalism, Ernest R. Sandeen, George M. Marsden, Paul Carter, Gregory H. Singleton, and Virginia

Gray have challenged the urban-rural model. Sandeen emphasized the urban "roots of fundamentalism" in the doctrines of British and American millenarianism of the nineteenth century. Marsden argued that fundamentalism was not distinctively rural but became identified with rural America in the popular mind as a result of the Scopes trial, which temporarily made fundamentalism "a focal point for the real hostility of rural America toward much of modern culture and intellect." Carter in a 1968 essay backed away from his earlier acceptance of an urban-rural interpretation of fundamentalism and warned scholars to apply the model "with caution" because fundamentalism "claimed many a strategic city pulpit" in the 1920s. Singleton has more specifically rejected the idea that fundamentalism had its base in rural areas by arguing that it had significant strength in cities and therefore two forms of fundamentalism thrived in the 1920s. Gray's unique study of voting in an antievolution referendum in 1928 found only slight correlations between ruralism and antievolution voting.[31] The importance of urban-rural cleavages to students of Prohibition and fundamentalism has declined, but they have retained the importance of some cultural conflict in the 1920s.

Perhaps the most pointed blow to the urban-rural argument came in Allan J. Lichtman's study of the 1928 presidential election. A number of scholars have seen in the Smith-Hoover contest a microcosm of the larger urban-rural tensions and struggles of the decade. Lichtman's *Prejudice and the Old Politics* discounted the urban-rural explanation through an intensive quantitative analysis of the voting patterns in the 1928 election. Lichtman decided that "religion is the best" explanation for the alignment of voters behind either the Catholic Al Smith or the Protestant Herbert Hoover.[32]

Influenced by the mounting monographic challenges, textbook authors by the early 1980s began to move away from a simple application of the urban-rural model to the 1920s. In *A People and a Nation*, for example, Howard P. Chudacoff discussed the decade as "a time of swift social change" that bred "waves of reaction" among "the Ku Klux Klan, immigration restrictionists, and religious fundamentalists," who wanted to "restore a society of simpler values." Cautiously, Chudacoff proposed that the reactionary "protests might be seen as the last gasps of a rural society yielding to modern industrial values," but he then pointed out that the "lines of defense" included many urban dwellers, too. Avoiding a clear urban-rural split, he cast the decade's conflicts into a "larger attempt to sustain old, local values in a fast-moving, materialist world."[33] Though more subtle and guarded, Chudacoff's analysis nonetheless demonstrated the persisting influence of the urban-rural interpretation.

Many writers have challenged the urban-rural model for events in the 1920s, but they have usually avoided explicitly substituting a new thesis in its place. Three exceptions have been Stanley Coben, Robert H. Wiebe, and Ellis Hawley, who have at considerable length offered new interpretations. In a 1973 textbook, ironically edited by Leuchtenburg, Coben reflected the growing interest among cultural historians in the concepts of Victorianism and modernism. He saw the 1920s as a time when traditional "Victorian culture" was undermined by economic and technological changes that created "modern America." In the place of urban-rural conflict, Coben proposed a clash of Victorian and modern cultures. The Ku Klux Klan, therefore, represented a defense of Victorian values, and fundamentalists and prohibitionists also "defended elements of the dominant Victorian culture during the 1920's."[34]

Robert Wiebe's section on post-1920 America in *The Great Republic* stressed the growth of "modern politics" and "modern culture" beginning in the 1920s. In the new politics of the 1920s, Wiebe saw a "division of interests between national and local affairs." Economic concerns prevailed in the former, while questions regarding "cultural sensitivities" dominated the latter. Immigration restriction and the KKK became for Wiebe examples of the power of local fears in the political system. The emerging modern culture of the 1920s, Wiebe perceived, contained a tension between modern mass society and the individual.[35] To replace urban-rural conflict, he seemed to propose conflict between national and local cultures, between the mass culture and the individual.

In *The Great War and the Search for a Modern Order*, Ellis Hawley in 1979 relied on the organizational synthesis to handle much of the 1920s; but when he examined the KKK, fundamentalism, Prohibition, and other issues usually associated with the urban-rural thesis, he drew on recent studies stressing ethnocultural forces to explain the decade's tensions. Without clearly identifying the significant ethnocultural groups, Hawley perceived conflicts in the 1920s as clashes between "modernists" and "traditionalists" or between "the 'genteel' traditions and standards" of the "established order of the Victorian age" and the "new attitudes emanating from cultural 'modernists' and promoters of the pleasure ethic."[36] Instead of urban-rural, therefore, he also suggested a Victorian versus modern dichotomy.

Several other alternatives to the urban-rural thesis have also been proposed. Warren Susman outlined a clash between a "producer-capitalist culture" and a "culture of abundance," and Daniel Horowitz has similarly seen a shift from a producer to a consumer culture. Daniel J. Singal has tentatively proposed an ideological paradigm for American history that would include a dialogue between a "market capitalist ideology" of the late nineteenth century and "a new bureaucratic ideology" of the twentieth century. In his study of political development from 1880 to 1940, Richard Franklin Bensel has tried to revive sectionalism as a major force. Drawing on the work of Immanuel Wallerstein, he has discovered conflict between "core" and "peripheral" economic areas. Though provocative and suggestive, the alternatives of Susman, Horowitz, Singal, and Bensel have been less well developed than the urban-rural model and less directly applied to the 1920s.[37]

Replacing a demographic dichotomy with a cultural or economic dichotomy certainly has made the distinctions appear more complex, if not more clear and precise. Nearly twenty years ago Robert K. Dykstra pointed out that "the conventional phrase 'rural-urban' conflict is lacking appropriate subtlety" and that scholars needed "a term that will reflect a division in attitude between farmers on the one hand, and 'urban' people (whether of town or city) on the other."[38] Use of Victorian and modern has seemed to add subtlety and has indicated more directly the importance of values and ideas involved in the conflicts of the 1920s, but the terms may be too vaporous to explain, for example, the resurgence of the Ku Klux Klan. More important, however, Coben, Hawley, and Wiebe still operate from a perspective hostile to rural, Victorian, local, or traditional forces.

The urban-rural thesis, however, has not been completely repudiated. As a recent text by Frank Freidel and Alan Brinkley has demonstrated, it remains useful and popular. Before the urban-rural thesis can finally be rejected, it (and its competitors) needs to be tested in more specialized studies similar to Robert Alan Goldberg's study of the Colorado Klan and Don Kirschner's examination of legislative voting in Illinois and Iowa.[39] Intensive investigations at the state and local levels will do much to substantiate or disprove the thesis of tension and conflict by discovering more about how urban and rural people viewed each other and the issues important to them in the 1920s. Urban historians, for instance, need to determine whether urbanites actually felt antagonism toward rural and small-town folk; otherwise the attitudes usually associated with the 1920s would simply reflect the anxieties and fears of nonurban people as they witnessed the growing power of American cities. On the national level, analysis of congressional voting on the supposedly urban-rural issues might also help to confirm or deny the thesis.

Though historians have paid scant attention to congressional reapportionment in the 1920s, conflict between urban and rural ways of life constituted a major theme in the reapportionment struggle. Repeatedly the issue appeared to pit cities against the country, industrial interests against agricultural concerns. The innumerable explicit references to urban-rural conflict in the discussion of reapportionment make the debate especially significant for historians of the 1920s. The rhetoric seems to reinforce the long-standing urban-rural interpretation by demonstrating that people at the time used exactly those concepts to understand the events of their own era; it provides for the first time concrete evidence that apparently confirms the scholars' theories by exploring a topic they have neglected. Reapportionment, furthermore, resulted from the very shift in population that has been crucial to the urban-rural interpretation. And, finally, the reapportionment debate appears to fit the model because the apparently reactionary forces opposing reapportionment of the House of Representatives claimed to defend rural America against the growing power of the cities.

2

Reapportionment before 1920

FOR THE FIRST and only time, Congress in the 1920s failed to reapportion the House of Representatives based on the latest decennial census. Nine years after the 1920 enumeration, Congress finally passed a reapportionment act, but it provided for reapportionment based on the upcoming 1930 census. The decade-long stalemate over reapportionment marked the culmination of over a century of recurrent controversy over the composition of the House of Representatives. The nation's rapid growth and expansion had caused numerous changes in the House membership. The enlargement of the House had been uneven and had occurred amid periodic disagreements, especially over the methods used to apportion seats. By 1912, when the last of the forty-eight states entered the Union, the House membership had reached 435, far from the original 65 seats provided by the Constitution in 1789.

The Constitution's provisions for representation grew out of compromises and concessions at the 1787 Constitutional Convention. In Philadelphia delegates favoring representation based on population for both houses of the proposed Congress battled other delegates insisting on equal representation for all states, perhaps in a unicameral legislature; generally the division fell between spokesmen for the larger states and those from the smaller states. The so-called Virginia Plan proposed a bicameral legislature in which representation would be based on the free inhabitants in each state; the people would elect the first house, which would then choose the second from nominations by the state legislatures. The New Jersey Plan suggested continuing the unicameral legislature of the Articles of Confederation with each state having equal representation chosen by methods determined by the individual state legislatures. James Madison and others soon realized that the "affair of representation" presented the greatest obstacle to agreement among the delegates, a judgment echoed by one historian of the convention when he labeled the fight over representation "the fiercest struggle for power of the entire summer."[1]

After considerable debate, the convention eventually resolved the issues. It proposed and the states later ratified a Constitution providing for a two-house legislature. To satisfy the interests of the smaller states, all the states would have equal representation in the Senate. The seats in the House of Representatives would be apportioned according to population, and that plan appealed to the larger, more populous states. Also as part of the large state–small state compromise, the convention agreed that money bills could originate only in the popularly elected House of Representatives. In the famous "three-fifths compromise," the Constitution provided that the population used to allot House seats would include all free citizens and three-fifths of slaves; free and slave interests accepted it because it applied to taxes as well as representation. The Constitutional Convention itself decided the makeup of the initial Congress. In the Constitution it called for Congress to have sixty-five members and distributed them, without benefit of reliable population figures, as follows: New Hampshire, three; Massachusetts, eight; Rhode Island, one; Connecticut, five; New York, six; New Jersey, four; Pennsylvania, eight; Delaware, one; Maryland, six; Virginia, ten; North Carolina, five; South Carolina, five; and Georgia, three.[2]

Except for calling for at least one representative per state and for no more than one for every thirty thousand in population, the Constitution made no explicit statement about how large future Congresses should be or about how the membership should be divided among the states. It did call for a census within three years of the first meeting of Congress and required that the enumeration be repeated every ten years. By implication, it suggested that Congress should use the census data to reapportion the House seats every ten years, but the document described no method to be employed. Similarly silent on how representatives were to be chosen, the Constitution left up to the state legislatures decisions on "the times, places, and manner of holding elections," but it did reserve to Congress the right to change the regulations.[3]

The vague constitutional provisions dissatisfied five state ratifying conventions, and they proposed amendments to clarify future reapportionments. Massachusetts, New Hampshire, Virginia, New York, and North Carolina agreed to maintain the ratio of one representative per thirty thousand population until the House reached two hundred members, but above two hundred they differed. Early in the fall of 1789, the first Congress responded to the states' concerns by approving and submitting to all the states a constitutional amendment for reapportionment. It provided for one representative per thirty thousand in population for a House of up to one hundred members, then the Congress could regulate the ratio of representation as long as it allowed at least one congressman for every forty thousand until the House reached two hundred and for no more than one for every fifty thousand in a House of more than two hundred members. The amendment was the first in a group of twelve sent to the state legislatures for ratification. Delaware alone rejected the reapportionment amendment. Only ten, however, did approve it, so it fell one short of ratification. Massachusetts, which had called for action on reapportionment, failed for some reason to act on the amendment. (Sufficient states did ratify amendments three to twelve, and they became the Bill of Rights.)[4] Without the clarifying amendment, the Constitution remained unclear about future reapportionments.

The second session of the First Congress followed the Constitution's directive and on March 1, 1790, enacted a law for the nation's first census of population. The 1790 census, which took a year and a half to complete, reported a population of 3.6 million. When the Second Congress considered reapportionment based on the census figures in November 1791, it soon confronted the sticky question of how to be fair to each state. Opting to avoid discriminating against smaller states by increasing the number of representatives, the House approved a bill that gave each state one representative for every thirty thousand in population for a total of 112 congressmen; it ignored any remainder left after dividing a state's population by thirty thousand. With the vice-president casting the deciding vote, the Senate changed the ratio to one representative per thirty-three thousand for a House of 105 members. Disagreeing about the best size for the House and about the most equitable way to distribute seats, the House rejected the Senate amendment. When the Senate refused to yield, the bill died, at least for the moment.[5]

After considerable debate lasting several months, the House again proposed a ratio of one seat per thirty thousand and added a provision for a census and reapportionment five years later. Once again amending the bill, the Senate deleted the 1797 census and added eight seats to be given to the states with the larger remainders for a total of 120. The House first rejected the amendment by one vote and then, when the Senate insisted, approved it by two votes. Congress submitted the reapportionment bill for the president's signature.[6]

When President George Washington asked his cabinet for advice, he found that Virginians Thomas Jefferson and Edmund Randolph opposed the bill, while Alexander Hamilton of New York and Henry Knox of Massachusetts favored it. The dispute reflected the growing disagreements between the sections, between the Republicans and the Federalists, and between farming and manufacturing concerns. Though the ratio of one per thirty-three thousand persons favored large states such as Virginia more than did the ratio of one per thirty thousand, southern interests objected because six of the additional eight seats went to northeastern states. Furthermore, the conflict grew out of two different approaches to computing reapportionment. Jefferson favored first fixing the ratio of population to representatives and then letting that determine the size of the House of Representatives; each state's population would simply be divided by the population per representative to fix how many congressmen the state would receive, with all remainders from the division ignored. Hamilton, however, wanted first to set the size of the House and then to multiply it by each state's percentage of the national population to determine representation; any remaining seats would go to the states with the largest fractions. Under Jefferson's method, Virginia's population of about 630,560 would be divided by 30,000 to produce 21 (or 21.019 exactly) representatives in a House that totaled 112 seats; but under Hamilton's plan, Virginia's population divided by the national total of about 3,615,900 and then multiplied by a predetermined 112 gave it only 19 (or 19.531 precisely) seats.[7] The 1792 controversy, therefore, involved politics, personalities, and statistics.

In the very first presidential veto, Washington rejected the reapportionment bill because he claimed that it unconstitutionally used two different ratios to allot representatives (30,000 to seven states and 27,700 to the eight states receiving an additional congressman each) and because he believed the ratio of 27,700 per representative violated the constitutional requirement of not more than one per 30,000.

The House failed to override the veto, but within ten days Congress passed and President Washington signed another reapportionment bill. It contained a ratio of one per 33,000, ignored all remainders, and created a House of 105 members. The crisis over the first reapportionment had ended.[8]

Jefferson's method involving rejected fractions was used in 1792 and in the following four reapportionments. As the nation grew, the House increased in size, though proportionally not as rapidly because the ratio also became larger. The 1802 reapportionment continued the thirty-three thousand ratio and allowed for 141 representatives, but nine years later Congress increased the ratio to thirty-five thousand, which yielded a House of 181 members. The ratio in 1822 grew again to forty thousand, and the House enlarged to 213, but for the first time four states had their number of representatives reduced—Connecticut, Delaware, Vermont, and Virginia each lost one representative. Ten years later the ratio again expanded to forty-seven thousand, and four states again lost one seat apiece. Under Jefferson's method the small states appeared to suffer and New England saw its power wane. In the first five reapportionments, Delaware, for example, should have received a total of 8.54 seats but actually got only 6 (one in each except for two after the 1812 reapportionment). New York, on the other hand, was entitled to a total of 123.58 yet was awarded 128 representatives.[9]

Opponents of Jefferson's method rightly charged that it favored the bigger states such as New York at the expense of smaller states like Delaware. To correct the inequities, some congressmen suggested changes in reapportionment, and controversies resulted. South Carolina's William Lowndes first sought to alleviate the unfairness by reviving a modified version of Alexander Hamilton's method. In 1822 he proposed following Hamilton's plan except that Lowndes wanted to assign remaining seats according to the average sizes of constituencies instead of according to the size of the remainder as Hamilton had. Although Congress defeated Lowndes's idea because it went too far in favoring the smaller states, his proposal had helped open the question of bias in Jefferson's method of apportionment.[10]

After the 1830 census, the controversy over reapportionment intensified. Several major politicians proposed different methods to reapportion the House more fairly. Upset over New England's loss of power, Representative (and former president) John Quincy Adams suggested fixing the size of the House and then finding a ratio that would produce the desired number of representatives when each remainder was rounded up to the nearest whole number; Adams, in other words, wanted to count *all fractions* of a representative whereas Jefferson had rejected all fractions. Adams's proposal came too late for the House had already passed a bill submitted by Representative James K. Polk, but Adams found an ally in Senator Daniel Webster. The Massachusetts Whig called for rounding off the remainders to the nearest whole numbers, or a method of accepting major fractions. Webster's plan fell between Adams's proposal favoring the smaller states and Jefferson's serving the interests of the larger states. In spite of Webster's objections, however, Congress once again adopted Jefferson's method in 1832.[11]

Ten years later Daniel Webster's arguments prevailed, but only after Congress had considered numerous ratios using the traditional method. The Senate insisted on a smaller House and on abandoning Jefferson's approach, in use since 1792. Instead it passed and the House approved a reapportionment bill that called for counting all major fractions resulting from dividing each state's population by the designated ratio of population per representative. The adopted ratio of 76,680 for the first time actually shrank the House of Representatives to only 223 members, 17 fewer than provided in 1832. Fourteen states lost seats in the new House; New England's delegations dropped by 6, but Jefferson's Virginia also lost 6 seats.[12] The adoption of Webster's major fractions formula for allotting representatives did not, however, once and for all end the controversy over congressional reapportionment.

In addition to drastically changing the method of reapportionment, the 1842 law also altered the way representatives were chosen. Since the First Congress, the states had followed no uniform method of electing congressmen. Numerous proposed constitutional amendments requiring individual congressional districts in multirepresentative states had failed, and Congress refused to exercise its constitutional power to regulate the elections. Some states with more than one congressman continued to elect them all at large, so in 1840 nine states with a total of thirty-three representatives still chose them in at-large elections. The 1842 law for the first time required that representatives be elected from individual districts "composed of contiguous territory."[13] Only a statutory provision, the requirement lacked the permanence of a constitutional amendment and would later be dropped.

As the sectional stresses increased in the mid-nineteenth century, Representative Samuel F. Vinton, a Whig from Gallipolis along the Ohio River in southern Ohio, tried to avoid having reapportionment exacerbate the North-South rivalry. In a proposed amendment to the bill providing for the census in 1850, Vinton argued for a permanent reapportionment law to prevent recurrent squabbles over the distribution of House seats. Vinton's bill not only provided for the 1850 census but also for a census every ten years thereafter. Even more boldly, it delegated to the secretary of the interior the power to allot seats in the House of Representatives using the census data and the method designated by Congress. Though it made no provision for individual congressional districts, the bill sought to settle the problems over reapportionment by making it unnecessary for Congress to act every ten years.[14]

In enacting Vinton's bill, Congress also incorporated a revived version of Alexander Hamilton's procedure for distributing seats among the states. Quickly known as the Vinton method, it set the size of the House of Representatives at 233 members, not the ratio of population to representatives as the Webster method did, and then divided the nation's population by the total number of representatives to determine the ratio. The population of each state was then divided by the ratio and the state given a representative for each whole number in the quotient. To reach the maximum of 233, additional seats were distributed to the states with the largest fractions of remainders but not necessarily to all or to all major fractions or only to major fractions. The size of the House had become more important than the size of congressional districts. The Vinton method remained the legal basis for reapportionment for the next fifty years, but Congress never applied it precisely. Just two years after approving the Vinton method, for example, Congress arbitrarily amended its own reapportionment act to give the booming gold-rush state of California an additional representative.[15]

After the 1860 census, the secretary of the interior applied the Vinton method to the population data and apportioned representatives so Congress enacted no general reapportionment law. The secretary apportioned the 233 members in July 1861. The secession of the southern states, however, meant that the Thirty-seventh Congress never had 233 members. The Alabama, Arkansas, Florida, Georgia, Mississippi, North Carolina, South Carolina, and Texas seats all remained vacant. From 1861 to 1865, the House of Representatives received more than thirty applications from men seeking admission to the House as representatives from the seceding states. The House accepted several from Virginia (later West Virginia), Louisiana, and Tennessee and rejected or did not act on the others. In July 1862, just one year after the secretary of the interior's reapportionment according to the 1850 law, the Congress passed a supplemental reapportionment act. The new law violated the Vinton method by arbitrarily adding eight seats to the House of Representatives, one new seat each to Illinois, Iowa, Kentucky, Minnesota, Ohio, Pennsylvania, Rhode Island, and Vermont, all northern states. The 1862 law also revived the requirement that congressional districts be made up of contiguous territory.[16]

In the wake of the Civil War and emancipation, Congress realized the impact of the end of the three-fifths compromise on the House of Representatives. Counting the former slaves as full persons was expected to increase the South's representation in Congress and in the electoral college by about fifteen votes. Worrying about this addition to Democratic power, Republicans considered ways to dilute what they saw as the possibly damaging political effects of emancipation. One proposal involved changing the population on which reapportionment was based to the voting population of the various states, which Republicans believed might ensure black suffrage. The solution reached by Congress came in the second section of the Fourteenth Amendment, which provided for reducing congressional representation for states that did not allow blacks to vote. Though the provision was never enforced, it demonstrated the willingness of Congress to tie the aims of Reconstruction to the reapportionment process.[17]

After the 1870 census, Congress agreed to a House of Representatives composed of 283 members because the Vinton method and the previously popular Webster method both agreed exactly on the distribution of 283 seats. As a result of the reapportionment, the South did not increase its power as Republicans had feared because most of the population growth had occurred in the West, because the South had suffered great casualties in the war, and because the census prob-

TABLE 2.1. The Alabama Paradox after the 1880 Census

State	Quota at 299	Allotment	Quota at 300	Allotment	Percent increase	Absolute increase
Alabama	7.646	8	7.671	7	.33	.025
Texas	9.640	9	9.672	10	.33	.032
Illinois	18.640	18	18.702	19	.33	.062

ably missed more than 1 million southerners. Less than three months later, however, Congress enacted another supplemental reapportionment law. It included a new provision that the congressional districts should as nearly as possible contain equal numbers of inhabitants. More important, the law again violated the principle of the Vinton method by awarding an additional congressional seat to each of nine states (Alabama, Florida, Indiana, Louisiana, New Hampshire, New York, Pennsylvania, Tennessee, and Vermont). Congress seemed to like the Vinton method but not enough to adhere to it strictly. One unintended result was that Rutherford B. Hayes won the presidency in 1876. If the Vinton method had been strictly followed, the electoral college also would have been apportioned differently and Samuel J. Tilden would have won.[18]

A major problem appeared when Congress began to consider reapportionment based on the 1880 census. When the Census Office reported the results of reapportionment using the Vinton method for Houses ranging from 275 to 350 members, it noted the paradox that Alabama received 8 congressmen in a House of 299 members but only 7 representatives in a House of 300. In a larger House, Alabama actually was entitled to one less seat (see Table 2.1). Under the Vinton method, remaining seats were distributed to the states with the largest fractions until the total allowed by law had been reached. With 299 seats available, Alabama got one additional seat but Texas and Illinois did not; with 300 seats, the fractions of Texas and Illinois surpassed Alabama so they received additional seats while Alabama lost one. Each of the quotas increased by .33 percent, but the larger quotas increased by a greater absolute amount; as a result, Alabama lost a seat in the larger House, while the larger states of Texas and Illinois each gained one seat (one coming from Alabama's loss and one from the overall increase from 299 to 300).[19]

The so-called Alabama paradox posed a major problem for Congress. Some congressmen in 1882 revived the charges used nearly a century earlier against Hamilton's similar method of apportioning representatives. They objected, for instance, that the Vinton method failed to abide consistently by the quotas and frequently favored the larger states (Illinois and Texas over Alabama). Once again Congress decided to avoid, not confront and solve, the problem. In February 1882, it passed an act calling for a House of 325 representatives. It settled on that size because the Vinton and Webster methods conveniently agreed on the apportioning of 325 seats so no state would lose and object. The law itself, however, neglected to specify the method to be used. A similar solution in 1891 again postponed dealing directly with the Alabama paradox. The Congress agreed to 356 seats in the House of Representatives to be allotted by the Vinton method because it gave a seat to every state with a major fraction, just as the Webster method would have.[20]

After the 1900 census the problem could no longer be avoided. Reapportionment figures for every size House of Representatives from 350 to 400 members revealed some startling inconsistencies. The Vinton method gave Colorado 3 representatives in each House between 350 and 400 except for a House of 357 members in which it got only 2 congressmen. A more glaring inconsistency involved Maine, whose representation fluctuated even more erratically (see Table 2.2). To solve the problem of the Alabama paradox, which now also affected Maine, Congress reverted to the Webster method for apportioning seats. At the 386 level, the Webster method prevented any state, even Maine, from losing a single seat. The congressional action finally seemed to settle the problem of the Alabama paradox by indicating that Congress would no longer accept any method that produced such an anomaly.[21]

In 1911 Congress further expanded the House by 47 seats to 433 and provided for 1 seat each for New Mexico and Arizona if they entered the Union, a total of 435. The enlargement meant that no state would lose a representative while twenty-four gained additional seats (New York, for example, added 6 for a total of 43). The 1911 law also continued the by then customary provisions for compact districts of contiguous territory and equal populations. More important, in enacting the reapportionment law, Congress followed the findings of Professor Walter F. Willcox of Cornell University, which demonstrated the superiority of Webster's method. Known increasingly as the method of major fractions, it received congressional endorsement

TABLE 2.2. The Alabama Paradox after the 1900 Census

House size	350–82	383–85	386	387–88	389–90	391–400
Maine representatives	3	4	3	4	3	4

and finally prevailed over the Vinton and Hamilton procedures that had been applied from 1850 through the 1890s.[22]

The first thirteen reapportionments up through 1911 involved considerable controversy. Most of the early disagreements, even the one in the Constitutional Convention, concerned the relative treatment of small and large states by various statistical procedures. The later discord focused on the Alabama paradox. Other rivalries such as the sectional jealousies of the mid-nineteenth century also played a role in the squabbles over reapportionment. In every instance, however, Congress managed to enact a reapportionment law within two years of the completion of the census. Sometimes the laws were amended and frequently the laws dissatisfied some, but the Congress did fulfill its apparent constitutional obligation every ten years. The pattern broke after the 1920 census.

3

The Controversy in the 1920s

THREE DAYS after Christmas in 1920, the Committee on the Census of the House of Representatives began hearings to consider legislation to reapportion the House based on the recently completed census. The nation's population had increased by nearly 14 million since the 1910 census to over 105 million, so some change in the distribution of representatives seemed necessary (see Appendix 1 for population changes). During the 1920s, however, the normally routine business of reapportioning the House of Representatives encountered numerous obstacles that together prevented any reapportionment employing the 1920 census data. The prolonged struggle over reapportionment occurred in four phases. First, in 1920–21 the House considered but rejected proposals for reapportionment. Second, Congress took no important action from October 1921 through 1925. Third, in the Sixty-ninth Congress (1925–27) the Census Committee once again held hearings but reported no bill to the House. Fourth, and finally, in 1928 progress began. After more hearings, the Census Committee reported a bill to the House in the spring of 1928, but it was recommitted. Toward the close of the Seventieth Congress, the House finally passed a bill only to have it die in the Senate. Early in the next Congress, a bill passed both houses and President Herbert Hoover signed it in June 1929; the new reapportionment act provided for reapportionment after the next census in 1930.

1920–1921

Even before the Census Committee's first meeting in 1920, problems had emerged. For example, the chairman, Republican Isaac Siegel of

New York City, observed that the House would need 60 more seats to follow the precedent of not reducing many states' representation. If the reapportioned House remained at 435, nearly a dozen states, including Indiana, Iowa, Maine, Missouri, Nebraska, and Vermont, would send fewer congressmen to the next House. Siegel noted, however, that the House floor was already crowded because since the 1911 increase to 435 the members no longer had individual desks in the chamber but instead sat at long tables. Enlarging the House, therefore, presented serious physical problems, and, perhaps more important, it threatened the House's efficiency. The *New York Times* and the *New Republic* each called for a smaller House. Describing the House as "unwieldy," the *New Republic* said it "functions badly enough" already and did not need more members to add "their oratory to the legislative babel." The *Times* agreed. In an early October editorial, it opposed adding members to the House because the existing "legislative machinery is cumbrous" and would only be worsened by more members; instead it suggested increasing the constituency of each representative. Some legislative leaders also objected to continuing the practice of enlarging the House. Two former Speakers, Joseph G. Cannon and James Beauchamp Clark, even favored a smaller House, and Clark endorsed a limit of 300 members.[1]

In the preliminary public discussions, opponents of an expanded House failed to appreciate fully the political difficulties involved in convincing states to accept fewer representatives. Even more difficult would be securing the cooperation of sitting representatives in the elimination of some of their own seats. Furthermore, the 1920 census returns clearly indicated that the losers would be the predominantly rural states because the states with large urban concentrations had gained significantly in population while the rural areas had declined. For the first time in the nation's history, the urban population exceeded the rural population.[2]

To avoid the problems involved in either reducing or maintaining the House's size, many advocated increasing the membership as had customarily been done. For example, Cordell Hull, a Democratic representative from Tennessee, proposed boosting the number of seats to 450. The most serious indication that the House would be increased, not reduced, came from a caucus of House Republicans shortly before the Census Committee opened hearings. The Republicans voted 106 to 61 to increase the size of the House from 435 to 483. Under the Republican plan as formally proposed by Representative Siegel, no state would lose a seat and twenty-five states would gain representatives. New York and Pennsylvania, for example, would each gain four seats, and Texas would add three. Disagreement over the appropriate size for the House continued, however, and constituted a major obstacle to any proposal for reapportionment.[3]

Another difficulty complicating attempts to reapportion Congress involved the right of southern blacks to vote. Adopted in 1868, the Fourteenth Amendment mandated a reduction in a state's delegation in the House as a penalty for denying any of its citizens the right to vote, and in 1920 defenders of the Negro argued that it should be enforced as a part of any reapportionment plan. Representative Siegel suggested applying the Fourteenth Amendment to southern states, but the idea received its strongest support from Representative George Holden Tinkham. The Boston Republican introduced a resolution in the House to authorize "the Committee on the Census to inquire respecting the extent to which citizens of the United States are denied the right to vote," and he spoke in support of his proposal before the Republican caucus. Although broadly worded, Tinkham's resolution clearly aimed at southern states that denied blacks the ballot. Tinkham and others continued to push his plan even after his party's caucus rejected it. Many Republicans instead preferred a more indirect attack on southern discrimination wherein representation would be based on the number of votes cast in presidential elections rather than on population. In eleven southern states, according to the editor of the *National Republican*, fewer people voted than in the state of Illinois, yet the southern states had five times the number of Illinois's representatives. Similarly, the *Nation* complained that only 153,990 of over 2 million Virginians voted in 1916, and it "hoped that the Reapportionment Committee will have the nerve to lay the situation wide open."[4] In 1920 discussion primarily concerned Negro voting and southern representation, but it soon expanded to include questions about counting northern urban aliens in the census data used to allot representatives even if the aliens could not qualify to vote for the congressmen.

The Committee on the Census began wrestling with the problems of reapportionment when it convened on December 28, 1920. The House committee had before it several bills for reapportionment. In addition to Representative Siegel's bill to increase the House to 483 members, Representative Henry E. Barbour (R.-Cal.) wanted the number to remain at 435, and Democrat Thomas L. Blanton of Albany, Texas, proposed a reduction to 304 members. The fourteen-member committee started by hearing from Joseph A. Hill, chief statistician of the Bureau of the Census. Using the statistical method adopted in 1910, Hill presented apportionment results based on a membership varying from 435 to 483. He acknowledged that Congress had not always used the method of major fractions to apportion representatives, but he assumed that after the 1920 census that system would be employed.[5]

In the Census Committee's first hearings, the major controversy involved the right of blacks to vote. In addition to Representative Tinkham's charges that earlier reapportionments had been "illegal" and "unconstitutional" because they failed to enforce the Fourteenth Amendment, a number of black witnesses, including James Weldon Johnson of the National Association for the Advancement of Colored People (NAACP) and Monroe Trotter of the *Boston Guardian* and the National Equal Rights League, alleged widespread discrimination against blacks in voting and demanded implementation of the Fourteenth Amendment. George H. Harvey, general counsel of the Colored Council of Washington, insisted that the committee conduct an investigation to determine where the suffrage had been withheld from Negroes. The field secretary of the NAACP declared that "colored people are discriminated against in the Southern States in the matter of color" and cited the example of Negro women certified by the state of South Carolina to teach yet denied the right to vote ostensibly because of illiteracy. Walter White, also from the NAACP, told of lawless actions in Florida to prevent blacks from voting and claimed that anyone who attempted to help blacks in isolated southern communities would "be subjected to mob violence."[6]

Southern representatives on the committee strenuously objected to the charges of discrimination. Congressman Carlos Bee of Texas even resented having "to sit here and hear a commonwealth [South Carolina] insulted by the witness" from the NAACP. With the backing of two other southern congressmen, Representative William W. Larsen (D.-Ga.) denied the charges of disfranchisement. "In my home 1,365, I believe is the number, niggers are registered," Larsen said. "We have a white primary, which has nothing to do with the general election. The nigger does not participate in the white primary." In the general election, he continued, the Republican party lacked strength to win so blacks did not bother to vote. Under questioning from a colleague from Illinois, Larsen declared "absolutely" that blacks had the same freedom to vote in the South as in the North and that election officials "do not permit such discrimination" as that described by the witnesses.[7]

The committee gave little heed to the Fourteenth Amendment and on January 6, 1921, approved a bill to increase the size of the House to 483, as proposed by its chairman. The bill provided that no state would lose a representative as a result of reapportionment and fifteen states would gain seats. California, for example, would add five congressmen, and Michigan, New York, Ohio, and Pennsylvania would each receive four more. Though it moved to expand the House, the Census Committee also acknowledged that the body could not continue to grow indefinitely and therefore recommended passage of a constitutional amendment to limit it to a maximum of five hundred members.[8]

A minority of the Census Committee opposed enlarging the House, and the minority report argued that the additional representatives would cost taxpayers as much as $1 million, an unnecessary and unjustified expense. The six dissenters contended, moreover, the forty-eight new members would not increase the House's efficiency but in fact would make it "more unwieldy and cumbersome." During the committee hearings, Representative Louis W. Fairfield (R.-Ind.) replied on the floor of the House to calls to expand the House by pointing out that "every Member of Congress represents not only the people of his own district but the people of the whole country. If the units are increased in number and the area diminished more and more would the representative become more provincial in his thought and confine his activities to the needs of a limited area." Fairfield found an "almost continuous judgment against increase."[9]

On January 18, 1921, the House of Representatives began two days' debate on the bill to increase the House to 483 seats. Managers of both sides of the debate tried to avoid the issues raised by Representative Tinkham by refusing to allot him time to speak, so four days before the actual debate began he had to secure thirty minutes from the chairman of the Appropriations Committee's Subcommittee on Indian Affairs. In soaring rhetoric he pleaded that the Fourteenth Amendment must be enforced or "the Republic is destroyed and democracy annihilated."[10] Once the debate commenced, the House paid little attention to Tinkham's argument. Instead the debate focused on whether the House should be increased.

The defenders of the Siegel bill for 483 members offered a wide variety of arguments. First, they addressed the general ability of congressmen to represent and serve their constituents. Siegel maintained that the larger population, especially with 4.5 million war veterans, required more representatives because the nation increasingly turned to Congress for action on a wide range of issues. In addition, the recent enfranchisement of women automatically doubled the voting constituency of each representative and added to his burdens. Even with 500 members, according to Siegel, the House would have far fewer members per population than European legislatures such as France's House of Deputies with nearly 700. An increase to 483 seemed moderate. Representative Jacob L. Milligan (D.-Mo.) thought that more representatives would allow each to maintain "close contact with the people he represents" and know their "needs and desires," and Rufus Hardy (D.-Tex.) believed that smaller districts would ensure better representation of minority interests. To counter the contention that a larger House would be too costly, a Louisiana Democrat claimed that the people "were more seriously concerned with service here than they are with the additional petty expense" and compared the added cost to the ready acceptance of expenditures for postal service, road building, and aid to disabled soldiers. One speaker even suggested that more representatives and smaller districts would enable men of modest means to run for Congress because the election campaigns would be less expensive.[11]

Second, proponents of the Siegel bill argued that a larger House would not hurt and might actually improve the internal operations of the House. Representative James B. Aswell (D.-La.) pointed out that the House's efficiency would not be harmed by adding members because "only about 40 Members do most of the talking anyway." To people worried about the effects size had on the work of the House, he asked why they even accepted 435 members and did not try to "make the membership 65, as the Constitution originally did." Other representatives voiced concern about the distribution of power in a smaller House. A representative trying to serve a large constituency would "feel compelled to trust to committee and to leaders," and the result would be the "concentration of power in the hands of a few," in the opinion of one Kansas Republican. Even worse, a rural Tennessee Democrat warned that "a lot of machine politicians" opposed enlarging the House because they worried that the "House is getting too big for their complete and perfect individual boss control and domination." He asked his colleagues, "Does not everybody know that those special interests that expect the most of Congress want the fewest number of Members?" Aswell summed up the fears of many when he declared that opposition to expanding the House was "an argument for the pernicious lobbyist here, against the will of the people; . . . it is an argument for autocracy and centralization against democracy and popular government."[12]

A third reason offered for enlarging the House involved concerns about the possible decline in the influence of rural areas in Congress and the apparent growth of urban power. As the New York City representative Isaac Siegel reminded the House, to remain at 435 and thereby reduce the number of representatives from some states would be to "strike at those states where the farmers predominate," and his bill guaranteed no such reductions. The effects of any decline in rural representation troubled Vermont Republican Frank L. Greene because he believed "the steadying influence of the countryside" provided "a moral influence," a "sheet anchor in sober second thought," a "restraint and check" in times of crisis. His fellow Republican Edward C. Little of Kansas agreed and further warned that the refusal to enlarge the House would be "to turn this government over to the cities where ignorance, poverty, vice, and crime are staring you in the face." He declared, "It is not best for America that her councils be dominated by semicivilized foreign colonies in Boston, New York, Chicago." Responding to Greene and Little with applause, many in the House appeared to agree with Maine's Ira G. Hersey when he said, "One of the greatest dangers that confront the Republic today is the tendency of the large cities to control the American Congress."[13]

Some congressmen refused to accept the findings of the 1920 census that clearly demonstrated that urban areas had grown faster than rural areas and had in fact surpassed them in total population. By challenging the accuracy of the census, they hoped to support their claims that rural areas should not lose seats in the House as a result of reapportionment or suffer a dilution of power in a larger House. Paul B. Johnson (D.-Miss.) and Oscar E. Bland (R.-Ind.) attacked the census because the Census Bureau paid insufficient salaries to obtain expert workers and conducted the census at "a peculiar time," which meant that many citizens were missed and the results were therefore inaccurate. Their most important objection was that the census was taken in the aftermath of disruptive World War I. As Bland said, "During the war the great activities in the big cities of this country drew men from the farming communities of the Nation like a magnet." In addition, Jasper N. Tincher (R.-Kan.) argued, the census caught some soldiers temporarily away from home. The defenders of rural America believed that the inaccuracies of the 1920 census would soon become apparent when many people naturally returned from the cities. The rural sections should not, they maintained, be forced to give up seats in the House of Representatives because of a temporary aberration in the population. To reapportion on the basis of the distorted 1920 census would, therefore, be unfair. The veteran James B. "Champ" Clark, a former Speaker of the House, who was only six weeks from death, had changed his mind, stopped arguing for a House of 300 members, and now supported "raising the number of Members to 483. . . . because this flow of people to the great cities is going to come back. The agricultural States proper will increase in population in the next ten years as compared with these great cities."[14]

In the House debate, opponents of the bill to enlarge the number of representatives strongly countered nearly every point made by its proponents. On a very basic level, Indiana's Fairfield declared that the Census Committee's majority had recommended "two things at this time diametrically opposed in principle. . . . If there is any justification for the number of Members to be permanently fixed at 500 there can be no possible justification for the increase to 483 at this time." He therefore supported retention of the 435 level. Another leading opponent of the bill, Representative Henry E. Barbour of California, reminded the House that nine of the thirteen previous reapportionments had involved the reduction of some states' representation and that a total of eighteen states had at various times lost seats. Thirteen had even lost seats in more than one reapportionment; for example, Massachusetts had lost seats on three occasions, Virginia six times, and Kentucky twice. If Congress had not reduced some delegations in past reapportionments, according to William R. Wood (R.-Ind.), New Hampshire would yet have 6 House seats and New York would have more than 100. The increase had to stop sometime, the 435 level was as good as any, and the necessary reductions in some states' delegations would not be unusual.[15]

Critics of the proposed increase to 483 also thought that a larger House would work less effectively than the already "extravagant, clumsy, and unwieldy body." Concerned about efficiency, Representative Barbour said that more members would mean more time for debates, longer roll calls, and larger committees. Marvin Jones of Texas doubted, however, that the half-dozen important committees would be expanded so the additional congressmen would exercise negligible influence in a larger House. Several opponents of the Siegel bill believed that it would lead to a more centralized and less democratic House. "The larger the lawmaking body the less the individual Member feels his responsibility," observed an Oregon Republican, "and the more he is tempted to pass it along to the leaders." Mississippi's Thomas U. Sisson predicted "boss rule," and Simeon D. Fess (R.-Ohio) argued that the "larger the House the more rigid must be the rules of the House, and with the increased rigidity of the rules the individuality of the membership is sacrificed." And the decreased efficiency and increased centralization of power would cost the taxpayers $4 million for office space and $1 million for salaries and expenses each year. North Carolina's Samuel M. Brinson proposed instead that Congress simply increase the clerical help provided existing representatives.[16]

Opponents of the Siegel bill also rebutted the claims that the United States House of Representatives was smaller in relation to population than European legislatures and that the enfranchisement of women made more congressmen necessary. James P. Glynn of Connecticut pointed out that many European legislators represented a landed aristocracy and not the people, and Representative Fairfield noted that the United States differed fundamentally from European nations because it had both state and national legislatures. Denying that the new women voters created a need for more representatives, a southern Democrat said that congressmen had guarded the rights of women before they received the vote just as carefully as the rights of voting men. Without mentioning disfranchised southern blacks, he further declared, "Representation is not legally or morally wrapped up in the question of voting population."[17]

To his colleagues worried about the declining rural power in the

House, Benjamin G. Humphreys (D.-Miss.) replied that the "representation of the cities will be increased whether we have 435 or 483, and Congress could not prevent it if we so desired." Others agreed that the size of the House would not affect the relative strength of urban and rural areas. As Eugene Black of Texas commented, Siegel's bill would save one seat for Mississippi by awarding four additional representatives to Siegel's New York. But Black went even further by suggesting that "it is erroneous to refer to hardly any one of our States as an industrial State and to another as an agricultural State"; New York and Illinois contained large urban populations, he conceded, yet they also ranked high in agricultural production. The cities in New York and Illinois did, however, elect "urban" representatives whom the rural congressmen had disparaged. A Chicago Republican rose in the House to defend himself and other urbanites against the charge that rural representatives were somehow superior. "I deny," Martin B. Madden insisted, "that the representation from the cities in this House is not as able or as patriotic as that which comes from the rural districts." The quality of representation would not be damaged by a reapportionment that necessarily reflected the population shift toward cities as shown by the census.[18]

Finally, several congressmen alleged that only self-interest, state pride, and personal friendship prompted many of their colleagues to support the Siegel bill. If the House did not expand, some states would surely lose one or more seats as a result of reapportionment, and many individual representatives would have to run in new districts. In addition, state pride might be injured by the reduction of a state's delegation. To avoid such inconvenience and embarrassment, the House could simply expand so that no district would be lost. "That legislation, however, should be based upon such consideration is not at all in keeping with the responsibility that rests upon Congress," declared Fairfield. "The fortunes of any one man in political life are not important enough to justify legislation having such far-reaching consequences upon the country."[19] Arguments against self-interest probably convinced few House members to change their votes, but the discussion undoubtedly struck at a key factor in the reapportionment battle.

After two days of stormy debate, the House on January 19, 1921, finally voted on reapportionment. First, it overwhelmingly rejected two amendments to the Siegel bill. An Iowa Republican proposed a compromise to enlarge the House to only 460, but he could muster few votes in support. Next, in the opposite direction, Marvin Jones tried with even less success to revive a fellow Texan's idea to cut the House to around 300 members. Finally, the House considered an amendment offered by Representative Barbour to retain the existing number of congressmen. By a margin of 279 to 76, the House ignored the advice of its Census Committee and the pleas of some rural representatives and approved the Barbour amendment.[20] The House then sent the reapportionment bill to the Senate.

The *New York Times* applauded the House's decision to remain at 435 members as "well judged and sensible." It contended that enlarging the House would not provide an advantage to any state, would not benefit the nation, would not produce better legislation, and would not add to the House's wisdom. In addition, it believed a larger House would probably be more disorderly and inefficient. Indicating widespread agreement with the *Times*, the *Literary Digest* declared that "every journal that has come to our attention" endorsed the House's vote. The *Baltimore American*, the *Dayton Journal*, the *Omaha World-Herald*, and the *Seattle Times*, among many, endorsed retention of 435 members for the House.[21] In its survey, however, the *Literary Digest* relied almost exclusively on the editorial opinions of urban newspapers.

The Senate failed to act on the House reapportionment bill before the end of the Sixty-ninth Congress. Howard Sutherland (R.-W.Va.), chairman of the Senate Census Committee, claimed to be unaware of any interest in the Senate to change the size of the House, yet he failed to secure passage of the bill. The Senate Census Committee did not even hold hearings on the bill in the six weeks between the House action and expiration of Congress in March 1921. According to the *New York Times*'s reports, however, some senators worked to block consideration and passage of the bill because their states would lose seats in a new House limited to 435 members. In any event, the reapportionment bill died in the Senate committee. Before the close of the Congress, the Senate Census Committee did take one significant action: it requested that a joint committee from the American Statistical Association and the American Economic Association study the various possible methods for reapportioning House seats and report its findings back to the Senate committee.[22]

The mathematical procedure to be used in reapportioning the

House had long been a subject of debate, and it reappeared in December 1920. In an address to the American Mathematical Society, Edward V. Huntington of Harvard University first proposed a new "method of equal proportions." The professor of mechanics and former president of the society claimed that his new technique would avoid the inequities he found in earlier methods, especially in the method of major fractions developed by Professor Walter F. Willcox, used in the 1911 reapportionment, and included in the Siegel bill.[23]

Huntington's challenge to Willcox set off a momentous clash among scholars in the 1920s. Educated at Amherst and Columbia, Willcox had been teaching philosophy, economics, and statistics at Cornell since 1891. As an early social scientist, he emphasized the practical application of statistics to specific problems. After the Spanish-American War, he had worked for the War Department on censuses from 1899 to 1901. He was the first to study seriously the statistical problems of reapportionment and in 1910 devised the method of major fractions. His professional accomplishments brought him the presidencies of the American Statistical Association in 1912 and the American Economic Association in 1915.[24] In the 1920s, therefore, he constituted a formidable foe for Huntington.

Huntington was thirteen years younger than Willcox and had been educated at Harvard and the University of Strasbourg and began his teaching career at Harvard in 1901. He worked in Washington during World War I as a statistician with the Census Bureau, where he became reacquainted with his old Harvard classmate Joseph A. Hill, a bureau statistician. In Washington, Huntington learned of Hill's criticisms of the method of major fractions; Hill thought the relative difference between the ratios of representatives per unit of population should be held to a minimum, not the absolute difference as the 1911 law had provided. When Hill's procedure for achieving his desired solution failed to provide consistently satisfactory results, Huntington discovered the flaws and corrected them and then proposed the refined version as his own method of equal proportions. The Harvard professor's humor, friendliness, and personal courtesy made him an effective advocate for his plan during the 1920s.[25]

Professor Huntington based his method of equal proportions on a key distinction regarding inequality. "There are," he claimed, "two measures of inequality in common use: (1) the *absolute difference* . . . (2) the *percentage difference*. . . . Since we are dealing here with

TABLE 3.1. Absolute Difference versus Percentage Difference

State	Population	Quota	Method I		Method II	
			No.	Reps./million	No.	Reps./million
New York	10,380,589	42.919	42	4.046	43	4.142
New Mexico	353,428	1.461	2	5.659	1	2.829
		absolute difference		1.613		1.313
		percentage difference		71.49		68.30

proportions rather than with absolute numbers, we shall adopt the second of these interpretations. . . . *By the inequality between two quantities, we shall mean their percentage difference.*" Two examples illustrate the principle stressed by Huntington and its effects on reapportionment. First, comparing two sets of numbers will show the basic differences. Between 3 and 5 the absolute difference is only 2, whereas between 45 and 50 it is 5. In percentage difference, however, 45 is closer (90 percent) to 50 than 3 is to 5 (only 60 percent). Second, an example from 1920 will demonstrate the importance of the differences in distributing seats in the House of Representatives (see Table 3.1).

Two methods for apportioning 435 representatives are shown. Under each, New York should receive 42.919 and New Mexico 1.416, but partial seats are impossible so the task is to come as close to the quota as possible. Under Method I, New York would receive 42 seats and New Mexico 2; in the other New York would be awarded 43 and New Mexico only 1. To determine the fairer method, either absolute or percentage difference could be used. The absolute differences were 1.613 representatives per million population (5.659 − 4.046) and 1.313 (4.142 − 2.829), so the fairer method using absolute differences would have been Method II. If percentage differences were stressed, the result would have favored Method I: 4.046 is 71.49 percent of 5.659, whereas 2.829 is only 68.30 percent of 4.142, so Method I produced more nearly equal ratios than did Method II. Professor Huntington believed his method of equal proportions, which emphasized percentage differences, would produce the fairest apportionment, and he made his ideas known in letters to Representative Siegel and the *New York Times*, in scholarly articles in 1921, and in his speech to the American Mathematical Society.[26]

After a request from Congress to settle the dispute over methods, the American Statistical Association and the American Economic Association's Joint Committee to Advise the Census Director examined the proposals and reported to the Senate Committee on the Census. Although Professor Willcox was a member of the committee but did not join the report, the committee endorsed Huntington's method of equal proportions as "logically superior" to Willcox's method of major fractions and superior also according to "purely technical criteria." The committee pointed out that apportionment involved ratios or proportions and agreed with Huntington that relative nearness took precedence over absolute nearness. It declared that "when the 'nearness' of ratios is measured on a relative scale, the results do not depend upon the particular form of the fractions by means of which the ratios are expressed." Although granting that the method of major fractions had the support of precedent, the committee nevertheless announced in December 1921 its preference for Huntington's new method.[27] Its verdict settled the technical battle only temporarily, for it reemerged later in the decade.

While the committee considered the technical aspects of reapportionment, politicians in 1921 continued their more practical debate. Opponents and proponents of a larger House of Representatives repeated many of their earlier arguments and added a few new twists during the House Census Committee hearings in the summer of 1921. Larsen of Georgia, an opponent of expanding the House, noted that in a reapportioned 435-member body neither New York nor Pennsylvania would gain seats, even though advocates of a larger House claimed that urban industrial states would increase their power unless the House grew. Also denying the need to add seats, Senator Theodore E. Burton (R.-Ohio) insisted in testimony before the committee that Congress had a constitutional obligation to enact reapportionment promptly. Supporters of a larger House seemed to sense that seats would not be added so they began to argue that the House should not be reapportioned. One Kansan, who even favored a House of up to a thousand members, claimed that the Constitution did not require a reapportionment every ten years and, therefore, Congress need not reapportion the House based on the 1920 census. Ira G. Hersey of Maine favored postponing reapportionment and suggested that a delay would be "simply a silent consent of Congress that they are satisfied with the present apportionment." Arguments for deferring reapportionment included contentions that the census had been "not correct," that "the country is too unsettled," that reapportionment would cause "endless trouble and expense," and that state legislatures would encounter "considerable trouble and inconvenience" in rearranging congressional districts before the 1922 elections.[28]

After three days of hearings in June 1921, the House Census Committee deadlocked on reporting a reapportionment bill to the full House. Half of the committee wanted to enlarge the House, while the other half sought to maintain the size at 435. To break the impasse and report a bill for House debate, two members of the committee who actually opposed expanding the House switched in July to support the new Siegel bill to set the House at 460 members. Under the bill reported by the committee, nine states were to gain one seat, four were to add two seats, three new representatives were to go to Michigan and Ohio, and California's delegation was to grow by four. Only Maine and Missouri were to lose one congressman each. Fortunately, at the 460 level the Willcox and Huntington methods for allocating seats agreed exactly, and a dispute over statistical techniques was avoided. The committe minority persisted in viewing any increase as unnecessary, unjustified, unpopular, inefficient, and wasteful.[29]

The House Republican caucus in the fall of 1921 endorsed the Siegel bill for a 460-member House but only after what the *New York Times* termed "vigorous opposition." More than 100 Republican representatives missed their conference, so the 94 to 76 vote for the Siegel bill did not guarantee overwhelming support for expanding the House, and a number of Republicans agreed with a minority of the Census Committee on the errors of expansion.[30] Nevertheless, the GOP caucus's stand affected the positions of some loyal Republican congressmen and augured well for eventual passage of the Siegel bill.

When the whole House considered the Siegel bill, the New Yorker himself led the supporters. He argued that the additional demands of the new veterans (averaging eleven thousand per district) and of new women voters required a larger House. In addition, Siegel said the growing number of controversial issues facing Congress and the lengthening sessions necessitated more members. To critics who charged that the expansion would be too costly, he simply pointed out that one additional secretary for each of the 435 members would cost half a million dollars but the total expenditures for 25 more representatives would amount to only $287,000. After his brief opening statement, Siegel yielded ten minutes to Representative Tinkham of Massachusetts, who brought up the explosive issue of enforcing the Fourteenth Amendment.[31]

The maverick heir to the abolitionist tradition opposed the "unconstitutional, unlawful, and unjust" Siegel bill because it "profoundly and fatally nullified the Constitution in one of its great and vital parts." The bill ignored the Fourteenth Amendment's requirement to reduce a state's representation in proportion to its disfranchisement of voters. "Franchise equality is fundamental and profound," Tinkham argued passionately, and "national elections can no longer be half constitutional and half unconstitutional. There can be no double standard of constitutional enforcement." Tinkham proposed an amendment to the Siegel bill to reduce representation in accordance with disfranchisement by poll taxes, property requirements, and literacy tests as determined by the Census Bureau. (He acknowledged a lack of evidence on disfranchisement through fraud, violence, and intimidation.) His amendment called for eleven southern states to lose a total of twenty-eight seats. Only Representative Wells Goodykoontz of West Virginia came to Tinkham's support by providing evidence of Negro disfranchisement. He pointed out that in November 1920 in his district 85,587 votes were cast yet at the same time only 67,737 South Carolinians elected seven congressmen and 70,657 Mississippians chose eight representatives. He too objected to this "discrimination and disfranchisement" and called for enforcement of the Fourteenth Amendment.[32]

Mississippi's John E. Rankin rebutted Tinkham. First, he claimed that the Fifteenth Amendment had by implication voided the part of the Fourteenth Amendment relied on by Tinkham because the Fifteenth specifically prohibited any denial of voting because of race or color. The provision for reducing representation had been in effect, according to Rankin, only until enactment of the Fifteenth Amendment. Although apparently suggesting that Tinkham should rely on the Fifteenth Amendment instead, Rankin did not call for strict enforcement of it. Second, Rankin confidently disparaged Tinkham's effort because "the time has passed when a man or a party can successfully make political capital by holding out to the Negro the hope or promise of social or political equality." Armed with the vote, the "white women of America are going to protect themselves at the ballot box against those irresponsible individuals who are willing to sacrifice them and their children by pandering to the baser passions of an inferior race."³³

The House easily rejected Tinkham's amendment, but other representatives raised objections that posed greater threats to the Siegel bill. Georgia's William Larsen led off the opposition by charging that the proposed increase would "lessen responsibility, destroy efficiency, and render the House unwieldy and its members abject tools in the hands of the chairmen and committees." Applause punctuated his remarks. Another representative agreed and suggested that more members would only "magnify and intensify" the institution's evils. After reminding his colleagues that earlier expansions had been in response to the nation's territorial growth, Larsen noted that no similar physical growth had occurred since 1911. Furthermore, he contended, "Highway extensions, automobile development, and telegraph and telephone communications have more than compensated for any increase in population. The mimeograph, the multigraph, and other labor-saving devices have all greatly multiplied our capacity for labor and communication" so no new members were needed.³⁴

On the sensitive topic of rural power in Congress, Larsen challenged his fellow rural legislators to explain to their constituents how they could protect agricultural interests by enlarging the House and giving two new seats each to urban industrial New York and Pennsylvania, as the Siegel bill provided. Texan Thomas L. Blanton, who favored reducing the House to 304 members, declared that even in his state the "big cities gobble up the new Members" under the Siegel bill, not the agricultural districts. Trying to assuage rural worries, a Cleveland congressman who opposed enlargement of the House as unnecessary observed that the "proportion will continue the same between country and city, whatever the reapportionment," and that the cities would more likely gain under the plan for 460 than would the rural areas. Such distinctions made little sense to Eugene Black of rural Clarksville, Texas, who thought it "hardly proper to refer to any of our States as agricultural States or manufacturing States." He said matter-of-factly that urban areas would gain because they had grown in population and the only solution would be a constitutional amendment to provide rural areas greater representation, but Black did not endorse such a move.³⁵

Congressmen differed, however, over the proper course to protect rural interests. In his maiden House speech, Cyrenus Cole of

Cedar Rapids, Iowa, revived the argument that the 1920 census came when rural areas had been depleted by wartime mobilization and so it did not accurately measure the rural population. To avoid penalizing agricultural areas, Cole supported the Siegel bill because it "at least does not deprive the great agricultural states of any part of their representation," which he considered "vital to the Nation." He passionately declared, "A home on the farm stands for something more than a tenement in a city. From the time when the poet's embattled farmers fired the first shot heard round the world the toilers of the land have been a large part of the safety and security of American institutions." To protect the nation, therefore, the rural representation must not be diminished, according to the Iowan. Congressmen from Louisiana, Illinois, and other states agreed, but rural representatives could not reach a consensus on the Siegel bill.[36] They agreed on the necessity of protecting the agricultural interests but not on how to do it.

The issue of urban-rural strength in the House was certainly controversial in the debate over the Siegel bill, but perhaps just as heated were charges that congressmen really sought only to protect their own self-interest. Maine Republican Carroll L. Beedy, a member of the Census Committee, accused the committee members of having abandoned principle in favor of protecting their own seats. Beedy opposed the Siegel bill and questioned, "By what process of ratiocination did the committee conclude to increase the membership of the House but to put the brakes at 460?" He explained that the committee contained two powerful congressmen from Kentucky and Iowa —John W. Langley, an eight-term veteran from Pikeville, Kentucky, who chaired the House Committee on Public Buildings and Grounds, and Iowa's Horace M. Towner, who headed its Committee on Insular Affairs. Beedy suggested that Langley "long since discovered that a House of 459 would save Kentucky a Congressman" and that Towner similarly knew that "a House of 460 would save Iowa a Congressman." A deal resulted. Beedy believed that the Siegel bill, "conceived in a spirit of petty politics and wrapped about with a cloak of party service, is dedicated to the proposition that else we save a Congressman for both Kentucky and Iowa our great party and the Nation itself is eternally damned." The House responded to Beedy's charges with "prolonged applause." In reply, however, Langley pointed out that the entire Maine delegation had in the previous Congress supported a

483-member House and suggested that, if the Siegel bill "carried 483, so as to save Maine from losing a Member, the gentleman from Maine [Mr. Beedy] would join readily and gladly the compact to which he had just referred." A colleague from Wisconsin retorted that representatives from several states, threatened with a loss of seats, not just Maine or Iowa or Kentucky, voted in their own self-interest and appealed to "fellow Members for sympathy and aid."[37] The debate, of course, failed to resolve the issue of self-interest, but it did succeed in bringing it into the open.

After nearly nine hours of wrangling and debating, the House neared a vote on the Siegel bill. Before deciding on a House of 460 members, it confronted an amendment offered by Henry Barbour to change the proposal to the current 435 level. William Vaile of Denver objected to Barbour's proposal and in doing so briefly discussed another difficult and controversial aspect of reapportionment. The Colorado Republican argued that a reapportioned House of 435 members would increase the representation from "districts of largely foreign make-up" and decrease it from districts of "more distinctly American population." Acknowledging that the Constitution called for allotting representatives by population and not citizens, Vaile suggested that circumstances had changed. At the Constitutional Convention and at the time of the Fourteenth Amendment, the unnaturalized aliens in the nation "had not become sufficiently noticeable to be recognized as a danger or an evil." In 1921 the eight states to lose seats under Barbour's amendment had a foreign-born population of only 5.9 percent, whereas the other thirty-eight states had a foreign-born population of nearly 15 percent. The eight losing states, moreover, were primarily agricultural and assimilated the aliens more quickly than the urban areas, where they often formed segregated ethnic communities. More specifically, Vaile compared several Kansas and New York congressional districts. He pointed out that the total votes in the last congressional election in three New York City districts totaled only 37,690, 18,866, and 13,904, and yet nearly 82,000 voted in one Kansas district; the difference resulted not from smaller populations in the New York districts but from majorities in them of unnaturalized aliens ineligible to vote. According to Vaile, the "alien elements will control the election of their Congressmen even if they do not vote. They will control it through the corner grocer, the tradesmen, the members of their families who are voters, through the entire sentiment of the community."[38] Coming at the close of the debate, Vaile's charges sparked little comment, though they did strike at a sensitive issue separating rural and urban representatives.

The House defeated Barbour's amendment and then easily disposed of yet another amendment dealing with at-large elections. Instead of voting directly on Siegel's bill, however, the entire House voted on a motion by Louis W. Fairfield to recommit the bill to the Census Committee. As a member of the committee, the Indiana Republican had opposed increasing the House to 460, and now he tried to defeat the Siegel bill, or at least delay enlarging the House, by sending the bill back to the committee. By the narrow margin of 146 to 142, with 3 voting present and 140 not voting, the House approved Fairfield's motion and recommitted the bill.[39]

Rejection of the Siegel bill ended a major phase in the struggle over reapportionment in the 1920s. In the three previous reapportionments, Congress had passed legislation within nine months of receiving the new census data, but by October 1921 nearly a year had passed without any significant progress. The defeat of the Siegel bill resulted from deep divisions within Congress. The lack of consensus reflected the general divisions in Congress that made any action difficult. As one historian concluded, the Sixty-seventh "Congress was still smarting from the bitterness of the League [of Nations] fight, and many members, Republicans and Democrats alike, had been so poisoned by that experience that they remained unable to cooperate on virtually any issue." The formation of many "greedy," "aggressive," and "ruthless" blocs further factionalized Congress. In considering reapportionment of the House, representatives could not agree, for instance, on the accuracy of the 1920 census, on the importance of rural representation, on the most efficient size for the House, on whether to consider aliens and disfranchised blacks, or on the statistical method to be used. The effort to reapportion the House seemed hopeless in the fall of 1921.[40]

1921–1926

During the second phase of the reapportionment controversy, from October 1921 through most of 1925, Congress took no action on reapportionment. Numerous important and controversial issues confronting Congress in the early and middle 1920s exacerbated legislative disharmony and contributed to the continuing neglect of reapportionment. In domestic affairs, the problems included reform of the tariff, immigration restriction, tax revision, farm credit needs, and a bonus for soldiers. Postwar international concerns involved treaties with the nation's former enemies, disarmament, and membership in the League of Nations. Presidential leadership failed to help overcome congressional difficulties because President Warren Harding, according to his chief historian, "viewed the presidency as primarily a ceremonial office" and "possessed neither the desire nor the ability to lead Congress."[41]

Under the chairmanship of Charles L. Faust of Missouri, the House Census Committee held no hearings and reported no bills to the whole House. Since his state of Missouri was expected to lose seats under most plans to reapportion the House, the chairman undoubtedly had little interest in pushing for reapportionment. The Senate, meanwhile, followed custom and waited for the House to act. Some legislators nevertheless did continue to propose reapportionment bills. A Georgia congressman suggested eliminating aliens from the allocation of representatives and awarding seats based only on citizenship. Others wanted to reduce the House to 304, 250, or even 217 members, and one senator proposed guaranteeing each state two representatives instead of just one. Tinkham of Massachusetts continued to press for a new census to measure the "scandalous" disfranchisement of Negroes. Objecting to "defiance and nullification of the Constitution," he considered recent elections "unconstitutional." Each proposal died in committee.[42]

In March 1924, the Census Committee's decision to drop all reapportionment plans angered some urban representatives. Henry E. Barbour, a member of the committee, believed the failure to reapportion struck "at the very foundation of our form of government" because some states had more or fewer representatives than their populations entitled them. As examples he cited California, Iowa, and Kentucky, each of which had eleven representatives, though his state of California had more than 1 million more residents than either of the other two. California actually had a larger population than Missouri but five fewer seats in the House. Deeming the present arrangement unfair and unjust, Barbour claimed that only local self-interest prevented reapportionment and called on the House to discharge the Census Committee if it failed to report a bill. Thirteen weeks later, Detroit's Clarence J. McLeod revived the attack on the House's inaction. He labeled it "the grossest disfranchisement" and "a national disgrace" and warned that congressional and presidential elections might be challenged as unconstitutional and void. His home city, he reminded the House, had only two congressmen for over 1 million residents while the nation averaged one per 243,013 inhabitants. In spite of the pleas of Barbour, McLeod, and others, however, nothing happened.[43]

A persistent Thomas L. Blanton from rapidly urbanizing Abilene took more direct action. A longtime advocate of a smaller House, Blanton offered an amendment to an appropriations bill to reduce the appropriation for Congress from $3.3 to $2.3 million and to reduce the membership from 435 to 304. Representatives from states losing seats would draw lots to see who kept them in the reapportioned House, and they would include Blanton because Texas would lose five seats. The presiding chair of the House ruled his maneuver out of order so it failed.[44] His effort demonstrated nonetheless the frustration felt by some representatives with the delay in reapportionment.

If some congressmen grew increasingly annoyed and irritated with the lack of reapportionment, the country seemed unperturbed. Congress avoided the question, and the nation's press ignored it. The press had spoken out during the initial activity in 1920–21, but after the congressional debate dissipated the press also lost interest. The *New York Times* in 1923 declared that the House was too big already and that a larger House would only increase, perhaps unwisely, the power of the cities. Representatives from the towns and cities controlled the House anyway, according to the *Times*, and it asked, "Why should there be any change?"[45] The *Times*'s lack of interest apparently reflected the sentiment of much of the nation. Few Americans seemed bothered that, in an unprecedented stalemate, three years had passed since the Congress had taken any significant action on reapportionment. Some members of the House of Representatives, however, refused to give up on a reapportionment based on the 1920 census.

1926–1927

The third phase of the battle over reapportionment occurred during the sixty-ninth session of Congress (1925–27). Although the Census Committee refused to budge, Representatives Clarence McLeod, Hart Fenn (R.-Conn.), and Henry Barbour waged valiant, though losing, fights to force the House to deal with reapportionment. As the deadlock over reapportionment continued, many of the old arguments over statistical procedures, aliens, rural representation, and the best size for the House resurfaced. All efforts in the Sixty-ninth Congress, however, failed.

As the Sixty-ninth Congress opened in December 1925, Detroit's McLeod called on President Calvin Coolidge to seek his support for a reapportionment at the 435 level, under which eight states would gain seats and eleven would lose them. He came away from the White House expecting Coolidge to support the scheme, but the president exerted little effort in its behalf or for any other plan for reapportionment. McLeod still hoped that the Census Committee, on which he was second-ranking member, would finally act.[46]

During the Sixty-ninth Congress, Hart Fenn of Connecticut, which expected to gain under a reapportionment, chaired the Census Committee and spurred it into action. For the first time in nearly five years, the Census Committee in February and March of 1926 held hearings on a variety of reapportionment proposals. In addition to bills by Barbour, McLeod, and Blanton, the committee considered a new proposal from Representative Roy G. Fitzgerald (R.-Ohio). Without taking sides in the argument over the size of the House, Fitzgerald suggested delegating the power to reapportion the House to the president or, if he failed to notify the states within fifteen days of the census report, to the clerk of the House. According to the Fitzgerald plan, Congress would continue to set the number of seats in the House but delegate only the administrative responsibility for reapportionment. He believed such a move would "destroy this ugly feeling, this contentiousness, and this danger of the subversion of representative government" by removing the "temptation" of losing states to block reapportionment. If enacted into law, his idea would be subject to court review, and the judiciary would offer protection because it, Fitzgerald thought, "will not enforce a fraud." Some members of the Census Committee found Fitzgerald's proposal troubling.

Mississippi's Rankin called it "dynamite to the Constitution," and Meyer Jacobstein of New York thought it put too much power in the presidency and threatened to make reapportionment an even more partisan issue. Though the committee refused to endorse the idea of delegating the power to reapportion, it did for the first time consider the important option that could prevent obstruction of future reapportionments.[47]

Old arguments about the census and reapportionment resurfaced during the hearings as opponents of reapportionment once again fought all proposals. Defending his state's imperiled representation, Ralph F. Lozier (D.-Mo.) called the 1920 census "viciously inaccurate, unreliable, and unfair." Edward R. Voigt (R.-Wisc.) claimed that an "abnormal distribution" of population had existed at the time of the 1920 census, and he believed the urban migration was slowing and would stop within six months. "I look for a remigration to the farm," he predicted. Kansas's Hays B. White generally agreed. When a New York City congressman asked if the 1930 census would not show even more movement to cities, White referred to the notion as "a little terror for the future" and refused to "seriously entertain that fear at all." Critical of the 1920 census, one representative even asked for a special census in 1927 solely for reapportionment purposes.[48]

Missouri's Lozier hit especially hard at suggestions that the House be reduced in size. In the larger districts required by a smaller House, rural areas would, according to Lozier, be merely "tails to the big cities." Using his own state as an example, he said that in fewer but more populous districts St. Louis and Kansas City would have "a preeminent power and influence which would absolutely dominate the agricultural groups."[49] For many representatives, reapportionment still meant less power for rural areas and greater power for urban areas. It boiled down to a conflict of urban versus rural interests.

Early in the spring of 1926, the Census Committee voted nine to four to table all four reapportionment bills before it. In addition to rural opponents, the *New York Times* found that conservative Republicans thought reapportionment was unnecessary and a larger House would be unwieldy, that other Republicans believed reapportionment would strengthen existing "blocs" in the House, and that some Democrats worried that reapportionment would benefit the Republicans in the Northeast.[50]

A few days after the committee's decision, a frustrated Henry Barbour attempted to force the House to consider reapportionment. Though no longer a member of the Census Committee, he offered as a constitutional privilege under the House rules a motion to discharge from the committee his reapportionment bill, which duplicated his proposal passed by the House in 1921. Claiming that the Constitution required reapportionment every ten years, Barbour condemned the apparent acceptance of the idea that "a committee of Congress is more powerful than the Constitution of the United States." The Republican leadership disagreed. Bertrand H. Snell of New York, chairman of the Rules Committee, denied that reapportionment qualified for consideration as a matter of constitutional privilege; he said, "There is no mandatory provision in the Constitution itself which provides for immediate reapportionment," though it did require a decennial census. The Republican majority leader agreed with Snell. Speaker of the House Nicholas Longworth, however, though admitting that House precedents upheld Barbour's right to offer his motion as a constitutional privilege, thought it was the wrong action for the House to take. Caught in a bind, he refused to rule on the question and instead referred it to the House for a vote. Barbour lost 87 to 265, and efforts at reapportionment failed once again.[51]

For the first time the delay in reapportioning the House caused a public clamor in the spring and summer of 1926, especially in urban areas. The *New York Times* expressed disappointment that the House disregarded 130 years of precedent in rejecting Barbour's motion and feared that "personal and partisan interests, and not constitutional scruples," blocked the equitable distribution of seats in the House. It urged Congress to act positively on reapportionment. "Tyranny in the Raw," trumpeted the *Chicago Daily News* after the House action. The *New York Evening Post* thought the House had defied the Constitution, and the *Raleigh News and Observer* considered the House's decision "unconstitutional and dishonest." A *Literary Digest* survey of press opinion found "no outburst of praise" but rather "a great volume of criticism" of the House's failure to reapportion itself. It quoted the *Detroit Free Press*: "There are honest members in the body, but as a whole it stands foresworn and unfaithful to its trust, a sad spectacle of moral weakness and ethical degeneracy." The *Literary Digest* argued that the spirit of the Constitution required reapportionment every ten years even if technically the Constitution did not.[52]

The *New Republic* led the periodical press's criticism of Congress. Calling the delay in reapportionment "deplorable," it charged that representatives from states with declining populations blocked reapportionment. "Rarely has the well known lust for power of the legislator been more strikingly—or reprehensibly—exhibited," declared an editorial. More specifically, the journal recognized that the effect of Congress's "disregard of the Constitution" had been "an overbalancing of country against city representation." Though the lack of reapportionment called into question legislation passed by a malapportioned House, the *New Republic* knew of no solution to the impasse except a reprimand by the voters in the next election because no other part of the government could compel Congress to act on reapportionment.[53]

An article by Ray T. Tucker of the *New York Evening Post* continued the *New Republic's* attack on Congress. The Washington correspondent observed that "our Congressmen are in a state of political terror" over reapportionment. In the debate and maneuvers, he saw "cowardice, hypocrisy, and complacency" in the nation's leaders. He believed that any child could see the inequities in Missouri's eighth district having 138,000 inhabitants while two Detroit districts had over one-half million apiece and Los Angeles had about 1.2 million, but "fear, distrust, selfishness, suspicion and pettiness" had prevented congressional action. Finally, Representative Barbour "rattled the skeletons and rent the shrouds," according to Tucker, because the Census Committee chairman came from the "rotten borough" of Connecticut and most of the committee opposed reapportionment for self-interested reasons. Moreover, the House majority leader also hailed from Connecticut, and the chairman of the Rules Committee came from a district with only 207,000 people. In the reapportionment fight, Tucker claimed, the "Constitution did not enter their heads; it was their own political skins they were thinking of most."[54]

Pettiness and self-interest, however, took many forms. According to Tucker, even representatives from states that would not lose seats might oppose reapportionment because the opposing party controlled their state legislature and might harm them in any reapportionment. Furthermore, reapportionment to correct urban-rural imbalance at the national level might spur similar state action in "states continually engaged in a city-country tug-of-war for control of the legislature"; congressmen from areas that would lose in the state battles might, therefore, vote against national reapportionment even though their own Washington seats were safe. Tucker also tied urban-rural disagreement over reapportionment to other contemporary issues that might be affected by changes in congressional strength. Under any reasonable reapportionment, urban areas known for opposing Prohibition would gain power so proponents of the Eighteenth Amendment hoped to protect it by blocking reapportionment. Similarly, according to Tucker, the farm bloc viewed reapportionment as a threat to its influence over agricultural policy.[55]

Tucker's emphasis on urban-rural conflict received confirmation from another Washington observer, Robert B. Smith of the *Philadelphia Public Ledger*. He argued that "subterranean cross currents of opposition" involving Prohibition and the Ku Klux Klan worked to prevent any reapportionment. In analyzing the failure to reapportion, Smith concluded, "The unwillingness of the rural sections to give up any of their power to the cities perhaps plays the most important part." He pointed out that "the rural sections are now in control," but reapportionment would put "the cities in control." Smith did not expect any reapportionment soon, and he worried that the urban-rural imbalance would only worsen and thereby increase opposition to a redistribution of power in the House. Inaction on reapportionment, according to Smith, "stands as a menace to the doctrine of representative government."[56]

In July 1926, the *Nation* agreed with a recent NAACP conference that Negroes were being disfranchised in violation of the Constitution but added its concern about the "virtual disfranchisement of millions of other voters by the rotten borough system" in the present Congress. The disfranchisement of city voters combined with the denial of the vote to southern blacks meant that in 1924 Los Angeles counted more votes for president than did Alabama, Georgia, and Mississippi combined, yet Los Angeles had only two representatives while the three southern states sent thirty representatives to Congress. The *Nation* concluded, "The Southern States are cheating."[57]

Another analysis of the reapportionment impasse came from historian Frederick L. Paxson. By the summer of 1926 he had concluded that it was "probable" that reapportionment would occur only after the 1930 census. Paxson pointed out that the Constitution contained "no explicit command" to reapportion the House of Representatives every ten years and provided no way to force the Congress to do anything except indirectly by electing "Representatives whose conscience and character are so good that they will do their honest duty even when it hurts." To explain congressional inaction, Paxson sensibly pointed out that representatives "are human, and have their share of selfishness, jealousy, and fear." Some states' reluctance to lose seats caused their representatives to oppose reapportionment. Moreover, some states especially feared losing power in Congress and in the electoral college to the Northeast and California or to urban states generally. Although Paxson disliked the resulting "misrepresentation," he noted that it resembled the situation in most states, where cities lacked fair representation in legislatures dominated by rural interests.[58]

In spite of the outcry over the delay in reapportionment, prospects for action remained slight. The Republican leader of the House, Connecticut's John Tilson, expected the House to postpone action on reapportionment until the Seventieth Congress, which would begin in December 1927. Advocates of reapportionment received no support from President Calvin Coolidge. In response to an appeal from Clarence J. McLeod, Coolidge refused to intervene in the reapportionment fight. Considering it a legislative matter, the president followed his practice of remaining aloof from affairs on Capitol Hill. He said only that he would not oppose the Republican congressional leaders who opposed reapportionment.[59]

When Congress convened in December 1926, Representative Hart Fenn pushed for a reapportionment bill. Fenn, chairman of the Committee on the Census, proposed a bill that would authorize the secretary of commerce to use the method of equal proportions to apportion 435 seats in the House immediately after the 1930 census. For six days in January and February, his committee held hearings on his reapportionment bill. Fenn had to defend the "novel feature" of his bill that would delegate to the secretary of commerce the responsibility for apportionment; he argued that the Constitution did not prohibit such a delegation and that precedents existed. For support he referred to the Legislative Reference Service's report that cited the 1850 authorization of the secretary of the interior to apportion seats based on the census and included numerous court decisions upholding similar delegations of power.[60]

During the committee's hearings in the winter of 1927, controversy focused on the statistical method to be used in reapportionment, not on the Fenn bill's delegation of responsibility for reapportionment or its anticipation of the 1930 census. Instead, for the first time the Census Committee confronted the statistical controversy that had emerged in 1920. Joseph A. Hill, assistant to the director of the Bureau of the Census, testified that he had "reached very definite conclusions on this question" and that he favored the method of equal proportions. Hill acknowledged that the method of major fractions had "the merit of greater simplicity" as well as popular appeal, but he thought it failed the key test of producing ratios of representation as nearly uniform as possible. He presented to the committee the application of each method to the Census Bureau's projection of the nation's population in 1930. The only serious objections to Hill's testimony came from representatives from states expected to lose seats. Representative Rankin of Mississippi claimed that Hill's figures did not reflect his state's growing population. Missouri's Lozier opposed both methods and instead proposed returning to "a hard and inflexible basis of representation" of one congressman for each set number of people; his suggestion would break the "straight-jacket" limitation of 435 seats and allow Missouri to retain its seats in an expanding House.[61]

On January 28, 1927, the central figures in the debate over the methods of reapportionment appeared before the Census Committee. Professor Walter F. Willcox came from Cornell to advocate the method of major fractions. Under questioning, he conceded that it gave "slightly more members to the large states than the method of equal proportions." Nevertheless, he favored the method of major fractions because it had in essence been used from 1850 to 1900, "it seems to hold the balance between the large State and the small State," and "it is much more intelligible." Harvard's Edward V. Huntington, of course, disagreed. "I am advocating an equal proportion method," he told the committee, "partly because I discovered it and partly because I think it is right." After the laughter subsided, he more seriously claimed that the method of equal proportions distributed seats among the states so equally that the shift of one seat from one state to another would not produce more equality of representation. The true measure of equality, according to Huntington, was the relative or percentage difference in the ratios of representation, not the absolute difference as used in the method of major fractions. Willcox and Huntington agreed that, once Congress decided which method would be used, it did not matter who did the actual statistical calculations.[62]

In questioning Willcox, Huntington, and other witnesses, the committee repeatedly confronted the vexing problem of rural representation in the House. Elbert S. Brigham (R.-Vt.) testified that he worried about the "continuing disparity in representation between those two different opinions," the rural and the industrial. One committee member shared his concern. Lozier wanted to "reduce to a minimum the disparity between the representation of industrial classes and the agricultural classes" by maintaining the current level of rural representation and expanding the House to accommodate more industrial representation. Lloyd Thurston of Osceola, Iowa, explained directly why he, Lozier, Brigham, and others feared increased urban power: "When power becomes centered in Rome, when the urban population controlled, ultimately and rather rapidly, disintegration took place and to such an extent that the inevitable fall of the government resulted." By contrast, he said, "The holding of the power in the rural districts tends to solidarity of government and prevents that control by the city population, which, directing the course of government, inevitably causes its fall."[63]

John E. Rankin brought up two other issues related to the rural-urban question. First, he demonstrated that the statistical methods treated small (in Rankin's view, rural) states differently. In responding to his probing, Professor Willcox did concede that the method of major fractions favored the states with large populations and worked slightly against the interests of small states such as Mississippi. Second, Rankin suggested that counting aliens as part of the population upon which representation would be based would be questionable. Two Kansans on the committee spoke out even more strongly than Rankin. Hays B. White claimed that counting 1 million aliens who "are probably technically subject to deportation . . . might vitiate the morality of the apportionment." James George Strong declared, "It would be a great pity to transfer a representative of our form of Government from an American State like Iowa to one where so many do not speak the English language."[64]

Observers expected the committee to report the Fenn bill to the House, which would then approve it. While the committee hearings proceeded, the *New York Times* reported that Speaker Longworth, Republican Majority Leader Tilson, and Chairman Snell of the House

Rules Committee had agreed on GOP support for the Fenn bill. The *Times* further announced that Longworth and Tilson would meet with the Republicans on the Census Committee to map strategy because a party-line vote was expected with the Democrats opposing the bill. In spite of the Republican leaders' efforts, however, the Census Committee refused to approve the Fenn bill and made no recommendation regarding reapportionment.[65]

A frustrated Hart Fenn moved on March 2, 1927, for the House of Representatives to suspend its rules and pass his bill providing for the reapportionment of 435 seats by the secretary of commerce after the 1930 census. Opponents of reapportionment reiterated their belief that the 1920 census had been unfair and inaccurate, but they added some new objections to the Fenn bill. One member called it "ridiculous" and "revolutionary" in its delegation of power to the secretary of commerce, and another denied that one Congress had the "power to bind a future Congress in its action" as the Fenn bill did. Missouri's Lozier charged that the Fenn bill "will get us nowhere" and was "a mere gesture designed and intended to enable the Representatives from California and Michigan to save their faces." After a brief, forty-minute debate, the House refused on a vote of 183 to 197 to suspend its rules and consider the Fenn bill.[66] An unconcerned public little noticed the quiet death of reapportionment in the last days of the Sixty-ninth Congress.

In the third stage of the reapportionment fight, several new ingredients appeared. Taking the initiative themselves without deferring to the Census Committee, congressmen attempted to maneuver with the rules of the House to force their colleagues to vote on reapportionment bills. Perhaps most encouraging for proponents of reapportionment, the press began in 1926 to voice irritation with Congress's irresponsibility, but the press's interest was fleeting. More substantively, the House began to consider ways to avoid future deadlocks by delegating the power to reapportion to the executive branch of the government.

1928–1929

The last phase of the long reapportionment struggle began nine months later in December 1927, when the Seventieth Congress opened. If Congress did not promptly pass a reapportionment bill, one did at least become law by the summer of 1929. One key to passage of the 1929 law was the intervention for the first time of the Senate in pushing for reapportionment, and freshman senator Arthur Vandenberg played the central role. The successful effort also involved the innovative idea of basing a new reapportionment on the upcoming 1930 census and delegating some responsibility for reapportionment to the executive.

Immediately when the new Congress convened late in 1927, more than a dozen representatives introduced reapportionment bills. Fenn, Barbour, McLeod, and Blanton resubmitted their plans that the House had previously considered. Others included calls for the exclusion of aliens from the population used for reapportionment and for a House of 435 members until 1940, when it would shrink to 300. The indomitable George Tinkham also renewed his call for an investigation of disfranchisement of Negroes in the South. "By his disfranchisement and the nullification of the Constitution," Tinkham charged, "the great Northern and Western States with their immense centers of population are deprived of their legal representation."[67]

For four days in February 1928, the Census Committee once again held hearings on reapportionment bills. Chairman Fenn expressed his hope that the committee and Congress would approve a bill to "rectify the error" of previous Congresses and to eliminate the criticism of Congress for not reapportioning after the 1920 census. The major points of controversy during the hearings involved delegating authority for reapportionment to the executive branch, passing anticipatory legislation, and, once again, using a particular statistical method to apportion seats. Lloyd Thurston of Iowa joined Rankin in objecting to giving power over the membership of the House to the secretary of commerce or any other part of the executive branch, and Lozier claimed that, once Congress gave the executive that power, the president could prevent Congress from retaking the power by vetoing later reapportionment bills. Fenn and others pointed out that in 1850 Congress had passed a law giving just that authority to the secretary of the interior, and later the law had been easily changed without presidential interference. With some reluctance, the committee appeared ready to delegate the reapportionment power to the executive.[68]

Committee members disagreed more over the proposal in several bills to provide in advance for reapportionment based on the future

1930 census. Legislation that anticipated future events troubled some representatives. Again Rankin objected most strongly to the proposal, but Meyer Jacobstein of New York had a ready reply. Granting that under "ordinary circumstances" he too would oppose anticipatory legislation, the New York Democrat argued, "We are passing through a period when the distribution of population is changing rapidly, in favor of the city against the country or rural districts. In 40 years the ratio has been reversed. It is now 60 percent of the people in the cities and 40 percent in the country, and it used to be the other way. Population has shifted that way."

"Whenever reapportionment is faced with a shifting population," he continued,

> you get injustice, and you will have a failure of apportionment unless you have anticipatory legislation because people who have authority never willingly relinquish it. . . . I can see how rural districts of the United States, losing out in population, may still refuse to surrender the power and authority they now have as to representation in Congress. I am not accusing them of selfishness; it is the inherent nature of political divisions to retain their power, and we are passing through a period of evolution in this country. We are becoming an industrialized Nation. We are going to accentuate the fight between rural and city districts, if you do not provide by anticipatory legislation a reapportionment which naturally takes care of this.

Though Rankin and others remained unconvinced, the House committee generally accepted Jacobstein's explanation of the need for anticipatory legislation. Lozier and Florence P. Kahn referred to similar situations in their state legislatures for Illinois and California as proof that Jacobstein was correct.[69]

Less controversial, because it had been so thoroughly debated in the 1927 hearings, was the statistical method to be used in reapportionment. Joseph A. Hill of the Census Bureau once again testified in favor of the equal proportions method, and Professor Walter F. Willcox marshaled evidence for the method of major fractions. Unlike the previous year, when the method of equal proportions gained the committee's approval, in 1928 the committee for unknown reasons switched to the method of major fractions.[70]

Early in March the Census Committee voted ten to eight to approve a bill keeping the House at 435, providing for automatic reapportionment by the Census Bureau after the 1930 census, and employing the major fractions method of apportioning seats. Under the bill, according to estimates by the *New York Times*, California would gain six seats, Michigan four, Ohio three, New Jersey and Texas two each, and several other states one apiece. Missouri, however, would lose four seats; five states, including Mississippi, Iowa, and Indiana, would lose two each; and ten states would lose one each.[71]

The *New Republic* hailed the committee-approved bill as "on the whole as good a compromise as we have any right to expect." Calling its method of reapportionment "fair and nonpolitical," the liberal journal hoped that the bill would prevent future impasses, which it considered illegal. Similarly, the *Review of Reviews* seemed pleased that Congress might correct its past defiance and dereliction of its constitutional responsibility by enacting a reapportionment law. If reapportionment did not occur, it warned, "some litigant in a particular issue, apparently affected by a close Congressional vote, would have a strong argument before the courts to the effect that continued failure to make reapportionment was producing genuine grievances." Remembering the election of 1824, which was decided by the House of Representatives, it suggested that a future presidential election might also be challenged.[72] Public interest in reapportionment seemed to be building.

The Fenn bill's prospects improved in the spring when the House steering committee unanimously called on the Rules Committee to give preferential status to the reapportionment bill. Moreover, Speaker Longworth and Majority Leader Tilson also pushed the Fenn bill. The reapportionment proposal was, therefore, reported out and placed on the House calendar early in April, and six weeks later the House considered it.[73]

In two days of debate, the Fenn bill encountered strong opposition on the House floor. Critics resorted to repetition of their reasons for objecting to reapportionment based on the 1920 census as if the arguments applied to the Fenn bill. They insisted on waiting until after a fair and accurate enumeration in 1930 before acting on reapportionment (though Rankin still refused to grant that the Constitution mandated reapportionment every ten years). By voting for the anticipatory legislation, according to William C. Ramseyer of Iowa, the House would accuse itself of being "too cowardly to face the situation when the time comes" and would be admitting that "the next Congress will not have the intelligence, courage, and patriotism to make a wise reapportionment." Lozier attacked the "sanctity" of a House limited to 435 members as in the Fenn bill and suggested that the House would properly grow within fifty years to more than 1,000 members. More specific objections to the bill related to its delegation of power to the Commerce Department. William B. Bankhead (D.-Ala.) and Virgil Chapman (D.-Ky.) considered it an "abdication" of congressional responsibility. More intemperately, Lozier charged that the bill would further the campaign to make Congress "impotent" and "a mere puppet to register the will of the President and department heads." Others less concerned with constitutional questions simply considered the bill "foolish and useless" and "an idle legislative gesture," and Hersey of Maine thought the bill deceptively sought to counter the popular prejudice against Congress for not reapportioning the House after the 1920 census.[74]

Opponents of the Fenn bill picked up surprising support from Emanuel Celler of New York City. Claiming that the bill sought to "break the deadlock by subterfuge," he insisted that the "issue underlying the deadlock must be faced. . . . The issues and the struggle underlying reapportionment is between the large States with large cities on one side and the rural and agricultural States on the other side. That thread of controversy runs through all of the political struggles evidenced in this House. That thread runs through immigration, prohibition, income tax, tariff. It is the city versus the country. The issue grows more and more menacing. This issue, in so far as it concerns reapportionment, must be faced squarely. This bill seeks to evade it, to cover it up."[75]

Advocates of reapportionment under the Fenn bill recognized a slightly different "irrepressible conflict" between congressmen unwilling to enlarge the House and representatives from states that would lose seats if the body remained at 435 members. Supporters emphasized that the problem could only worsen after the 1930 census. New York's Jacobstein called it "a germ disease which becomes more and more malignant" because only eleven states would have lost seats based on the 1920 census but seventeen would probably lose after the 1930 count. Proponents of the Fenn bill admitted that it was only a "gesture" or a "formula" that would not bind future reapportionments. To critics concerned about the delegation of power, Michigan's Earl C. Michener merely mentioned the Tariff Commission, the

Interstate Commerce Commission, and the 1850 reapportionment act as precedents; and Jacobstein called the statistical process "simple, accurate, and air-tight," leaving no room for discretion by the Census Bureau.[76]

The most impassioned plea for the Fenn bill came from Robert H. Clancy of Detroit. Calling his opponents "ambitious Caesars bent on tyranny," he charged that they would continue to "deprive citizens of their representation in Congress and voice in Electoral College." He compared them to the "vote thief" and the "political gunman" because they held seats in the House that should not have belonged to them after the 1920 census. They maintained their illegal power "by brute strength and recourse to rape of the Constitution." Clancy believed their real reason for opposing the Fenn bill was "to save their own political hides or the hides of some of their political friends." The Detroit representative wanted reapportionment because it would give his city more seats in the House.[77]

Before the House voted on the Fenn bill, Beedy of Maine tried to substitute the method of equal proportions for the bill's method of major fractions. He claimed that the latter favored large states so the change would save at least three seats for the smaller states. In reply, Fiorello LaGuardia argued that "the principle of equal representation divided among the whole country is more important than the distribution of three members among the 48 States." The New York City representative pointed out that his seat "will be the first to be wiped out under this reapportionment" because of its location, its population, and his popularity in his party, yet he believed reapportionment was "far more important to representative government than the political interests of any individual." The Beedy amendment lost on a voice vote.[78]

Late on April 18, Representative John Rankin moved to have the House of Representatives recommit the Fenn bill to the Census Committee. The House voted 186 to 164 to send the bill back to the committee.[79] Once again the House failed to reapportion itself, but this attempt to provide for reapportionment after the 1930 census at least got to the House floor. The momentum for passage of some reapportionment bill seemed to be growing in Congress.

During the congressional recess from May to December 1928, public pressure for reapportionment increased. The *Saturday Evening Post*, for instance, expressed confusion over the "extremely complicated and controversial" technical parts of reapportionment and recognized the problems involved in either enlarging the House or cutting the representation of some states to maintain a 435-seat House. More important, however, the *Post* worried about the "misrepresentative government" caused by the failure to reapportion. The lack of "fair and equitable representation" for perhaps 20 million Americans in the current Congress greatly troubled the editors of the *Post*. To avoid "a great injustice," reapportionment would have to occur, and the *Post* trusted the Census Bureau to do it. A more ominous comment about the legislature's "disregard for the Constitution" and about the representatives' neglect of their oaths to support and maintain it came from a Princeton University professor of politics. William Starr Myers pointed out the possible connection between the eight-year delay in reapportionment and the fast-approaching 1928 election. He wondered if voting would yield "an unconstitutional President." Writing in the *North American Review*, he declared that Congress's inaction would "vitally increase or decrease the legitimate power and influence of many of our States in the election next November," especially in a close election, and would cause the electoral college to be "unconstitutionally composed." The result, Myers warned, might be "a crisis of utmost gravity" because one candidate might be officially elected yet the apparent loser would be "rightfully entitled to the office." Myers demonstrated how Alfred E. Smith, the Democratic candidate, could win with two more than the minimum electoral votes by carrying states that included five thought to have one vote each more than they deserved plus Missouri with two more than justified and at the same time winning four states with one fewer vote apiece than warranted; the result would be a Smith victory based on a malapportioned House and electoral college when in fact his opponent should be elected. Not only could the constitutionality of the result be challenged, but the professor feared that "even revolutionary action" might occur because the issues in the campaign "strike so deeply into the consciences and prejudices of the American people."[80] Congress certainly could not reapportion before the election, and the election did not conform to Myers's scenario, but his example did argue forcefully for the need to reapportion the House soon before disaster did strike.

At the opening of the second session of the Seventieth Congress, reapportionment activity increased. Speaker Longworth, Majority Leader Tilson, and Rules Committee Chairman Snell announced their support for the Fenn bill and promised action on it. Representative McLeod warned the leadership of a possible filibuster against the Fenn bill if the House did not pass it promptly. Even supporters of the Fenn bill had become disgusted; one Ohio Republican expressed his frustration by protesting "the transaction of business by the House on the ground that it is illegally constituted." The Republican steering committee of the House agreed that the House ought to act and promised a vote on the Fenn bill near January 10.[81]

A new force emerged in the reapportionment battle late in 1928. The recently elected junior senator from Michigan, Arthur H. Vandenberg, had pledged during his campaign to fight for automatic reapportionment after each census. He had first introduced such a bill in May 1928, only weeks after being appointed to a Senate vacancy. In a Senate speech in December, he renewed his efforts by saying the lack of reapportionment after the 1920 census amounted to "a gross contempt of the Constitution and a violent trespass upon the right of representation." He asked the Senate to delay action on a pending census bill until he could add an amendment calling for automatic reapportionment, and the sponsor of the census bill agreed. On January 3, he presented such an amendment. Three days later he spoke on a Washington radio station and claimed that 32 million people were virtually disfranchised by the failure to reapportion. Pointing to the threat to the electoral college, Vandenberg said, "It is insufferable folly to permit such a hazard to exist."[82] In the coming months Vandenberg, a novice at legislative maneuvering, would play a significant role in the final passage of reapportionment legislation.

During the second week of the new session, the Census Committee met and voted to retain the controversial method of major fractions in the Fenn bill. Four days later the committee appeared ready to endorse the bill, but five members had the flu and could not attend so the committee lacked a quorum. On January 5, the committee met again and had a quorum, in part because Tilson had threatened to have the sergeant at arms round up any absent members. In addition, Senator Vandenberg's actions spurred the House committee. In the committee meeting one opponent of the Fenn bill agreed to be paired with an absent supporter so the committee narrowly voted to approve the bill. The seven-to-six margin came from seven Republicans supporting the bill while one Republican and five Democrats opposed it.

The *Nation* called the action "good news" and endorsed the Fenn bill because it would end the "most notorious and inexcusable anomaly in our democracy . . . the failure to reapportion the membership of Congress."[83]

As the Fenn bill started to progress, old controversies surrounding reapportionment reappeared. Professors Huntington and Willcox sparred over the best statistical method to allot seats in the House, and representatives introduced proposals to protect small and rural states. Vermont's Elbert S. Brigham, for example, wanted all states to have at least two congressmen. The most controversial proposal came from a Kansas Republican, Homer Hoch. He suggested a constitutional amendment to provide for apportioning representatives according to the number of citizens in a state, not the entire population. During debate on an agriculture bill, Hoch took the floor to argue that justice called for excluding aliens. He knew no reason why his "state should lose one member and New York gain one member through inclusions of thousands of unnaturalized aliens in the country," and he audaciously pointed out that the New York constitution excluded aliens when it apportioned seats in the state legislature according to population. To charges that he wanted taxation without representation for aliens, Hoch reminded the House that aliens could not vote so they were already taxed without representation. As an aside, he said, "If such people come here and do not become citizens and yet want representation, let them hire good lawyers to represent them." The Kansan emphasized that his own grandfather had been an alien, that he recognized their contributions to the nation, and that he "made no attack on the aliens."[84]

Hoch's proposal outraged Fiorello LaGuardia, John C. Schafer (R.-Wisc.), and others. Claiming that Hoch's idea was known as the Evans plan after the head of the Ku Klux Klan, Hiram Wesley Evans, LaGuardia declared that "aliens are rapidly becoming citizens," except where blocked by "the Ku Klux Klan administering the naturalization department." He sadly suggested that the recent immigration restriction legislation would make Hoch's plan unnecessary because so few immigrants would be entering the nation, but the New York City representative feared that the Hoch scheme constituted only the "first step in getting away from popular and constitutional government of free men" until finally only "a small privileged class" controlled the government. Schafer reminded the House that aliens paid taxes and served under the selective service in World War I. He believed the KKK and the Anti-Saloon League supported the Hoch proposal. Though the controversial Hoch suggestion sparked heated debate, it quickly faded as a serious idea.[85]

When the House took up the Fenn bill on January 10, prospects for passage seemed very good. The Pennsylvania House delegation had decided in caucus to support the bill, and the Maine delegation also voted to support it even though their state would lose one seat. Each side seemed confident, but Representative McLeod, the ad hoc leader of the bill's supporters, worried that "the vote is going to be dangerously close." More impartial observers had a difficult time predicting the outcome. The *New York Times,* for instance, claimed on January 5 that opponents of the Fenn bill would include "rural and dry members of other states who fear an increase in the Congressional strength of wet, populous centers." Four days later the same newspaper reported that drys would support the bill because their insistence on obedience to the Eighteenth Amendment required that they also abide by the Constitution's mandate for reapportionment.[86]

Special House rules limited debate on the Fenn bill to three hours and compelled a vote by the time of adjournment on January 11. No new arguments appeared as the House wrangled over reapportionment. Opponents claimed that the bill delegated too much power to the secretary of commerce, that it denigrated the will of the future Congresses to act on reapportionment, that it unfairly used the method of major fractions, that it failed to exclude aliens, that it hurt rural states, that it accomplished nothing, that it undermined popular government, and that the Constitution did not require reapportionment every ten years. The rhetoric escalated. Rankin called the bill "an abdication bill . . . the most ignominious capitulation I have ever seen the House attempt to make," and Lozier said it contained many "invalid, specious, and unconstitutional provisions." Two Kentucky congressmen opposed the bill as "unsound, unnecessary, and wrong" and "foolish" and "vicious." In response, Representative Robert Luce (R.-Mass.) declared that the opponents gave "pretexts, not reasons," for voting against the bill.[87]

Several representatives attempted to revive their amendments to the Fenn bill. Tinkham wanted to enforce the Fourteenth Amendment, but the House again refused. It also rejected Hoch's wish to exclude aliens from the population for reapportionment. Dissatisfied with the method of major fractions, Lester Jesse Dickinson (R.-Iowa) first suggested unsuccessfully that the method of equal proportions be substituted and then switched to a vague provision allowing future Congresses to determine the method. After hearing the arguments against the bill and the suggestions for changing it, New York's Emanuel Celler observed, "Everybody seems to be in favor of reapportionment, but nobody wants to do anything."[88]

Supporters of the Fenn bill similarly repeated their arguments. They stressed that the Constitution required reapportionment and allowed the delegation of power to the secretary of commerce. Michigan's Carl Mapes provided the most concrete argument for adopting the Fenn bill by reminding the House of the inequality in congressional districts. Michigan's sixth had a population of 1,350,000 and California's tenth had 1,250,000 inhabitants, whereas ten of the sixteen Missouri districts contained fewer than 180,000. Quoting the *Philadelphia Public Ledger*, Mapes said that "all this measure does is to restore the system of equal representation in the House according to the population of the States. . . . This is a measure for justice to all."[89]

In an inexplicable move at the end of the debate, Fenn himself moved successively to strike the third, fourth, and fifth sections of his bill. The third section would have required that each congressman be elected from an individual district "composed of contiguous and compact territory" and that each district would "contain as nearly as practicable the same number of individuals." The other sections allowed states losing or gaining seats to elect at-large representatives until the state legislature approved new congressional districts. Fenn's moves took from the bill significant requirements that had been in effect since the reapportionment after the 1870 census. The resulting bill apparently would have left the creation of congressional districts completely up to the state legislatures, and it opened the possibility that gerrymandering would return and that some districts would be significantly larger than others. The House approved the deletions without any debate on the floor, and the action prompted no comment in the press.[90]

Fenn left the basis for his move unstated, and the lack of debate over the changes in the bill and the lack of roll-call votes obscured the reasoning of his colleagues. Their actions may have been part of a behind-the-scenes compromise to attract more supporters for the bill by leaving its results more unclear than ever. For example, a rural congressman from a state scheduled to lose seats could, under the amended Fenn bill, still hope that his state legislature would leave his district intact, even if it had a small and dwindling population. Similarly, any congressman whose party controlled his state's legislature could hope that partisan pressures would protect his district.

Minutes after accepting Fenn's motions to strike three sections of the bill, the debate ended. The House then voted first not to recommit the bill to the Census Committee by a margin of 134 to 226. It then passed the Fenn bill by a simple voice vote.[91] For only the second time since the 1920 census, the House passed a reapportionment bill. The Senate had less than two months to act on it before the Seventieth Congress expired.

Public sentiment for passage of the Fenn bill seemed to be growing. The *Philadelphia Record* observed that, because the "issues at stake do not concern the Senate," it too should pass the reapportionment measure. "No argument of any weight can be advanced against legislation so wholly consonant with justice and common sense and demanded by the Constitution," declared the *Cleveland Plain Dealer* in supporting Senate approval of the Fenn bill. Similarly, the *New York Telegram* argued that the "senate should let nothing interfere with adoption" of "this wise measure." Others doubted the Fenn bill would survive the crowded Senate calendar as the Seventieth Congress came to a close, and a few hoped it would be killed. The *Des Moines Tribune Capital* worried that basing representation on population meant "it is the country that will stand the losses." A Richmond daily called the Fenn bill "pernicious" because "it delegates the plain duty of Congress to a coordinate branch of the Government, the Department of Commerce." Although Missouri seemed sure to lose under the reapportionment, the *St. Louis Post-Dispatch* denied that the loss "involves any calamitous results" and recognized that the House could not always be enlarged because it would thereby "soon resemble the audience at Yale-Harvard football games." The *Outlook and Independent* maintained that enactment of the Fenn bill would revive the House of Representatives and make it "a Constitutional body" again.[92]

The *Review of Reviews* found the lack of reapportionment in the 1920s "a violation of the clear intent of the Constitution" and of "every principle of common justice." The automatic provision of the

Fenn bill appealed to the magazine because it meant the "computation could be made in an hour and the results announced on the same day." Calling it "preposterous that we should have chosen Presidential electors as well as Congressmen in November, 1928, under a reapportionment based upon the census of 1910," the *Review* reminded its readers of the problems that could arise in elections and how a malapportioned House would affect them. It recalled the controversial election of 1876, the death of Horace Greeley just before the 1872 election, and the death of a vice-presidential candidate right before the 1912 vote. Although recognizing that controversy surrounded reapportionment, the *Review* thought Congress had a duty to pass the Fenn bill.[93]

Without holding any hearings on the bill, the Senate Commerce Committee reported it to the entire Senate. The chairman of the Republican Steering Committee opposed the bill because his state of Kentucky would lose a representative under its reapportionment so he assigned the bill a low priority on the Senate calendar. Michigan's Arthur Vandenberg took on the responsibility for shepherding the bill through the Senate. On January 24 Vandenberg managed to secure by a vote of 53 to 23 a brief consideration of the Fenn bill by the Senate. Referring to the failure to reapportion as "an ugly constitutional default," he contended that the Fenn bill was the most important legislation pending before the Senate. He agreed with the limit of 435 members, endorsed the delegation of power to the secretary of commerce, and accepted the method of major fractions. Refusing to "follow detours into irrelevant matters," Vandenberg avoided discussions of the difference between citizens and people, enforcement of the Fourteenth Amendment, and which states might gain or lose. He urged immediate adoption of the bill. Massachusetts's David I. Walsh supported Vandenberg and directly attacked the opponents of reapportionment. The failure to reapportion amounted, in Walsh's opinion, to a "plain, deliberate, intentional nullification, disregard, and disrespect for . . . the Constitution. Some of the people claiming to be 'holier than thou' in Americanism," he declared, "are the very persons who are responsible for this outrageous nullification." In spite of the efforts of Vandenberg and Walsh, the Senate cut short its debate on the reapportionment bill and returned its attention to a bill providing for the construction of cruisers for the navy.[94]

Vandenberg, however, continued to press. On February 14 he lost another attempt to have the Senate debate the Fenn bill, and he complained of the Senate's indifference. When the Senate finally took up the reapportionment bill in the last week of the session, it could muster a quorum only after the sergeant at arms rounded up senators for the evening session. The critics then attacked. Hugo Black (D.-Ala.) called the bill "unjust and unrighteous." In particular, he objected to the delegation of power to the secretary of commerce and criticized the method of major fractions as deliberately extending "the Representatives in the large States to the detriment of the small States and the rural communities." Claiming he would support a fair reapportionment based on the 1920 census, he proposed that the Fenn bill be rewritten entirely. Mississippi's Byron Patton Harrison simply stated that it would be "impossible to pass" the reapportionment bill. "We have before us now the second deficiency appropriation bill of 200 pages which touches every agency of the Government," he told Vandenberg. "If an explanation of the innumerable items therein contained is demanded, I think it would take six weeks at least for us to get through with that measure." Irritated at the "perversity" of Harrison and his allies, Vandenberg proposed to recommit his bill to committee. He claimed to have assurances that the bill would reappear for an early vote in the special postinaugural session of Congress. Though defeated, disillusioned, and disappointed, Vandenberg refused to give up.[95]

Planning for congressional action in the upcoming Congress, Vandenberg began to court the congressional leadership and rewrote his proposal. He met with Charles Curtis, the outgoing Senate majority leader and next vice-president, with Charles E. Watson, the probable new GOP leader in the Senate, with Nicholas Longworth, the Speaker of the House, and with John Tilson, the House majority leader; all assured Senator Vandenberg that Congress would again consider reapportionment in the special session after the inauguration of Herbert Hoover. In his address to the special session, President Hoover directly called for action on reapportionment. Two days later Vandenberg reintroduced his bill, which differed in three ways from his earlier one. No longer "An Act for the Apportionment," the new bill carried the title "An Act to Provide for Apportionment" because it provided only for future reapportionments instead of actually designating how they would be carried out. More important, the revised proposal substituted the president, a constitutional officer, for the secretary of commerce as the agent charged with implementing reapportionment. Finally, the new bill replaced specific provisions for a House of 435 members and the method of major fractions with the more accommodating phrases "the existing number" and "the method used in the last preceding apportionment"; the new wording allowed for future changes by Congress without altering the intent of Vandenberg's bill.[96]

The Senate Commerce Committee immediately held one day of hearings on bills for the 1930 census and for reapportionment. Hiram Johnson (R.-Cal.) shouted "Mirabile dictu!" when Vandenberg announced virtual unanimity among statisticians for his bill (for unknown reasons Professor Huntington remained silent). The committee devoted most of its time to considering and approving November 1 as the date for the census, instead of January 1 as had been the case in 1920. The only controversy arose over excluding aliens from the population considered for apportionment, and the committee easily rejected that idea. On April 20, the committee approved the Vandenberg bill.[97]

For five weeks in April and May, the Senate for the first time since 1911 thoroughly debated a reapportionment bill, combined with a census bill. The bill and its sponsor, Senator Vandenberg, immediately came under attack. The opponents repeated many of the complaints against earlier bills but also discovered new concerns about the bill. Senator Hugo Black charged that the bill whittled away at congressional power and centralized it in the executive branch. Unimpressed with the claims that reapportionment would be more efficient under the Vandenberg bill, Black alluded to the "sentiment all over this Nation in favor of Mussolini running Italy, because, they say, he established order and security." Black preferred liberty. The Alabamian also objected to the "iniquitous" method of major fractions because it favored the large states. More generally, Black denied that the Constitution required reapportionment every ten years (though he preferred it) and even suggested that Congress wait until after the 1930 census to consider reapportionment. Though not original, Black's arguments received support from many senators, such as Mississippi's Pat Harrison and Virginia's Claude A. Swanson. The Senate, however, defeated Black's amendment to allow the president only to report the results to Congress and leave the actual reapportionment to the legislative branch. Although it also rejected Black's attempt to substitute equal proportions for major fractions, the Senate did agree to an amendment by Key Pittman (D.-Nev.) to require the president to furnish reapportionment figures using both statistical methods. The Senate also defeated two proposals by Walter George (D.-Ga.) to drop the automatic reapportionment provisions of the bill.[98]

Coleman L. Blease of South Carolina revived the issue of including aliens in the population figure used for reapportionment, and then Frederic M. Sackett (R.-Ky.) introduced an amendment to the Vandenberg bill to exclude aliens. The aliens concentrated in the cities, according to Sackett, and thereby exacerbated the "decided drift from the country to the city." Appealing directly to "those from the rural communities," he hoped to block the concentration of political power in the urban areas by "confining representation to those who are citizens of the United States." Many rural senators agreed. Arkansas's Thaddeus H. Carraway considered it "unthinkable" that aliens could not be president or serve in Congress yet "vote indirectly" for those officials. Kenneth McKellar (D.-Tenn.) protested that aliens would have almost forty representatives in the House, and Kansas's Arthur Capper pointed out that the aliens in five northeastern states would have strength in the electoral college equal to his entire state. An intemperate James Thomas Heflin (D.-Ala.) referred to aliens as crooks, criminals, kidnappers, bandits, terrorists, racketeers, and "refuse of foreign countries" and claimed that most came to the United States illegally. More calmly and simply, Harry B. Hawes of Missouri suggested calling them "visitors" or "temporary residents" instead of aliens and pointed out that because they could always return to their overseas homes, they should not be included in the population for reapportionment.[99]

Sackett's amendment provoked considerable opposition. A Wisconsin Republican criticized "the nativistic philosophy that seems to be permeating many sections of the country" and claimed that aliens, in fact, represented "the very cream of civilization." Furthermore, John J. Blaine believed that aliens should be counted because each congressman represented "every single human being residing within the State of which he is a Representative," not just citizens. Senator David I. Walsh of Massachusetts suggested that if Sackett's amendment succeeded, others might try to bar additional groups. He pointed out that any reason for excluding aliens could be used against "that large class of citizens who possess the rights of American citizens, but through crass ignorance, negligence, inexcusable indifference, and illiteracy, decline to assume the responsibility of citizenship." Conceding the futility of arguing against prejudice, Walsh nonetheless contended that aliens worked hard, obeyed the laws, fought for the United States in wartime, and were thrifty. After listening to the defense of aliens offered by Walsh, Blaine, and others, the Senate voted down the Sackett amendment.[100]

Opponents of the Vandenberg reapportionment bill raised new objections. Some worried about possible error and fraud in the census. To prevent a spoils system, New York's Robert F. Wagner proposed that census enumerators be hired under the civil service system, and the Senate accepted his amendment. It similarly approved an amendment to allow Congress to reapportion later if it discovered fraud in the census figures.[101]

Although they agreed to several changes in the original bill, proponents of the Vandenberg bill stood firm in its defense. Vandenberg justified the Senate's consideration of the reapportionment bill before the House passed it because the Senate had previously killed two bills passed by the House. Pointing to the "last eight years of constitutional trespass," he argued that the bill's automatic provisions would make it unnecessary "to leave the problem to the voluntary instincts and attitudes of Congress itself," though he readily acknowledged that Congress could still reapportion the House if it wanted to act before the automatic provisions went into effect. Supporters of the bill also denied that it delegated any real power to the president because it only allowed him to conduct mathematical calculations without giving him any discretionary authority. As for the proper statistical method to be used, Vandenberg said, "Camouflage never aspired to larger confusion than in this irrational effort to magnify the choice of methods." As Frederick H. Gillett (R.-Mass.) summed up the complaints against major fractions, "the real purpose of the opposition is to defeat the bill, no matter what system of apportionment is adopted." More concerned with reapportionment than with the particular method to be used, Vandenberg and his allies, therefore, accepted without much discussion Pittman's amendment to have the president report using both methods.[102]

Finally on May 29, 1929, the Senate passed the Vandenberg bill by a vote of 57 to 26. The bill then went to the House, where debate began on June 3. Writing in *Commonweal*, William C. Murphy, Jr., expressed hope that a reapportionment bill would be passed in spite of "sordid, selfish political interests." He contended that the House of Representatives had been the real obstacle to earlier bills, even though the Senate had defeated two; the bills would not have passed the House except that representatives expected the Senate to reject them. The lack of reapportionment, according to Murphy, "means that the ballot of the bucolic citizen is worth, in some instances, the ballots of ten city voters . . . at a time when a certain rivalry between urban and rural districts is noted." The *Review of Reviews* also predicted that Congress would finally enact reapportionment. It saw some irony in a special session that "will bring some economic relief to the farmer and at the same time, through the reapportionment bill, . . . bring some political relief to urban regions now grossly under-represented in Washington."[103]

As the House considered the Senate-adopted bill, Professor Zechariah Chafee of the Harvard Law School entered the debate with a major essay in the *Harvard Law Review*. He contended that Congress was "permitting the streams of legislation to become poisoned at the source" by ignoring reapportionment. In addition, Congress had "a mandatory constitutional duty to reapportion." Chafee acknowledged, however, that the courts lacked the power to order a reapportionment and would probably not void legislation or elections based on a malapportioned House. Further delay would mean, Chafee predicted, that "the moral support of law will gradually weaken." Reapportionment based on the 1930 census appeared to Chafee to be a "political obligation," if not a strictly legal or constitutional one. With the assistance of Professor Huntington, also of Harvard, Chafee reviewed the proposed statistical methods and concluded that the method of equal proportions made the most sense. If Congress designated a specific size for the House and authorized a precise method to be used, the president would be left with "no discretion whatever." Such a delegation of power did not trouble Chafee, and he believed the courts would accept it too.[104] Without specifically mentioning the Vandenberg bill, Chafee added his authoritative voice to the call for a reapportionment bill.

During the House debate on the Vandenberg bill, opponents of the reapportionment bill again called for excluding aliens, for postponing any reapportionment, for keeping in Congress the power to allot House seats, and for ignoring civil service in employing enumerators. On the second day of the debate, the House considered a flood of controversial amendments to the bill. "Rarely has the House chamber presented such a scene of wild confusion," noted one observer. After a "sharp fight," the House approved an amendment offered by Alabama's Bankhead to require census takers to list the names and addresses of all aliens and to explain how each got into the country. George Tinkham again unsuccessfully proposed an amendment to enforce the Fourteenth Amendment in places where Negroes could not vote, and later the House did approve his idea to omit from the census all individuals barred from voting for reasons other than rebellion and other crimes (i.e., Negroes). It also accepted Homer Hoch's amendment to define persons to be included in the census so as to exclude aliens.[105]

The changes dealing with aliens and Negroes "stirred bad blood and were subject of angry disputes wherever members congregated to discuss them on the House side of the Capitol," according to the *New York Times*. The House leadership feared a defeat for a reapportionment bill containing the Hoch and Tinkham amendments, even though each amendment separately appeared to have majority support in the House. The leaders decided that the only way to defeat them and pass the bill would be to combine them for a single vote. The *New York Times* considered it "a shrewd piece of parliamentary strategy" that "shows what can be done when old hands in the House take advantage of the rules to get rid of a troublesome matter." On June 6, therefore, Majority Leader Tilson offered an amendment that in effect struck both the Hoch and Tinkham amendments. After prolonged parliamentary wrangling, the chair ruled Tilson's proposal in order, and the House approved it overwhelmingly. One legal scholar, however, saw humor in the House action because "the House in doing so at once vindicated and nullified the Constitution."[106]

In the debate over the Senate-passed bill and amendments to it, the House made no attempt to restore the requirements for compact, contiguous districts of nearly equal populations. Representative Daniel Alden Reed (R.-N.Y.), however, did argue that Section 21 of the bill threatened to repeal the earlier laws pertaining to districts. It declared that the 1919 census law "and all other laws and parts of laws inconsistent with the provisions of this act are hereby repealed." To remedy the situation, Reed offered an amendment explicitly stating that the 1929 bill did not invalidate the provisions of the 1911 reapportionment law that called for contiguous, compact, and equal districts. The presiding officer, Carl Richard Chindblom (R.-Ill.) ruled that the amendment was not germane because the bill contained nothing related to actions by state legislatures. Undeterred, Reed repeated his motion in a slightly different form. Without his proposal, argued the congressman from upstate New York, if his state legislature deadlocked on reapportionment, all the state's representatives would be elected at large and "the entire representative power of the State of New York may be thrown into the cities. On the other hand, the entire representative power might be thrown into the rural portions of the State. In either event a very large portion of the population of the State would be without representation as contemplated by the Constitution." Reed knew that New York City could control the election of all at-large congressmen, and "these men would not accurately reflect the sentiment of the rural section of the great State regarding prohibition, immigration and other important public questions." The chair ruled Reed's revised amendment not germane, and the House dropped the issue of the nature of congressional districts.[107] The bill omitted any requirement that the districts be compact, contiguous, and equal.

The House of Representatives then approved the reapportionment bill by a vote of 271 to 104. The House bill differed, of course, from the Senate's, and the upper house refused to accept the lower house's changes. To settle the differences, each body named four members to a conference committee; among them were Senators Hiram Johnson and Arthur Vandenberg and Representatives Hart Fenn, Clarence McLeod, and John Rankin. The major points at issue involved the time of the census and the statistical method to be used in reapportioning seats. The Senate provided for taking the census on November 1, 1929, and for the president to report the results of reapportionment by using the last method employed in a reapportionment and by applying the method of equal proportions. The House called for the census to be taken on May 1, 1930, and the president to report using two methods provided for in the Senate bill plus the method of major fractions. On June 8 the conferees quickly agreed to November 1, 1929, for the census and for all three possible methods for reapportioning the House seats. Representatives Rankin and Lozier refused to sign the conference report.[108]

In the further "stormy" debate in the House on June 10, the compromise bill came under heavy attack because many members believed the November 1 census date threatened rural interests. Rural representatives assumed that in November many farm workers would have temporarily left the agricultural areas to spend the winter in cities. The House's members of the conference committee led the debate. The November 1 census would, according to Rankin, "increase the power of the large alien-congested centers [cities] of this country by reducing the number of Representatives from agricultural sections of the United States." Lozier predicted that agricultural states would lose twenty to thirty seats so he believed "no greater calamity could befall the agricultural group than to have its population enumerated in November. . . . The future of agriculture is involved in these dates. If the agricultural States lose these Members now, we will never get them back." William V. Gregory of Kentucky saw in the conference report "another plan to increase urban representation . . . another scheme to further stifle the voice of the American farmer in the affairs of the Government of which he is the chief bulwark and support." Rankin even warned his colleagues from rural areas of the states with large urban centers that the November 1 date for the census would increase the power of the cities in their state legislatures and in their delegations to Congress. In reply, Hart Fenn reminded the House that early November sufficed for voting so it should for the census. And McLeod pointed out that all major farm organizations supported November 1 as the best date for the census. The opponents of the conference report carried the day, however, when they adopted Rankin's motion to recommit the bill.[109]

The House and Senate conferees quickly met again and agreed that the census should be taken on April 1, 1930. After minimal debate, the House on June 11 agreed to the new compromise on a voice vote. Representative Edward Everett Denison (R.-Ill.) commented, "I hope it will turn out there is no April fooling about this census." When the Senate two days later considered the conference report, it promptly approved it by a vote of 48 to 37. On June 19 President Hoover signed the census and reapportionment bill.[110]

In analyzing the recent "row over reapportionment," the noted journalist Mark Sullivan detected, "beneath the surface, a tug of war" between the slowly growing, mainly farming states and the rapidly growing urban states. The former contained primarily native-born Americans and generally supported Prohibition, whereas the latter had a much larger percentage of recent aliens and opposed Prohibition. Other observers agreed. The *Seattle Times*'s Washington correspondent thought agricultural representatives "saw control of the House slipping from their hands," Prohibition supporters feared more "wet" votes from the urban areas, and the Ku Klux Klan opposed giving more power to Catholic aliens in the cities. The rural population, W. W. Jermane of the *Times* concluded, "opposed reapportionment because it would take House memberships from the country districts and give them to the cities." The *Baltimore Evening Sun* concurred and saw larger implications in the new reapportionment bill's effects. "The cities," it said, "which gain new representatives, have a powerful weapon in their hands, and, once having tasted blood, they are not likely to submit as tamely to rural domination as they have submitted heretofore."[111]

Two months after Congress finally passed the reapportionment bill, Oliver McKee, Jr., of the *Boston Evening Transcript* examined the "clash and conflict of interest between two protagonists, pretty evenly matched." He detected a major "conflict in contemporary American politics between town and country, or as some would rather have it, between rural and urban areas." According to the Washington correspondent, a special "philosophy, a trend of thinking and an economic interest all its own" set urban America apart from rural America. What he described as a "cleavage in thought and feeling between city and country" did not conform to sectional or partisan lines; in fact, the "participants on either side are not always conscious of the alignment." McKee saw an urban-rural division in the reapportionment fight and especially in the battle over counting aliens where the battle clearly involved tangible political power. Rural representatives "did not perhaps conceive of themselves as spokesmen for the country, and as champions of its cause and ascendancy against the city, but that is precisely how they were acting."[112]

To a number of observers, therefore, as well as many of the participants, the decade-long dispute over reapportionment involved a decisive shift in congressional power from the rural sections of the country to the growing urban areas. Rural representatives managed to avoid reapportionment based on the 1920 census and thereby postponed any decrease in their power. Even the mandate of the Constitution for reapportionment failed to compel them to support reapportionment. As the *New Republic* commented, only when "the scandal had become too notorious" did a majority in Congress finally succeed in enacting the 1929 reapportionment bill.[113]

4

Voting on Reapportionment: A Test of Urban-Rural Conflict

THE INTENSITY AND VOLUME of the urban-rural rhetoric in the public debate over congressional reapportionment lends some credence to the popular urban-rural interpretation for the 1920s. Scholars heretofore, however, have offered scant contemporary testimony of urban-rural conflict; their interpretation has been imposed on the events of the decade without much specific evidence from the time specifically suggesting such a conflict. In the controversy over reapportionment, substantial evidence emerged for the first time that people in the 1920s did talk explicitly of urban-rural conflict. The distinct possibility arises that the voting in the House of Representatives may have followed the urban-rural rhetoric and divided on reapportionment along urban-rural lines.

For all the work on the 1920s and the urban-rural concept, few scholars have used quantitative techniques to test the urban-rural model, and none has analyzed roll-call voting in the House of Representatives. Of course, not all supposedly urban-rural issues can be so examined; neither fundamentalism nor the Ku Klux Klan, for example, ever came to a vote in the House of Representatives. The ostensibly urban-rural issues that did receive considerable congressional attention (Prohibition and immigration restriction) have only recently been examined by means of roll-call analysis.[1] Though ignored by historians, especially by scholars concerned with urban-rural conflict, reapportionment in the 1920s will provide a new test through an examination of congressional voting. Proving or disproving such a broad historical interpretation has been difficult, and an analysis of voting patterns on eight roll-call votes in the House of Representatives will not provide any conclusive answer. At best, a roll-call analysis of voting on reapportionment will determine whether on this one issue rhetoric and action followed each other and thereby whether the urban-rural thesis can in a small way be confirmed or denied.

Any analysis of congressional voting immediately confronts a myriad of underlying problems. For example, what a congressman represents and how he represents it remain problematic. A congressman can endeavor simply to reflect the wishes of his constituents, but then the definition of his constituency becomes crucial. The constituents can be understood to include just the voters who elected him, only the members of his party in his district, all the voters back home, all the residents of his district, or primarily influential or powerful groups back home. In any case, the representative determines their preference and votes accordingly as their agent in Washington. Seeing the responsibility quite differently, a congressman can assume the voters elected him to use his best judgment in voting. Such a representative considers his constituents' desires but also what he considers to be good for his district or state, what he thinks is in the national interest, or what he simply believes to be right: he reaches his own independent judgment about how to vote. Many factors can affect how a congressman views his job, but certainly his security might play a large role. A veteran legislator from a safe one-party district, for example, could feel more freedom than a first-term congressman elected by a slim margin.[2]

Congressional voting involves much more than just whether a representative follows his own thinking or the preferences of his constituents. Pressures within the House of Representatives, for instance, also can play a major role in determining how a congressman votes. Loyalty to a party's announced position, personal friendship with other congressmen vitally involved in an issue, the influence of powerful committees or leaders, and trading of votes for other considerations can influence a particular vote. A congressman may, moreover, respond to pressure from special interest groups, the president, or other parts of the government. Since all issues do not have the same importance for all congressmen and their constituents, the factors involved in a single roll call can vary widely among the members of the House of Representatives, and they can change from vote to vote for an individual congressman.[3]

The following analysis assumes that if the urban-rural rhetoric really reflected congressmen's attitudes on reapportionment, the tension and conflict between urban and rural areas would have been so great and intense that it would have played a major role in determining the voting on reapportionment legislation. Congressional reapportionment seemed to have for representatives not just intrinsic but also symbolic importance as an example of the clash of urban and rural ways of life in the 1920s. The significance of reapportionment within the context of the urban-rural conflict would therefore have generally outweighed the personal preferences of individual representatives, partisan pressures, and other incentives inherent in the institution of the House in determining voting patterns. The urban-rural divisions would not, of course, have been perfect and complete, but they would have been so significant as to be observable if the voting in the House of Representatives followed the lines of the debate.

Measuring urban-rural conflict in voting in the House of Representatives requires careful definitions of urban and rural. The Census Bureau provides some assistance. For the first time, in 1920 it defined as urban any incorporated place with a population of twenty-five hundred or more; the remaining incorporated places of fewer than twenty-five hundred and all unincorporated areas constituted rural areas.[4] Accepting the census definition of rural presents the least difficulty—certainly most unincorporated areas and towns smaller than twenty-five hundred can hardly be considered urban. In the examination of roll calls, rural will refer to districts that had less than 50 percent of their population in towns of twenty-five hundred or more; in other words, rural will mean districts in which at least 50 percent of the population lived in unincorporated areas or in towns of fewer than twenty-five hundred people. Using this definition, 254 congressional districts qualify as rural according to the 1920 census. The remaining 181 districts can be considered urban according to the census standard because more than 50 percent of the population in each lived in towns of more than twenty-five hundred people. One test of urban-rural conflict, therefore, will be to compare the votes of congressmen from the 181 urban districts with the votes of the representatives from the 254 rural ones.

The census designation of urban contains serious weaknesses. A population of only twenty-five hundred seems inappropriately small for any meaningful definition of urban. Using the twenty-five hundred level for urban, for example, the fifth district of Maryland according to the 1920 census had an urban population of only 9.72 percent, yet it was directly adjacent to both Washington, D.C., and Baltimore. At the same time, Iowa's second district contained Clinton, Davenport, and Muscatine, which with other smaller towns gave it an urban population of 52.91 percent.[5] Even in the 1920s the area between Baltimore and Washington must have seemed more urban than small-town Iowa, in spite of the census. Yet to treat only large cities as urban would exclude some areas considered heavily urban by the census, such as eight of Massachusetts's districts that were heavily urban according to the census.[6]

To discriminate more carefully between urban and rural, standards different from the ones provided by the census had to be created. A standard had to be employed, for example, that allowed for areas close to big cities to be considered urban also. The Census Bureau's new 1920 classification of metropolitan districts provided just such an alternative. Deemphasizing the importance of official city boundaries, the census ranked metropolitan districts including urban and suburban territory surrounding the core cities.[7] For example, parts of the twenty-second district of Illinois fell in the eighth largest metropolitan district even though it was across the Mississippi River from St. Louis, Missouri. The eleven largest metropolitan districts with a total of ninety-three congressional districts (see Appendix 2) will be used to compare a second type of urban, or "metro," congressional districts with rural ones in the voting in the House of Representatives.

To highlight any possible urban-rural conflict, the votes of congressmen from these metro districts will be compared with the votes of representatives from the "most-rural" districts. The latter will be defined as the 104 congressional districts that in 1920 had less than 20 percent of their populations in incorporated areas of twenty-five hundred or more (that is, at least 80 percent of the populations were rural according to the census definition; for a list, see Appendix 4). By eliminating from consideration the marginally urban and rural districts, the metro and most-rural categories should reveal what is usually called urban-rural conflict, if there is any.

The several definitions of urban, rural, metro, and most-rural then have to be applied to the particular congressional districts before the roll calls can be analyzed for urban-rural conflict. Two sources provide descriptions of all congressional districts. Each session of

Congress issued a *Congressional Directory* that explained the boundaries of each district, and Kenneth C. Martis's more recent *Historical Atlas of United States Congressional Districts, 1789–1983*, provides the same information all in one large volume.[8] Most districts had rather simple descriptions because they fell completely within a large city or were composed of several entire counties. For instance, New York City alone contained more than a dozen districts (all indisputably urban), and more than a score of counties made up the much larger fourth district of western Colorado. Other districts posed difficult problems because they contained only part of a county or city. The first, second, sixth, and thirteenth districts of Michigan each included part of Wayne County, whereas Hampden County fell into three Massachusetts districts; in each case the populations of individual towns or townships had to be employed to determine the district population. A final complication in recreating the congressional districts involved changes in district lines. Though Congress failed to reapportion the House of Representatives between 1912 and 1932, nine individual states on occasion redrew some district boundaries between 1917 and 1929, and three states made changes involving representatives elected at large. Tennessee, for example, adjusted the lines for its seventh, eighth, ninth, and tenth districts; Pennsylvania dropped its four at-large representatives and redrew many district lines.[9] Each change had to be taken into account, though none materially affected the results.

Determining which congressional districts actually fit the various definitions of urban and rural proved, for the most part, fairly simple. Under the census definition of metropolitan areas, the eleven largest metropolitan areas included parts of one hundred districts. Applying the census definition of twenty-five hundred for urban, however, required a much closer use of the census data to solve some problems. The census listed the urban population for each county so the total of the county figures produced an urban population for each district that followed exact county lines. The total urban population divided by the total district population yielded the district's percentage of urban population. When district lines followed other than county lines, the task became more complicated. The second and sixth districts of Michigan, for example, contained parts of Wayne County not in Detroit in addition to other counties; computing their urban populations required the summing of urban populations for some individual towns and townships in Wayne County. Sometimes approximations had to be used. Three Pennsylvania districts in and around Pittsburgh, for instance, had boundaries that were difficult to trace, such as part of Pittsburgh plus "boroughs and townships lying north of the Ohio and Allegheny rivers" in Allegheny County; several of the very small boroughs and townships listed in the census could not be definitely located so arbitrary judgments placed them in the most likely districts.[10] The estimates all involved heavily urban areas and probably made little difference because all of the districts would have qualified as urban with more than 50 percent urban population.

Finding the most-rural districts meant computing the urban population by census standards for all districts and determining which were less than 20 percent urban. The districts all followed county lines and always included more than one county. Districts in Kansas, Nebraska, Montana, Texas, and the Dakotas, in fact, frequently consisted of more than a score of counties each.

All calculations to determine urban and rural congressional districts relied on the 1920 census. The prolonged controversy over the 1920 census and the congressional reapportionment to be based on it made representatives unusually sensitive even nine years later to their districts' status according to the 1920 enumeration.

To analyze the voting in the 1920s on congressional reapportionment, two sets of statistical procedures have been used. The manipulation of the quantitative data has been kept as simple as possible to facilitate understanding. The first involves simple percentages supporting reapportionment and indexes of disagreement between different categories of congressmen. The second probes for the major components of the coalitions opposing reapportionment.

In the first, neither the simple percentage nor the index of disagreement can prove the causes for a particular voting result, but they can suggest explanations. A simple percentage has been employed to determine how many of a particular category of congressmen voted similarly on a specific issue; if, for example, 150 out of 200 rural Republicans voting on a measure all voted No, then the percentage of rural Republicans opposing it would be 75. The lowest possible percentage would be 0 when all votes opposed it; the highest would be 100 when all votes favored it.

An index of disagreement next measures the difference between two groups of congressmen on a single roll call; an index of 100 indicates total disagreement (that is, all of one group voting Yes and all of the other voting No); an index of 0 means no disagreement existed between the two groups (for example, 58 percent of each group voted for a particular measure). The index of disagreement has been used to compare urban congressmen with rural ones, Democrats with Republicans, northern and southern congressmen, metro representatives with the most-rural ones, and multiple combinations of those categories (e.g., urban Republicans versus urban Democrats).

When using the index of disagreement, no specific level can be characterized as particularly revealing a threshold of significant disagreement, but any index of disagreement lower than 50 would indicate that both groups supported (or opposed) the particular measure; for example, 95 percent support by Republicans and 51 percent support by Democrats would produce an index of disagreement of 44, which shows that they both gave majority support to the measure. On the other hand, an index of disagreement higher than 50 would result when a large majority of one group votes in favor of a measure and a large majority of the other group opposes it (e.g., 75 and 25 percent for) or when one group overwhelmingly supports it and another narrowly opposes it (e.g., 95 and 45 percent for). Although levels of disagreement near or over 50 would indicate serious disagreement, the index here will attempt first to find the greatest levels of disagreement, determine if they are urban-rural, and then see if they are generally significant.[11]

The tables listing the percentage support also list the average size of the various groups. The groups do not include congressmen paired or not voting on the issue, vacant seats in the House, or the few members who were not in the Democratic or Republican parties. Some of the groups are rather small, especially the metro Democrats, the metro Republicans, and the most-rural Republicans. Although data for the small groups may be less reliable because of the exaggerated impact of absences or pairings, those very groups are precisely the ones that would be expected to be most committed and most united in their voting if urban-rural conflict exists. Only when a group's size falls below ten has it been excluded from the tables.

Eight roll-call votes on reapportionment are examined.[12] They span the decade from early in 1921 until the middle of 1929, when Congress finally passed a reapportionment bill. The eight votes include two votes on the actual passage of reapportionment bills, three

92   DEMOCRACY DELAYED

TABLE 4.1: Percent Support* by Urban/Rural Categories

Legislator Groups	Average No. in Groups	Roll Calls							
		1	2	3	4	5	6	7	8
All†	353	78	51	24	48	47	85	62	72
Urban	137	82	50	28	64	61	95	81	92
Metro	71	89	38	35	69	62	99	89	100
Rural	211	75	51	22	37	37	79	49	59
Most-rural	78	68	51	18	20	24	65	32	46

*Support means voting as follows on each of the roll calls:
1. For measure to retain House of 435.
2. For recommital of bill for House of 460.
3. For motion to force from committee a bill for House of 435.
4. For motion to suspend rules to consider a bill for House of 435.
5. Against recommital of bill for House of 435 after 1930 census.
6. For resolution to form Committee of the Whole House to consider reapportionment.
7. Against recommital of bill for House of 435.
8. For bill for House of 435 based on 1930 census.

†All includes every representative voting on the measure; the other categories include only Democrats and Republicans and exclude congressmen in minority parties.

votes on motions to recommit bills to committee, and three special procedural votes involving reapportionment proposals; the voting margins ranged from a close 4 votes to an overwhelming 245 votes. The variety in the eight roll calls permits tests for urban-rural conflict in a number of different circumstances, all pertaining to reapportionment. If urban-rural conflict provides a key to the voting alignments, then such divisions should appear in the voting.

Table 4.1 reports the percentage of support for reapportionment in each of the eight roll calls and lists the issue involved in each. Supporters of reapportionment obviously would have voted for the two reapportionment bills (Roll Calls 1 and 8) and against attempts to recommit bills (5 and 7), though they supported recommittal of the 1921 proposal for a 460-seat House (2) because they still hoped to repass the bill for a 435-member House that had been approved earlier in the year. Supporters of reapportionment would also have favored parliamentary maneuvers to have the House consider reapportionment, even if it meant forcing the bill from a committee or suspending the House's rules (3, 4, and 6). Of course, some representatives may have supported reapportionment and yet have voted differently; for example, a congressman could have opposed calling a bill from committee because he had too much respect for the committee or had

TABLE 4.2: Indexes of Disagreement by Urban/Rural Categories

	Roll Calls							
Legislator Groups	1	2	3	4	5	6	7	8
Urban/rural	7	1	6	27	24	16	32	33
Metro/most-rural	21	13	17	49	38	34	57	54

personal ties to the committee members. If urban-rural conflict was powerful in the House on reapportionment, however, it should have outweighed and overcome other considerations.

According to Table 4.1, the rural and most-rural representatives gave the lower levels of support to reapportionment, except for the 1921 recommittal of a bill to committee, and urban and metro congressmen more consistently supported reapportionment. The exception involved a bill to increase the size of the House to 460 members, and some rural representatives may have favored the larger House (and hence opposed shelving the proposal) because it would have given additional seats to rapidly growing states without taking many from the more static states, which were often rural ones. Table 4.2 highlights the disagreement along urban/rural lines and metro/most-rural lines. Table 4.2 reveals an absence of significant urban-rural conflict on reapportionment. The metro/most-rural indexes are much higher, yet even they do not reveal complete disagreement between metro and most-rural congressmen. Even on the relatively noncontroversial question of forming a Committee of the Whole House to consider reapportionment on May 18, 1928 (6), however, the metro/most-rural index of disagreement is 34. Both sets of indexes reach their greatest levels on the last two roll calls, when the passage of the final bill was clearly at stake and after a decade of strong urban-rural rhetoric. The lines of division over reapportionment, therefore, were probably not simply urban/rural or even metro/most-rural, though the disagreement between the groups appeared to be growing as the decade ended.

In *The Politics of Provincialism*, David Burner argued that the Democratic party experienced urban-rural divisions in the 1920s, regardless of whether the Republican party did. The possibility exists, therefore, that the indexes in Table 4.2 hide considerable conflict *within* the Democratic party. In addition, partisan differences may

TABLE 4.3: Percent Support by Party and Urban/Rural Categories

Legislator Groups	Average No. in Groups	Roll Calls							
		1	2	3	4	5	6	7	8
DEMOCRATS	144	80	69	16	19	27	75	41	56
Urban	39	85	53	18	22	38	90	69	90
Metro	24	88	20	27	27	36	96	81	100
Rural	105	78	72	15	17	22	69	29	43
Most-rural	64	75	65	15	13	16	63	22	37
North	61	77	35	16	25	32	81	57	86
Urban	29	87	37	17	26	38	90	81	100
Metro	24	88	20	27	28	36	96	81	100
Rural	32	66	33	14	24	28	75	33	64
Most-rural	20	53	20	17	6	14	65	21	60
South*	83	82	77	16	14	19	66	27	38
Urban	10	80	71	20	8	40	90	33	43
Rural	73	82	78	16	14	19	66	27	38
Most-rural	48	83	71	15	15	18	61	23	33
REPUBLICANS	204	77	43	30	72	62	93	80	81
Urban	98	80	49	32	82	71	97	87	93
Metro	47	89	40	40	92	77	100	94	100
Rural	106	73	37	28	61	53	90	72	71
Most-rural	25	53	31	25	43	50	74	65	60

*South contains no metro districts and so few Republicans as to be unimportant.

have been greater than urban-rural conflicts. Table 4.3 presents the support for reapportionment by party and by urban-rural groups within the parties. In addition, because southern Democrats played such a strong role in the Democratic party, the Democrats are subdivided by North-South to determine whether the South skewed the results for the party as a whole.

In Table 4.3 the unanimous support given final reapportionment by metro congressmen of both parties and by northern urban Democrats appears striking, as do the low levels of support from Democrats for the effort to suspend the rules of the House in Roll Call 4. Table 4.4 lists the disagreements over reapportionment by party, region, and urban-rural categories and thereby refines the distinctions contained in the previous table. No strong partisan divisions distinguish the voting on reapportionment, but four examples of significant disagreement partially along partisan lines occurred on the fourth roll call. The simple Democrat/Republican index of 53 on Roll Call 4

TABLE 4.4: Indexes of Disagreement by Party
and Urban/Rural Categories

	Roll Calls							
Legislator Groups	1	2	3	4	5	6	7	8
DEMOCRATS								
Urban/Rural	7	19	3	5	16	21	40	47
Metro/Most-rural	13	45	12	14	20	33	59	63
North/South	5	42	0	11	13	15	30	48
Urban	7	34	3	18	2	0	48	57
Rural	16	55	2	10	9	9	6	26
Most-rural	30	51	2	9	4	4	2	27
REPUBLICANS								
Urban/Rural	7	12	4	21	18	7	15	22
Metro/Most-rural	36	9	15	49	27	26	29	40
DEMOCRATS/REPUBLICANS	3	26	14	53	35	18	39	25
Urban	5	4	14	60	33	7	18	3
Metro	1	20	13	65	41	4	13	0
Rural	5	35	13	44	31	21	43	28
Most-rural	22	34	10	30	34	11	43	23
Dem. Urban/Rep. Rural	12	16	10	39	15	0	3	19
Dem. Metro/Rep. Most-rural	25	11	2	16	14	22	16	40
Rep. Urban/Dem. Rural	2	23	17	65	49	28	58	50
Rep. Metro/Dem. Most-rural	14	25	25	79	61	37	72	63

exceeds all the other party-line divisions yet also fails to confirm any significant, overall partisan splits, and, in fact, greater partisan disagreements occur on Roll Call 4 between urban and metro congressmen. Although Table 4.4 also fails to find any consistently significant urban/rural conflict, the last line reveals important divisions between metro Republicans and Democrats from most-rural districts on four of the last five votes. In addition, on the last roll call, urban/rural, metro/most-rural, and North/South conflicts among Democrats reached relatively high levels. Table 4.4, however, fails to reveal any definite pattern of urban/rural conflict or any general metro/most-rural conflict. The urban-rural thesis would seem discredited.

If urban-rural conflict and partisanship fail to explain voting on reapportionment, then some other factor must or the voting conformed to no pattern. Inherent in congressional reapportionment lies one possible explanation for the voting. Reapportionment necessarily involves either adding (or subtracting) seats in the House of Representatives or shifting the existing seats from some states to others. From the beginning of the debate in 1921, adding or subtracting House seats seemed unlikely, even though many congressmen proposed increasing the size of the House so no state would lose a single seat. If, as most probably expected, the House remained at the 435-seat size, then some states would lose seats and others would gain, and the winners and losers were well known.[13] As early as December 19, 1920, the *New York Times* reported that a 435-seat House reapportioned on the basis of the 1920 census would include the following changes:

> California *gains* 3 seats
> Michigan and Ohio *gain* 2 seats each
> Connecticut, New Jersey, North Carolina, Texas, and Washington *gain* 1 seat each
> Indiana, Iowa, Kansas, Kentucky, Louisiana, Maine, Mississippi, Nebraska, Rhode Island, and Vermont *lose* 1 seat each
> Missouri *loses* 2 seats.

The gain or loss of seats under reapportionment would occur, of course, by states, not by individual districts, but the changes could affect the lines of each district in a state gaining or losing even one seat. Congressmen in the involved states could be affected, whether they represented growing urban districts or declining rural ones. In Missouri, for example, the loss of two seats could easily cause the redrawing of district lines in St. Louis and Kansas City, as well as the state's less populous rural regions. Reapportionment would have significantly different results in states gaining and losing at least one seat each. In a state gaining, a congressman might well face an easier reelection campaign because the district would be smaller and because the state's new district would open election possibilities for would-be opponents. In a state losing at least one seat, however, a congressman might face a more difficult reelection race because the district would grow and because the new district might include the home of another incumbent congressman. More generally, a state gaining a seat would increase its power and influence in Washington, whereas losing a seat would have the opposite effect. Representatives from states expecting to gain seats under reapportionment could be expected, therefore, to support reapportionment, and congressmen from states expecting

TABLE 4.5: Percent Support by Expected Gain,
No Change, or Loss in Seats

Legislator Groups	Average No. in Groups	Roll Calls							
		1	2	3	4	5	6	7	8
Gain	77	94	80	62	80	95	96	94	96
No change	191	93	58	18	51	45	88	67	78
Loss	80	25	13	2	7	6	69	15	31

to lose seats might understandably oppose reallocating seats in the House. With political survival at stake, the members of the House of Representatives may have been strongly influenced by the expected impact of reapportionment on their states and on themselves. The key to voting on reapportionment may have been the expected gain or loss of seats.

Table 4.5 shows the support given reapportionment by congressmen from states expecting as a result of the 1920 census to gain or lose seats and from states that anticipated no change in their numbers of representatives. The representatives from states expecting more seats under reapportionment gave nearly unanimous support to reapportionment on five of the eight roll calls. A majority of congressmen from states predicted to lose seats voted affirmatively only on the procedural question of forming a Committee of the Whole House to consider reapportionment (Roll Call 6), and even then nearly one-third of them apparently hoped to avoid any reapportionment by voting against the procedural motion. On five of the other seven roll calls, the expected losers gave 15 percent or less support to reapportionment. Only on the first roll call (when the question of self-interest had perhaps not become clear) and on the last (when the result probably seemed inevitable) did as much as one-fourth to one-third of the losers support reapportionment. The differences in voting between the gainers and the losers appears more striking in Table 4.6. The indexes of disagreement reach 60 or more on seven of the eight votes on reapportionment measures and go as high as 89, which is nearly total disagreement. Only on the relatively noncontroversial procedural question in Roll Call 6 does the disagreement fall to a low level. The indexes of disagreement strongly suggest that the expected gainers and losers opposed each other on the question of reapportion-

TABLE 4.6: Indexes of Disagreement
by Expected Gain, No Change, or Loss in Seats

Legislator Groups	Roll Calls							
	1	2	3	4	5	6	7	8
Gain/No change	1	22	44	29	50	8	27	18
No change/Loss	68	45	16	44	39	21	52	47
Gain/Loss	69	67	60	73	89	27	79	65

ment. Self-interest on each side provides the obvious explanation for the voting: the expected gainers sought reapportionment because it would increase their states' power, whereas expected losers tried to avoid any reapportionment that would keep the House at 435 members and thereby reduce their states' power and their own security.

Most congressmen, however, came from states that expected after reapportionment to retain the same number of seats in the House of Representatives unless the total membership changed. Unaffected by any obvious political self-interest in reapportionment, the no-change representatives seemed to follow an independent path on the eight roll calls; they generally voted with neither the gainers nor the losers. Only on the first roll call did they vote nearly identically with the expected gainers (an index of disagreement of only 1), but thereafter they failed to side consistently with either gainers or losers. The decisions of the congressmen in the no-change category, however, had great importance for the fate of reapportionment legislation. When they voted strongly for a reapportionment measure, as they did on Roll Calls 1, 2, 6, 7, and 8, it passed; when they opposed one or only a slim majority supported it, however, the House defeated the measure (Roll Calls 3, 4, and 5).

To probe for the possible reasons for the voting of no-change representatives and possibly to clarify the slight divisions within the gainers and losers, Table 4.7 considers a combination of partisan factors and expected results of reapportionment. Partisan influence alone and in combination with urban-rural categories fell short of adequately explaining voting on reapportionment (see Table 4.4), but partisanship may have occurred along gain/no change/loss lines. Table 4.7 confirms that gainers in both parties invariably gave reapportionment majorities and losers (with the exception of the pro-

TABLE 4.7: Percent Support by Party
and Expected Gain, No Change, or Loss in Seats

Legislator Groups	Average No. in Groups	Roll Calls							
		1	2	3	4	5	6	7	8
Gain									
Democrats	28	97	91	57	54	91	95	88	93
Republicans	49	92	72	65	98	96	96	98	98
No change									
Democrats	81	91	84	8	13	24	76	42	56
Republicans	110	95	47	26	80	63	97	88	93
Loss									
Democrats	35	38	14	0	0	0	61	0	22
Republicans	45	16	12	4	15	14	78	31	36

cedural Roll Call 6) consistently opposed reapportionment. Among no-change representatives, the Republicans very strongly backed reapportionment on six of the eight roll calls, while Democratic support varied more widely. Except for the first two roll calls, Republicans in each category gave a higher percentage of support to reapportionment than did the Democrats. Most striking in Table 4.7 is the unanimous opposition of Democratic losers on Roll Calls 3, 4, 5, and 7. The indexes of disagreement in Table 4.8 show that the gain, no change, and loss groups failed to divide significantly along partisan lines. On the fourth roll call, which involved suspending the House rules to reconsider a reapportionment bill, partisan differences among representatives expecting no change for their states reached a level of 67, yet the partisan differences among losers remained insignificantly low (index of 15). Except for the first roll call, the Democratic-Republican disagreement among no-change representatives exceeded the corresponding disagreement between gainers and between losers; partisanship apparently had a greater impact on congressmen not directly affected by reapportionment, but even among them it stayed at relatively unimportant levels.

More important, Table 4.8 reveals the greatest disagreement between Republican gainers and Democratic losers. The average index of disagreement between the two groups is 73, and on three roll calls the disagreement is nearly complete. The Republican gainers gave reapportionment the strongest support and Democratic losers pro-

TABLE 4.8: Indexes of Disagreement by Party
and Expected Gain, No Change, or Loss in Seats

Legislator Groups	Roll Calls							
	1	2	3	4	5	6	7	8
DEMOCRATS/REPUBLICANS								
Gain	5	19	8	44	5	1	10	5
No change	4	37	18	67	39	21	46	37
Loss	22	2	4	15	14	17	31	14
Dem. Gain/Rep. Loss	81	79	53	39	77	17	57	57
Rep. Gain/Dem. Loss	54	58	65	98	96	35	98	76
DEMOCRATS								
Gain/No change	6	13	45	41	67	19	46	37
No change/Loss	53	70	8	13	24	15	42	32
Gain/Loss	59	74	57	54	91	34	88	71
REPUBLICANS								
Gain/No change	3	25	39	18	33	1	10	5
No change/Loss	79	35	22	65	49	19	57	57
Gain/Loss	76	60	61	83	82	18	67	62

vided the most opposition. Further analysis of the gain/no change/loss groups within the two parties points to the very high and consistent levels of disagreement between gain/loss Republicans (average index of 70) and the only slightly lower disagreement between Democratic gainers and losers (average index of 66). Only on the procedural question of Roll Call 6 did the gain/loss differences within the parties fall below an index of 50. The large and crucial no-change groups in the parties, however, displayed important dissimilarities. The no-change Democrats tended slightly to side with the Democratic losers (average index of 32, compared to an average index of 34 between gain/no change), while Republican no-change congressmen voted more closely with the Republican gainers (average index of 17, compared to an average index of 48 for no change/loss). Tables 4.7 and 4.8, therefore, suggest some differences within the parties but highlight few partisan differences.

Since the combination of partisanship and expected results of reapportionment added little to an understanding of the voting divisions, perhaps urban-rural categories when considered with expected gains, no changes, and losses in seats will clarify the voting patterns. The urban-rural categories, however, should include most urban

TABLE 4.9: Percent Support by Urban/Rural Categories
and by Expected Gain, No Change, or Loss in Seats

Legislator Groups*	Average No. in Groups	Roll Calls							
		1	2	3	4	5	6	7	8
Gain									
Urban	35	93	67	54	87	100	100	95	100
Metro	20	88	53	53	91	100	100	100	100
Most-urban states	22	89	71	35	91	100	100	100	100
Rural	42	95	89	67	76	89	92	89	93
Most-rural	11	80	90	67	79	89	90	92	100
No change									
Urban	83	92	49	20	65	55	96	85	95
Metro	49	90	33	28	61	44	98	86	100
Most-urban states	64	91	40	18	64	57	99	91	97
Rural	108	94	65	17	39	63	81	53	64
Most-rural	46	94	76	17	12	26	68	35	50
Most-rural states	55	93	20	12	9	24	74	24	44
Loss									
Urban	19	25	22	10	19	16	79	22	41
Rural	61	25	10	0	3	3	66	13	24
Most-rural	30	22	7	0	3	3	52	3	17
Most-rural states	17	41	14	0	0	0	33	0	0

*Members in the following groups were too small in number to be significant: Gain most-rural states, Loss metro, and Loss most-urban states.

states and most rural states because a congressman's consciousness of representing an urban or rural constituency may have been tied more to his state than to an individual district, especially when involving reapportionment (see Appendixes 3 and 5 for lists of the most urban and most rural states).

Table 4.9 displays the support given reapportionment according to urban/rural categories who expected gains, no changes, or losses in seats. Legislators from states anticipating gains generally voted overwhelmingly for reapportionment; even the gaining rural and most-rural representatives gave six of the eight measures more than 80 percent support. Contrarily, the congressmen from states predicted to lose seats usually opposed reapportionment measures, except for the procedural Roll Call 6. The urban representatives from losing states opposed reapportionment, though their opposition shrank to 59 percent on the passage of the final reapportionment bill in 1929. The three categories of rural losers overwhelmingly opposed reapportionment; on eleven of their combined twenty-four votes, they gave 3 percent or less of their votes to reapportionment.

The pattern among no-change congressmen in Table 4.9 is more complex. On the initial roll call in 1921, each category backed reapportionment by at least a nine-to-one margin. Over the course of the decade, however, their support fragmented. Their votes on the next half-dozen roll calls fell roughly between the strong support from the gainers and the nearly united opposition of the losers. By the time of the last two votes in 1929, the urban categories of no-change representatives had come to advocate reapportionment by margins as wide as their original support, and the rural ones provided much less support than in 1921. The representatives from the most-rural districts and the most-rural states even failed to give the measures a majority, which the rural ones at least did.

Table 4.10 emphasizes the splits occurring along urban-rural lines within and between the gain, no change, and loss categories. Little disagreement exists between urban and rural or between metro and most-rural representatives within the gain group, and even less occurs between urban and rural in the loss group. Clearly, the self-interest involved in one's state gaining or losing under reapportionment outweighs any demographic differences. Within the no-change category, however, considerably more disagreement shows up between metro and most-rural congressmen and between those from most-urban states and most-rural states. The indexes of disagreement in the no-change category hit near or above the fifties on the fourth roll call and the last two roll calls. Nonetheless, no overwhelming tendency prevails within the no-change category.

The indexes in Table 4.10 also point out the disagreement between gain, no change, and loss groups and the urban-rural classifications within them. In the gain/no change comparison, only the most-rural groups display significant disagreement with any consistency; on five of the roll calls the index hit at least 50. The disagreement suggests that the most-rural representatives who expected no change probably voted more similarly to the most-rural losers than did any of the others in the no-change group. In a similar way, the urban–no-change representatives must have tended to vote more like the urban gainers than the urban losers, though the tendency is less pronounced than in the gain–no-change comparison. Such slight differences, though, pale in comparison to the gain/loss disagreements.

TABLE 4.10: Indexes of Disagreement by Urban/Rural Categories and Expected Gain, No Change, or Loss in Seats

	Roll Calls							
Legislator Groups	1	2	3	4	5	6	7	8
Gain								
Urban/Rural	2	22	13	11	11	8	6	7
Metro/Most-rural	8	37	14	12	11	10	8	0
No change								
Urban/Rural	2	16	3	26	8	15	32	31
Metro/Most-rural	4	43	11	49	18	30	51	50
Most-urban states/								
Most-rural states	2	20	6	55	33	25	67	53
Loss								
Urban/Rural	0	12	10	16	13	13	9	7
Gain/No change								
Urban	1	18	34	22	45	4	10	5
Metro	2	20	25	30	56	2	14	0
Most-urban states	2	31	17	27	43	1	9	3
Rural	1	24	50	65	63	22	57	50
Most-rural	14	14	50	65	63	22	57	50
No change/Loss								
Urban	67	27	10	46	39	18	63	54
Rural	69	55	17	36	60	15	40	40
Most-rural	72	69	17	9	23	16	32	33
Most-rural states	52	6	12	9	24	41	24	41
Gain/Loss								
Urban	68	45	44	68	84	21	73	59
Rural	70	79	67	73	86	26	76	69
Most-rural	58	83	67	76	86	38	89	83
Gain metro/Loss								
most-rural	66	46	53	88	97	48	97	83
Gain most-urban states/								
Loss most-rural states	48	57	35	91	100	67	100	100

Except for the relatively noncontroversial Roll Call 6, the gain/loss indexes topped 50 in nineteen of the twenty-one comparisons, and in the other two the indexes reached in the forties. When the gainers and losers are compared between metro and most rural and between most-urban states and most-rural states, the levels of disagreement are even higher. In fact, the disagreement on the last three votes is complete between the most-urban states expecting to gain and the most-rural states expecting to lose. Table 4.10 suggests, therefore, that the urban-rural categories have some marginal impact on the gain/no change/loss groups, but the more important factor remains the expected effects of reapportionment on a congressman's state.

Although the indexes of disagreement for gain/loss alone showed significant disagreement on seven of the eight roll calls (see Table 4.6), further analysis that considered the effects of party (see Table 4.8) and of urban-rural categories (see Table 4.10) failed to uncover any additional important disagreement not tied directly to the gain/loss comparison. In addition, the extended analysis revealed no particularly powerful pattern for the crucial no-change representatives. Perhaps a simultaneous consideration of party, urban-rural, and expected changes in seats will reveal patterns of disagreement hidden in previous comparisons.

Table 4.11 shows the percent supporting reapportionment by gain/no change/loss, by appropriate urban-rural categories within them, and by party within each urban-rural group. As must by now be expected, the gaining representatives provided extraordinarily high support. Except for the rural gainers, they backed reapportionment unanimously on the last five roll calls, and the rural gainers voted in favor of reapportionment by at least four-to-one margins except for two cases. Similarly, the loss category yields few surprises. Its members generally voted overwhelmingly against reapportionment; the only exceptions were the noncontroversial sixth roll call and urban Republicans, and even a majority of the latter opposed reapportionment. Among the no-change group, the nearly unanimous support for the final reapportionment bill among congressmen of both parties in all urban categories stands out in Table 4.11. Also apparent from Table 4.11 is the decline of support for reapportionment among Democrats in all three rural categories; initially more than 90 percent of them voted for reapportionment, but by the last two roll calls their support had fallen to about one-third.

To probe for important variations within the large and crucial group of congressmen who expected no change in their states' representation, Table 4.12 examines only the no-change group. It reports in yet more detail the various indexes of disagreement to see if a pattern emerges that suggests why they voted as they did. Among Republicans very little disagreement occurred between urban/rural, metro/most-rural, or most-urban states/most-rural states; only twice did the indexes go as high as the forties, and usually they remained

TABLE 4.11: Percent Support by Party, Urban/Rural Categories, and Expected Gain, No Change, or Loss in Seats

Legislator Groups*	Average No. in Groups	Roll Calls							
		1	2	3	4	5	6	7	8
Gain									
Urban									
Republicans	28	89	64	52	100	100	100	100	100
Metro									
Republicans	16	82	53	50	100	100	100	100	100
Most-urban states									
Republicans	19	83	71	32	100	100	100	100	100
Rural									
Democrats	21	95	90	54	59	88	94	83	90
Republicans	20	95	87	84	95	91	90	95	95
No change									
Urban									
Democrats	27	88	56	11	23	33	93	71	87
Republicans	56	94	48	26	86	67	98	93	98
Metro									
Democrats	20	83	20	25	78	29	95	80	100
Republicans	29	94	36	30	88	58	100	91	100
Most-urban states									
Democrats	20	93	0	13	29	30	95	88	100
Republicans	44	90	43	21	83	71	100	93	96
Rural									
Democrats	54	93	91	7	8	19	67	24	39
Republicans	54	95	46	27	74	59	96	83	88
Most-rural									
Democrats	33	95	90	12	3	14	61	21	34
Republicans	13	93	54	33	45	58	91	75	82
Most-rural states									
Democrats	42	93	96	5	2	18	69	16	33
Republicans	13	91	53	33	36	50	91	60	75
Loss									
Urban									
Republicans	14	20	21	14	29	23	85	31	46
Rural									
Democrats	29	25	12	0	0	0	60	0	9
Republicans	32	26	9	0	7	8	75	31	33
Most-rural									
Democrats	21	32	8	0	0	0	54	0	7
Most-rural states									
Democrats	13	54	20	0	0	0	40	0	0

*Members in all groups not listed were too few in number to be significant.

TABLE 4.12: Indexes of Disagreement by Party,
Urban/Rural Categories, and Expected No Change in Seats Only

Legislator Groups	Roll Calls							
	1	2	3	4	5	6	7	8
Democrats/Republicans								
Urban	6	8	15	63	34	5	22	9
Metro	11	16	5	10	29	5	11	0
Most-urban states	3	43	8	54	41	5	5	4
Rural	2	45	20	68	40	29	59	49
Most-rural	2	36	21	42	44	30	54	48
Most-rural states	2	43	28	34	32	22	44	42
Urban/Rural								
Democrats	5	35	4	15	14	26	47	48
Republicans	1	2	1	12	8	2	10	10
Metro/Most-rural								
Democrats	12	70	13	75	15	34	59	66
Republicans	1	18	3	43	0	9	16	18
Most-urban states/								
Most-rural states								
Democrats	0	96	8	27	12	26	72	67
Republicans	1	10	12	47	21	9	33	21
Urban Democrats/Rural								
Republicans	7	10	16	51	26	3	12	2
Urban Republicans/Rural								
Democrats	1	43	19	78	48	31	69	59
Metro Democrats/Most-rural								
Republicans	10	34	8	33	29	4	5	18
Metro Republicans/Most-rural								
Democrats	1	54	18	85	44	39	70	66
Most-urban states Democrats/								
Most-rural states								
Republicans	2	53	20	7	20	4	28	25
Most-urban states Republicans/								
Most-rural states								
Democrats	3	53	16	81	53	31	77	63

near or below 20. Among Democrats, however, considerable disagreement did appear on several occasions between metro/most-rural and most-urban states/most-rural states (the index of 96 on Roll Call 2 in the latter category is an aberration caused by only three most-urban states Democrats voting). On the last two roll calls, the vital ones for final passage of the final reapportionment legislation, the division within the Democrats hits its strongest levels. The Republicans, therefore, showed little variation according to urban-rural categories and generally supported reapportionment; the Democrats, however, divided to a much greater extent, with rural representatives opposing reapportionment and urban ones supporting it.

The isolation of rural Democratic voting on reapportionment emerges more clearly in interparty comparisons. Though never hitting high levels of significance, the disagreements between Democrats and Republicans in the rural, most rural, and most-rural states groups hovered around the 40 to 50 range, except for the first vote. Also, as the comparisons in the last six rows in Table 4.11 demonstrate, Democrats in the rural categories repeatedly differed with Republicans in the urban categories; the indexes often were near 50 or above and on the last two roll calls averaged 66. Rural Republicans, on the other hand, showed little disagreement with urban Democrats, just as they had differed only slightly with other Republicans. The Democrats in the three rural categories were the odd ones out among the representatives expecting no change in their states' representation. The isolation of the rural, most rural, and most-rural states Democrats apparently increased through the decade. On the first roll call the indexes of disagreement involving the three groups of rural Democrats remained quite low. They increased over the next several votes until they hit the upper fifties, sixties, and, in some cases, seventies on the last two roll calls. On the last two roll calls, the highest levels of disagreement always involved rural Democrats of one category or another.

Tables 4.11 and 4.12 suggest that the no-change representatives started out supporting reapportionment fairly uniformly, but by the end of the decade the no-change Democrats had become split along urban-rural lines. In 1929, all groups of urban Democrats in the no-change category joined the no-change Republicans to vote for reapportionment just as did the representatives from states expecting to gain seats. The rural categories of Democrats alone within the no-change group, however, sided by 1929 with the congressmen expecting to lose under a new reapportionment. The key division was gain/loss for congressmen expecting to gain or lose, and within the no-change group urban-rural splits occurred only among Democrats.

No single factor, therefore, seems to explain congressional voting on reapportionment in the 1920s. For congressmen from states expecting to gain seats, the prospect of additional power and influence for their states and perhaps smaller districts and easier elections for themselves probably prompted them to support reapportionment overwhelmingly. The reverse held true for representatives from states predicted to lose seats from a new reapportionment; they voted consistently against reapportionment as not in their own or their states' best interests. For the majority of congressmen who expected no change in the size of their states' delegations to the House of Representatives, other factors must have decided their votes. Partisanship and simply a belief in reapportionment every ten years may have encouraged no-change Republicans to endorse reapportionment, whether they came from urban or rural areas. For no-change Democrats, however, urban-rural pressures apparently exerted a decisive influence.

Although the indexes of disagreement point to some potentially important differences between the voting of urban and rural congressmen on reapportionment, another approach may further clarify the nature of divisions in the 1920s. The urban-rural conflict thesis emphasizes the rural resistance to change more than urban advocacy of progress. Rural areas have been portrayed as hotbeds of fundamentalist Christianity, as the source of efforts to restrict immigration, and as the strongest advocates of Prohibition; though by implication the urban areas have been just the opposite, the stress has been on the reactionary qualities of rural folk. The urban-rural interpretation for the 1920s would, therefore, lead to a greater emphasis on who actually opposed reapportionment legislation than on who supported it. In addition, congressmen may well have supported reapportionment because they believed the Constitution required it, but few would have opposed reapportionment on constitutional grounds.

The second step in analyzing the voting on reapportionment, therefore, focuses exclusively on the opponents of reapportionment. The following analysis will examine the voting on the eight roll calls on reapportionment to determine whether any group or bloc of con-

TABLE 4.13: Percentages of Total Vote
in the Opposition to Reapportionment by Urban/Rural Category

Legislator Groups	Average No. in Groups	Roll Calls							
		1	2	3	4	5	6	7	8
Urban	137	30	39	35	28	29	14	21	11
Metro	71	11	22	15	13	14	2	7	–
Rural	211	70	61	65	72	71	86	79	89
Most-rural	78	39	25	28	38	35	58	44	48

gressmen clearly and consistently formed the bulk of the opposition and support. All possibilities cannot be exhausted but some can be eliminated and others suggested as possible sources of serious resistance to reapportionment in the 1920s. Although the same data will be used, the emphasis will now be on the percentage of the opponents who belonged to a particular group (instead of the percentage of a particular group who opposed reapportionment). For example, even though rural Republicans did not unanimously oppose reapportionment in the 1920s, they may have provided a large part of the opposition to the various reapportionment measures considered by the House of Representatives in the decade. On one hypothetical roll call, a rather small minority of 35 of the 106 rural Republicans may have voted against reapportionment; if only 70 congressmen voted against the measure, their 35 votes may have amounted to half of the opposing votes. The rural Republicans would therefore in this case have constituted a major source of the opposition even though most of them actually supported the measure.

Table 4.13 reports the percentage of the total vote in opposition to reapportionment supplied by various groups of congressmen on the eight roll calls. It also supplies the average number of representatives in each group, and the size of the groups must be kept in mind. A small group voting unanimously against a reapportionment bill might supply only a small percentage of the opposition, whereas a relatively small part of a large group could make up a sizable percentage of the opponents.

An examination of Table 4.13 reveals some general contours within the opposition to reapportionment. Throughout the 1920s, the urban and metro categories provided a diminishing part of the opposition to reapportionment. On the final roll call urban representatives

TABLE 4.14: Percentages of Total Vote in the Opposition
to Reapportionment by Party and by Urban/Rural Category

Legislator Groups	Average No. in Groups	Roll Calls							
		1	2	3	4	5	6	7	8
DEMOCRATS	144	38	19	48	70	61	74	70	58
Urban	39	8	5	12	18	14	8	11	4
Metro	24	4	3	6	11	9	2	4	–
Rural	105	30	14	35	51	47	66	67	55
Most-rural	64	21	11	21	32	30	48	39	35
REPUBLICANS	204	62	81	52	30	39	26	30	42
Urban	98	22	35	23	10	15	6	10	8
Metro	47	7	19	9	2	5	–	2	–
Rural	106	39	46	29	21	24	20	21	34
Most-rural	25	18	14	7	6	5	10	5	13

provided only 11 percent of the opposition to passage of the reapportionment bill, although they had made up about one-third of the opposition earlier in the decade. The rural and most-rural categories, on the other hand, made up a slowly increasing part of the opposition. Rural congressmen, who at first were about two-thirds of the opponents, supplied almost 90 percent of the opposition to the final bill in 1929. Though not contradicting the findings in Table 4.1, the figures in Table 4.13 highlight the importance of the rural opposition. On the last roll call, for example, 41 percent of the rural representatives opposed reapportionment, but they contributed nearly 90 percent of the total opposition.

Similarly, the Democratic role in the opposition grew while the Republican share of the opposition shrank, according to Table 4.14. At the start of the 1920s, most of the opposition came from Republicans, but by the end most came from Democrats. When compared to the percentage of each party supporting reapportionment, however, their respective shares of the opposition are somewhat surprising. On the first roll call, for instance, 20 percent of the Democrats and 23 percent of the Republicans voted against reapportionment, but they made up respectively 38 and 62 percent of the opposition. The Republican opposition was obviously more significant early in the decade. By 1929, when 44 percent of the Democrats and only 19 percent of the Republicans cast votes against the final reapportionment bill, their respective shares of the total opposition were remarkably close—58 and 42 percent. The GOP opponents of reapportionment still played a key role in the opposition, even though they were a distinct minority within their own party. Crucial to the change in Democratic voting was the growing opposition among rural and most-rural Democrats. On the last three roll calls, rural Democrats alone constituted more than half the opposition. Among Republicans, however, rural and most-rural congressmen maintained a fairly steady role in opposition to reapportionment, usually between one-fourth and one-third of the total. Among urban and metro congressmen in each party, opposition to reapportionment declined, particularly among the Republicans. Tables 4.13 and 4.14 suggest, therefore, that rural Democrats supplied the bulk of the opposition to reapportionment, but rural Republicans played a greater role in the opposition to reapportionment than had been expected after the first step in the analysis.

According to Table 4.15, representatives from states expecting to gain seats under a new apportionment contributed very little to the opposition to reapportionment. Except for the second roll call that involved an expanded House and the third and fourth roll calls that involved controversial procedural points, the representatives expecting to gain seats under a new reapportionment provided only marginal opposition, usually about 5 percent or less. In fact, nearly half of the urban-rural classifications of expected gainers in Table 4.14 contributed nothing to the opposition to reapportionment (in some cases, obviously, because there were no gainers in the categories—such as Democrats from most-rural states). Even more significant, a majority of the expected gainers (average of 42 of 77) came from rural districts (according to the census definition), and even they provided very little of the opposition to reapportionment; self-interest clearly overruled any rural ties. The major sources of opposition to reapportionment were the no-change and losing representatives, each of which made up about half of the opposition.

Congressmen from states that expected to lose seats in a reapportioned House of Representatives were as crucial to the opposition to reapportionment as the no-change representatives were, even though there were many fewer of them (average 80 losers and 191 no-changers). When the vote was lopsided and the opposition to reapportionment was small, the losers made up a significantly large percentage of the opponents. For example, the first, sixth, seventh, and eighth roll calls saw the supporters of reapportionment win easily

TABLE 4.15: Percentages of Total Vote in the Opposition to Reapportionment by Expected Gain, Loss, or No Change in Seats, by Urban/Rural Category, and by Party

Legislator Groups	Average No. in Groups	Roll Calls							
		1	2	3	4	5	6	7	8
Gain	77	5	10	18	9	2	6	4	3
Democrats	28	1	1	5	8	1	2	3	2
Republicans	49	4	8	6	1	1	4	1	1
Urban	35	3	7	6	3	–	–	–	–
Democrats	7	–	–	1	3	–	–	–	–
Republicans	28	3	7	5	–	–	–	–	–
Metro	20	3	5	3	1	–	–	–	–
Democrats	4	–	–	–	1	–	–	–	–
Republicans	16	3	5	3	–	–	–	–	–
Rural	42	3	3	5	6	2	6	4	3
Democrats	21	1	1	4	6	1	2	3	2
Republicans	20	1	1	1	1	1	4	1	1
Most-rural	11	3	1	2	2	1	2	1	–
Democrats	9	1	1	2	2	–	–	1	–
Republicans	3	1	–	–	–	1	2	–	–
No Change	191	17	42	57	52	58	46	47	45
Democrats	81	9	5	29	41	37	40	38	37
Republicans	110	8	37	29	12	21	6	10	8
Urban	83	8	23	22	17	20	6	10	5
Democrats	27	4	3	9	12	11	4	7	4
Republicans	56	4	20	13	5	10	2	3	1
Metro	49	7	15	12	11	13	2	6	–
Democrats	20	4	3	6	9	8	2	4	–
Republicans	29	3	13	6	2	5	–	2	–
Rural	108	9	20	35	35	37	40	37	41
Democrats	54	5	2	20	28	26	36	30	33
Republicans	54	4	18	15	7	11	4	7	8
Most-rural	46	4	6	14	22	19	28	22	25
Democrats	33	3	1	11	19	16	26	20	22
Republicans	13	1	4	3	3	3	2	2	3
Loss	80	78	48	31	39	40	48	49	52
Democrats	35	28	13	14	21	23	32	29	20
Republicans	45	50	35	17	18	17	16	20	32
Urban	19	20	10	7	9	9	8	10	7
Democrats	5	4	2	2	4	3	4	4	–
Republicans	14	16	8	5	5	5	4	7	7
Metro	3	1	1	0	1	1	–	1	–
Democrats	1	–	–	0	1	1	–	1	–
Republicans	2	1	1	–	–	–	–	–	–
Rural	61	58	38	25	30	32	40	39	45
Democrats	29	24	11	12	17	20	28	25	20
Republicans	32	34	27	13	13	12	12	13	25
Most-rural	30	33	18	12	14	16	28	21	24
Democrats	21	17	8	8	11	14	22	18	13
Republicans	9	16	10	4	3	2	6	3	10

with 78, 85, 62, and 72 percent of the votes, and on the four roll calls the expected losers of seats made up 78, 48, 49, and 52 percent of the opponents (compare Tables 4.1 and 4.15). On the third roll call the expected losers fell to a low of only 31 percent of the opposition because the motion in question was soundly defeated with 76 percent of the House voting against it. Within the expected loss category, Democrats and Republicans each provided an average of about one-fourth of the opposition to the various proposals concerning reapportionment.

Very few representatives expecting their states to lose House seats under reapportionment came from urban areas. Neither urban Democrats nor urban Republicans in the losing group, therefore, contributed much of the opposition to reapportionment. The bulk of the opponents in the expected loss category hailed from rural districts; in fact, rural congressmen expecting their states to lose seats made up around 40 percent of the opposition to most of the reapportionment measures. No significant partisan disparities appeared among opponents in the losing rural categories.

Finally, no-change congressmen provided very little of the opposition on the initial reapportionment measure in 1921. Nine months later, however, they constituted nearly half the opposition to recommitting a bill for a House of 460 members. For the remainder of the decade-long controversy, no-change congressmen made up around half of the opposition, even though a substantial majority (67 to 88 percent) of the no-change group actually supported reapportionment on the last three roll call votes (see Table 4.5). The voting within the no-change group was not uniform. Democratic no-change representatives were a growing percentage of the opposition on the first four roll calls and then maintained a level of approximately 40 percent, while Republican no-changers composed a dwindling part of the opposition after the second roll call. By the final vote on the bill in 1929, Democrats were more than four times as important to the opposition than were Republicans. The partisan differences occurred in the no-change category even though Republicans outnumbered Democrats by about one-third.

Among the no-change representatives, the ones in the urban categories were only a small percentage of the opponents. The bulk of the no-change opponents of reapportionment fell in the rural groups. Rural no-change congressmen made up 35 percent or more of the opponents on the last six roll calls, while the most-rural and most-rural states representatives each composed about one-fourth of the opposition, even though they were much smaller groups. Within the rural categories, partisan differences mirrored the partisan splits within the larger no-change group: though initially indistinguishable, by the later roll calls the Democrats were a much larger percentage of the opposition than were the Republicans in each rural category.

In the rural no-change category the differences become especially evident because each party had an average of fifty-four congressmen in it; the rural Republican contribution to the opposition hit its peak on the second roll call at 15 percent and declined on subsequent votes, while the Democratic part of the opponents of reapportionment grew from 5 and 2 percent on the first two roll calls to reach 36 percent on the sixth roll call and 33 percent on the last one. Democrats in the most rural and most-rural states categories followed similar patterns. Among the representatives expecting no change in their states' representation under a new reapportionment bill, therefore, the congressmen in the rural categories, and particularly the Democrats, made up a sizable and growing percentage of the overall opposition.

The examination of only the opponents of reapportionment clearly indicates that rural representatives made up the overwhelming majority of the congressmen resisting reapportionment, and their share of the opposition grew gradually over the decade. Democrats, particularly in the rural no-change group, appeared more influenced by urban-rural forces than their Republican colleagues, but otherwise rural opposition seemed unaffected by party. When combined with the indexes of disagreement from the first phase of the roll-call analysis, the evidence from the opposition confirms that personal political self-interest was the primary consideration of most congressmen in voting on reapportionment. Since most representatives expecting to lose from reapportionment came from rural districts, rural losers constituted a large part of the opposition. They joined with rural representatives expecting no change, especially Democrats, to constitute nearly 80 percent of the opponents on the final four roll calls.

Although rural representatives constituted most of the opposition to reapportionment, not all of them voted against the various reapportionment measures that came before the House of Representatives in the 1920s. Rural congressmen from states expecting to gain seats under reapportionment tended to support reapportionment, and their colleagues from states expecting to be unaffected by reapportionment divided somewhat along partisan lines. The most important factor determining the voting would seem, therefore, to be the expected gain or loss of seats in the House, which is completely understandable. Urban-rural influences would seem to have been at best secondary. Partisan factors played a tertiary role in the voting.

Conclusion

NEVER BEFORE or since the 1920s has the United States Congress failed to reapportion the House of Representatives after a decennial census of population. Despite debates over statistical procedures, the proper size of the House of Representatives, and the ways congressmen were chosen, Congress had always overcome controversies and passed reapportionment legislation within a couple of years of the census. Even the sectional jealousies of the nineteenth century had not prevented the congressional reapportionment everyone believed the Constitution required. After the 1910 census, Congress had readily enacted reapportionment legislation that increased the size of the House to 435 and provided thereby for representation for the soon-to-be-admitted states of Arizona and New Mexico. Once again after the 1920 census, the House Committee on the Census began to consider bills to reapportion the House. Only after a decade-long struggle, however, did Congress finally enact legislation for reapportionment after the 1930 census. The unprecedented procrastination in reapportionment provoked some controversy among the public and in the press, but no major uproar occurred. No individual or group, for instance, challenged in the courts the constitutionality of laws passed by an unreapportioned Congress or the results of presidential elections decided by an unfairly apportioned electoral college. The deadlock in the 1920s nevertheless denied many Americans their just representation in Congress for a decade.

The failure to reapportion the House based on the 1920 census resulted from many controversies that divided the Congress. Although the 1920 census had occurred without any special controversy, its results soon sparked strenuous disagreements. The 1920 census showed that the population had grown by nearly 14 million and that most people for the first time lived in urban areas, but some questioned the accuracy of a census taken so soon after the socially disruptive World War I. The population shifts revealed by the census meant that some changes in the apportionment of congressmen would be necessary; to prevent any state from losing a representative, sixty new congressmen would have to be added to the House. Physical limitations of the House chamber, however, made more congressional seats unlikely, and some representatives argued that the House's efficiency would decline if it grew in numbers. Others pointed out that the larger number of voting constituents after women's suffrage made smaller districts and more representatives necessary. An additional controversy involved whether representation should be based on a population that included Negroes and aliens who could not vote. Finally, congressmen disagreed over the proper statistical procedure to use to allot seats in the House.

The law finally enacted by Congress in 1929 rendered unlikely any recurrence of the unprecedented delay in reapportioning seats. The automatic features of the new law meant that congressional action would no longer be necessary every ten years. After the 1930 census, the House of Representatives was reapportioned easily, in part because the two statistical methods agreed on the distribution of House seats among the states. The first reapportionment in twenty years expanded the delegation from California from eleven to twenty, gave Michigan four more representatives, and provided for two more congressmen each for New York, New Jersey, and Ohio. After the 1940 census, however, the two statistical methods included in the 1929 law yielded slightly different results; the method of major fractions shifted one seat from Arkansas to Michigan, and the method of equal proportions left each state the same. To save a sure Democratic seat in Arkansas, the Census Committee moved to adopt the method of equal proportions for future reapportionments and to make it apply retroactively. Congress agreed to the change, saved the seat for Arkansas, and made the method of equal proportions the sole method for reapportioning the House of Representatives in the future. After the 1929 law and its amendment in 1941, the regular reapportionment of the House of Representatives has proceeded without much controversy or public notice.[1]

The major legal challenge to congressional reapportionment after 1930 came from citizens who wanted to restore the requirements that congressional districts be compact, consist of contiguous territory, and have, as nearly as possible, equal populations. Though the three requirements had been in the 1911 reapportionment law and earlier ones, the 1929 law had omitted them. By allowing the state legislatures freedom to draw district lines, the federal courts permitted malapportioned congressional districts, and the discrepancies usually benefited small-town and rural districts at the expense of urban ones. One urban New York district, for example, had 799,407 people while a rural one in the state had only 90,671. For three decades, the federal courts acquiesced in the malapportionment that favored rural areas. In 1963, however, the Georgia case of *Wesberry v. Sanders* questioned the omission from the 1929 reapportionment law of any requirement that districts have nearly equal populations. In its ruling in *Wesberry v. Sanders*, the United States Supreme Court finally restored one of the pre-1929 mandates when it ruled that districts did have to be equal in population "as nearly as practicable."[2] In spite of the 1941 change in the reapportionment process and the 1963 court decision, congressional reapportionment after the 1920s has occurred routinely. The experience in the 1920s was truly an anomaly.

Running through many of the specific points of disagreement over reapportionment in the 1920s and, more important, pervading the entire debate in the House of Representatives and much of the press's commentary were explicitly stated conflicts between urban and rural interests and between their representatives. For example, the rapidly growing areas were usually cities and the declining ones rural so the states that would lose seats in a new House of only 435 members would more likely be rural than urban. The rural areas also naturally challenged the accuracy of a census that showed a drop in rural population. In addition, aliens also lived predominantly in urban areas, though blacks resided overwhelmingly in the rural southern states. Even the statistical aspects of reapportionment impinged on urban-rural concerns because one procedure favored states with smaller populations, which were usually rural ones, and another benefited states with larger populations, which were usually urban.

Even more significant for rural interests were the feared legislative results of reapportionment. Any reapportionment based on the 1920 census would give more congressional power to urban areas at the expense of rural areas. Rural representatives worried that the larger number of urban congressmen would then vote to repeal prohibition and immigration restriction legislation, two measures seen as protecting traditional rural America's way of life. Rural representatives made innumerable invidious comparisons of urban and rural ways of life, and they frequently fired stinging attacks at urban inhabitants and the evils they seemed to embody. The urban-rural conflict over reapportionment was a manifestation primarily of rural resentments of urban growth and dominance; urban representatives seldom engaged in any overt verbal attacks on rural America.

The urban-rural rhetoric of the debate over reapportionment supplies important support for the dominant historical interpretation of the 1920s. For more than a generation, scholars have viewed much of the 1920s in terms of urban-rural tension and conflict. In an ironic inversion of popular attitudes in the 1920s, they have almost invariably displayed hostility toward the rural interests. They have, however, borrowed their analysis from the social sciences and imposed it on the decade without offering any significant evidence that people in the 1920s themselves perceived an urban-rural conflict or were even aware of such tension. An examination of the congressional debate over reapportionment for the first time provides from the 1920s just such extensive concrete examples of people's perceptions of urban-rural conflict. The examples mean that urban-rural conflict need no longer remain an abstraction applied to the 1920s; historians now have contemporary evidence confirming the existence of urban-rural tension.

Like the rhetoric in the debate over reapportionment, an examination of the voting in the House of Representatives on reapportionment cannot conclusively confirm an urban-rural interpretation. Many representatives decided how to vote on reapportionment primarily on the basis of whether their state expected to gain or lose seats in a reapportioned House of Representatives. The clear self-interest of the congressman and his state prevailed, but that should not be surprising on an issue so crucial to political survival. If predictions indicated his state would gain one seat or more, for example, the congressman did not feel endangered and usually voted for reapportionment. If, however, his state expected to lose at least one seat in a reapportioned House, the representative worried that his seat might be affected and most likely opposed all efforts to reapportion the House. A state's expected gain or loss, therefore, overcame the urban or rural qualities of a congressional district in influencing the votes of most congressmen.

Among representatives from states expecting neither to gain nor lose seats from a reapportionment, urban-rural factors were very important, though not as uniformly decisive as the strongly urban-rural rhetoric may have suggested. Republicans expecting no change in their states' allotment in the House generally voted for reapportionment, perhaps because they simply believed in reapportionment every ten years or because they hoped their party would benefit from reapportionment. Among the no-change Republicans, no significant differences in voting on reapportionment appeared between the urban and rural representatives. For Democratic congressmen in the no-change group, however, urban-rural pressures apparently did eventually exert a decisive influence. As the decade-long debate over reapportionment progressed, the urban-rural rhetoric may have convinced the rural no-change Democrats that something important to rural interests needed to be protected by voting against reapportionment. By the end of the decade, urban and rural Democrats in the no-change group divided to a significant degree with the more urban ones supporting and the more rural ones opposing reapportionment. More specifically, the urban-rural division was not between congressmen from districts more than half urban and others from districts more than half rural (according to the census definitions), but the split really occurred between congressmen from metropolitan districts and their colleagues from very rural areas and between representatives from heavily urban states and those from very rural states.

Consideration of just the opponents of reapportionment in the 1920s reinforced the real importance of rural representatives. Nearly all the opposition to reapportionment came from rural congressmen, and many of the other opponents were urban congressmen from states expecting to lose seats in a new House of Representatives. Certainly not all rural congressmen voted against all reapportionment measures, but the bulk of the opponents came from rural areas. The rural representatives were the ones most likely to fear reapportionment and its effects and, therefore, the ones who most consistently resisted any changes in the distribution of seats in the House.

Analysis of the congressional voting on reapportionment, as a result, suggests that the ubiquitous urban-rural interpretation does indeed apply, even if somewhat imperfectly. Urban-rural tensions seem, as David Burner has argued in *The Politics of Provincialism*, a vital explanation for the behavior of the Democrats who expected to be unaffected by reapportionment. Among the Democrats predicted to gain from reapportionment, political self-interest naturally augmented any urban sentiments and outweighed rural loyalties. Mostly from rural areas, Democrats who expected their states to lose seats found their self-interest reinforced by urban-rural arguments. For the Republican congressmen urban-rural factors apparently had less impact.

Although the urban-rural model's utility in partially explaining the voting behavior on reapportionment suggests that the urban-rural interpretation has some validity, the repeated use of urban-rural themes by congressmen trying to convince colleagues in debate much more clearly demonstrates the importance of urban-rural conflict. The fact that some politicians thought urban-rural arguments would be powerful and persuasive testifies to their perceived importance at the time. Furthermore, the journalists' ready use of urban-rural conflict to explain the stalemate over reapportionment showed that they too accepted urban-rural conflict as a reality in their society. Urban-rural tensions may not have dominated the decade as some historians have suggested, yet they clearly did play a significant role for some people on some issues, including congressional reapportionment.[3]

The study of reapportionment alone, however, can neither completely confirm the urban-rural thesis nor disprove competing arguments that stress clashes between modern and Victorian cultures, producer and consumer cultures, core and periphery areas, or various ethnocultural groups. The struggle over reapportionment did not exactly pit urban interests against rural ones so students should realize that other conflicts of the time may not have been simple struggles either. The Ku Klux Klan, Prohibition, immigration restriction, and fundamentalism also were probably not simple examples of conflicts between urban and rural peoples, modern and Victorian cultures, producer and consumer interests, or various ethnic and religious groups. After all, immigrants in urban areas who liked to drink alcoholic beverages could have fought Prohibition out of self-interest without being examples of a modern consumer culture struggling against a Victorian culture.[4]

Before historians of the 1920s can more confidently evaluate the importance and validity of the urban-rural thesis, more work needs to be done. In politics, for instance, the Republicans deserve a study as revealing as Burner's examination of the Democrats to determine whether urban-rural forces ever divided them and, if not, why. Economic, labor, and cultural historians need to plumb the relationships between economic functions and values. Urban historians should explore the attitudes of urbanites toward rural areas to see whether they reciprocated the rural hostility toward cities.[5] Scholars also need to study more sympathetically Americans who lived in small towns and rural areas to determine why they felt so defensive toward and threatened by cities.

More generally, historians should refine their definitions of urban and rural to include more than demography, though it certainly should not be ignored. The study of reapportionment employing urban and rural in their crude demographic meanings has suggested the validity of the urban-rural thesis. The necessary and accessible demographic data on each congressional district made analysis of the roll-call voting in the House of Representatives possible, but it should be only the first step in reevaluating the urban-rural thesis.

Scholars have too cavalierly used the urban-rural model without considering the substance, development, and refinement of Ferdinand Tonnies's conceptions of *Gemeinschaft* and *Gesellschaft* from which the use of urban and rural have usually derived. Thomas Bender has suggested that "by returning to the nineteenth-century origins of this theory, particularly to Ferdinand Tonnies's *Gemeinschaft-Gesellschaft* typology, one finds a surprising complexity and sensitivity to actual historical processes that is absent in many modern theories that derive from the work of Tonnies."[6] A more careful and rigorous use of Tonnies's categories might, therefore, revive a more sophisticated, less static version of the urban-rural thesis, especially if historians can emulate Tonnies's unprejudiced approach to both urban and rural societies.

As Bender has proposed, a greater awareness that urban and rural can mean more than just the number of people living in a particular incorporated or unincorporated area ought to lead scholars to examine the real lives of urban and rural people to determine whether they have different sets of ideas, values, attitudes, and behavior patterns. After further study, scholars may conclude that urban and rural categories that include more than just demography can supplement or even supplant the strongest recent competitors, which see conflict between modern and Victorian cultures, between consumer and producer cultures, between core and periphery regions, or between ethnocultural groups. The analysis of urban-rural congressional voting on reapportionment, however, should at least alert historians to the complexities, including some urban-rural conflict, probably also hidden within the alternative models. In addition, students of the 1920s should be ever mindful of possible congruences among what are now variously called urban, modern, consumer, and ritualist cultures, and conversely among rural, Victorian, producer, and pietist cultures—demographic, intellectual, economic, and ethnic factors may reinforce one another in producing conflicts in American society —and the interplay of various forces would need to be analyzed.

Scholars need also to be prepared to discover few pure examples of urban and rural cultures.[7] Great variety exists, for example, among urban cultures because of the particular city's circumstances, including its economy, its history, its ethnic and racial composition, its geography, and its relationship to the surrounding countryside. Among rural cultures a similar variety exists because of differences in crops, in size of farms, in farm populations, in trade patterns, and in historical development. Furthermore, considerable overlapping of urban and rural cultures may occur among the same people as they exhibit some characteristics of both ideal cultures.

And finally, students of the 1920s ought to expand their vision to include the years before and after that decade because it has become a historical cliché that should probably be avoided. Unlike the struggle over congressional reapportionment, most issues in the 1920s usually explained by the urban-rural model have histories before and after that decade. The controversies over Prohibition, immigration restriction, and fundamentalism had longer lives than just the 1920s. The alternate modern-Victorian and consumer-producer models have pointed to the inadequacy of the 1920s by suggesting that analysis should move beyond the decade because forces did not suddenly appear in 1920 and then disappear in 1930. Investigators of urban-rural tension need to follow the lead of students of its competitors and expand their work beyond the 1920s to examine possible urban-rural conflicts as they gradually emerged and declined.[8]

Analysis of the controversy over reapportionment—limited conveniently to the 1920s, whether that decade has significance itself or not—suggests the importance of the urban-rural model. Without conclusively proving the urban-rural thesis, the analysis can serve to reawaken historians to the possible significance of urban and rural forces in the early decades of the twentieth century. Before scholars rush to reject the urban-rural thesis and embrace modern-Victorian or consumer-producer explanations, they should beware that urban-rural conflict may still remain an important part of American life, even if it is not the whole story.

Appendixes

APPENDIX 1: Population Figures for 1910, 1920, and 1930

	1910	1920	1930
United States	91,972,266	105,710,620	122,775,046
Alabama	2,138,093	2,348,174	2,646,248
Arizona	204,354	334,162	435,573
Arkansas	1,574,449	1,752,204	1,854,482
California	2,377,549	3,426,861	5,677,251
Colorado	799,024	939,629	1,035,791
Connecticut	1,114,756	1,380,631	1,606,903
Delaware	202,322	223,003	238,380
Florida	752,619	968,470	1,468,211
Georgia	2,609,121	2,895,832	2,908,506
Idaho	325,594	431,866	445,032
Illinois	5,638,591	6,485,280	7,630,654
Indiana	2,700,876	2,930,390	3,238,503
Iowa	2,224,771	2,404,021	2,470,939
Kansas	1,690,949	1,769,257	1,880,999
Kentucky	2,289,905	2,416,630	2,614,589
Louisiana	1,656,388	1,798,509	2,101,593
Maine	742,371	768,014	797,423
Maryland	1,295,346	1,449,661	1,631,526
Massachusetts	3,366,416	3,852,356	4,249,614
Michigan	2,810,173	3,668,412	4,842,325
Minnesota	2,075,708	2,387,125	2,563,953
Mississippi	1,797,114	1,790,618	2,009,821
Missouri	3,293,335	3,404,055	3,629,367
Montana	376,053	548,889	537,606
Nebraska	1,192,214	1,296,372	1,377,963
Nevada	81,875	77,407	91,058
New Hampshire	430,572	443,083	465,293
New Jersey	2,537,167	3,155,900	4,041,334
New Mexico	327,301	360,350	423,317
New York	9,113,614	10,385,227	12,588,066

(Continued)

Appendix 1—(Continued)

	1910	1920	1930
North Carolina	2,206,287	2,559,123	3,170,276
North Dakota	577,056	646,872	680,845
Ohio	4,767,121	5,759,394	6,646,697
Oklahoma	1,657,155	2,028,283	2,396,040
Oregon	672,765	783,389	953,786
Pennsylvania	7,665,111	8,720,017	9,631,350
Rhode Island	542,610	604,397	687,497
South Carolina	1,515,400	1,683,724	1,738,765
South Dakota	583,388	636,547	692,849
Tennessee	2,184,789	2,337,885	2,616,556
Texas	3,896,542	4,663,228	5,824,715
Utah	373,351	449,396	507,847
Vermont	355,956	352,428	359,611
Virginia	2,061,612	2,309,187	2,421,851
Washington	1,141,990	1,356,621	1,563,396
West Virginia	1,221,119	1,463,701	1,729,205
Wisconsin	2,333,860	2,632,067	2,939,006
Wyoming	145,965	194,402	225,565

APPENDIX 2: Eleven Largest Metropolitan Districts (1920 Census)

District	Congressional Districts
1. New York City	New York 1–25
	New Jersey 3, 5–12
2. Chicago	Illinois 1–11
3. Philadelphia	Pennsylvania 1–8 (1–9)*
4. Boston	Massachusetts 5–14
5. Pittsburgh	Pennsylvania 25, 31–36 (22, 24, 29–32)*
6. Detroit	Michigan 1, 6, 7, 13
7. Cleveland	Ohio 20–22
8. St. Louis	Missouri 10–12
	Illinois 22
9. San Francisco–Oakland	California 1, 3–6, 8
10. Los Angeles	California 9, 10
11. Baltimore	Maryland 2–5

*Individual states redrew some district lines during the 1920s. The initial figure is for the original district and the figure in parentheses is for the redrawn district.

APPENDIX 3: Seven Most Urban* States (1920 Census)

State	Percent Urban	No. Congressional Districts
1. Rhode Island	97.5	3
2. Massachusetts	94.8	16
3. New York	82.7	43
4. New Jersey	78.4	12
5. California	68.0	11
6. Illinois	67.9	27
7. Connecticut	67.8	5
		117

*Census definition of urban.

APPENDIX 4: 104 Most-Rural* Districts (1920 Census)

State and District	Percent Urban*	State and District	Percent Urban*
1. Alabama 5	1.7	40. Tennessee 9	11.4
2. Missouri 16	1.8	41. North Carolina 1	11.5
3. Kentucky 4	2.4	42. South Carolina 6	11.7
4. Mississippi 2	2.8	43. Minnesota 9	12.0
5. South Carolina 2	3.4	44. Kentucky 9	12.1
6. Alabama 10	3.5	45. Kentucky 11	12.2
7. Vermont 2	4.1	46. Louisiana 8	12.3
8. Kentucky 10	4.5	47. Tennessee 5	12.4
9. Kansas 6	4.9	Virginia 5	12.4
10. Tennessee 4	5.0	49. Tennessee 8	12.5
11. Maryland 2	5.7		(9.7 and 10.0)†
12. Tennessee 7	6.1	50. Florida 2	12.6
	(5.9)†	51. South Carolina 3	12.8
13. Alabama 6	7.0	52. Mississippi 7	12.9
14. Louisiana 5	7.3	Texas 3	12.9
15. Arkansas 2	7.4	54. Kentucky 8	13.1
16. South Dakota 3	7.8	55. California 2	13.2
17. Georgia 9	8.1	56. Georgia 8	13.4
18. Arkansas 3	8.2	57. South Carolina 5	13.5
19. North Dakota 2	8.4	58. Missouri 14	13.6
20. Mississippi 3	8.5	Nebraska 6	13.6
21. Georgia 12	8.6	60. West Virginia 5	13.8
22. Minnesota 7	9.1	61. Georgia 3	14.0
Missouri 6	9.1	Virginia 7	14.0
24. Texas 9	9.2	63. Maryland 1	14.3
25. Arkansas 7	9.4	Nebraska 4	14.3
26. Maryland 5	9.7	Texas 6	14.3
27. Missouri 3	9.8		(16.1)†
28. Oklahoma 7	10.5	66. Virginia 10	14.4
29. Virginia 8	10.6	67. Illinois 24	14.5
30. Mississippi 4	10.7	North Carolina 3	14.5
31. Nebraska 3	10.8	69. North Carolina 10	14.7
Virginia 9	10.8	Texas 18	14.7
Alabama 7	10.8	Tennessee 1	14.7
34. North Carolina 7	10.9	72. North Carolina 2	14.9
35. Kansas 4	11.0	73. Georgia 2	15.1
North Dakota 2	11.0	North Carolina 4	15.1
37. Kentucky 3	11.2	75. Georgia 7	15.2
Mississippi 5	11.2	76. Mississippi 1	15.3
Missouri 13	11.2	77. Missouri 9	15.4

(Continued)

Appendix 4—(Continued)

	State and District	Percent Urban*		State and District	Percent Urban*
78.	Alabama 3	15.5	92.	West Virginia 2	18.5
79.	Arkansas 1	15.6	93.	Missouri 1	18.7
80.	Iowa 8	15.7	94.	Louisiana 3	19.0
81.	Virginia 4	16.0	95.	Oklahoma 6	19.1
82.	Arkansas 6	16.5	96.	Louisiana 6	19.3
83.	Minnesota 2	17.1	97.	Georgia 4	19.4
84.	Texas 1	17.4		Kentucky 1	19.4
85.	Louisiana 7	17.6		West Virginia 3	19.4
	Alabama 8	17.6	100.	Nebraska 5	19.6
87.	Oklahoma 4	17.8	101.	Florida 3	19.7
88.	New Mexico 1	18.0		Nevada 1	19.7
	West Virginia 6	18.0		Wisconsin 10	19.7
90.	South Dakota 2	18.2	104.	Ohio 5	19.9
91.	South Dakota 1	18.4			

*Census definition of urban, with rural being everything else.
†Individual states redrew some district lines during the 1920s. The initial figure is for the original district and the figure in parentheses is for the redrawn district.

APPENDIX 5: Fourteen Most Rural* States (1920 Census)

	State	Percent Urban*	No. Congressional Districts
1.	Mississippi	13.4	8
2.	North Dakota	13.6	3
3.	South Dakota	16.0	3
4.	Arkansas	16.6	7
5.	South Carolina	17.5	7
6.	New Mexico	18.0	1
7.	North Carolina	19.2	10
8.	Nevada	19.7	1
9.	Alabama	21.7	10
10.	Georgia	25.1	12
11.	West Virginia	25.2	6
12.	Tennessee	26.1	10
13.	Kentucky	26.2	11
14.	Oklahoma	26.6	8
			97

*Census definition of urban, with rural being everything else.

APPENDIX 6: Seats in House of Representatives in 1910 and 1930

State	1910	Expected Change	1930	State	1910	Expected Change	1930
Alabama	10	–	9	Nebraska	6	–1	5
Arizona	1	–	1	Nevada	1	–	1
Arkansas	7	–	7	New Hampshire	2	–	2
California	11	+3	20	New Jersey	12	+1	14
Colorado	4	–	4	New Mexico	1	–	1
Connecticut	5	+1	6	New York	43	–	45
Delaware	1	–	1	North Carolina	10	+1	11
Florida	4	–	5	North Dakota	3	–	2
Georgia	12	–	10	Ohio	22	+2	24
Idaho	2	–	2	Oklahoma	8	–	9
Illinois	27	–	27	Oregon	3	–	3
Indiana	13	–1	12	Pennsylvania	36	–	34
Iowa	11	–1	9	Rhode Island	3	–1	2
Kansas	8	–1	7	South Carolina	7	–	6
Kentucky	11	–1	9	South Dakota	3	–	2
Louisiana	8	–1	8	Tennessee	10	–	9
Maine	4	–1	3	Texas	18	+1	20
Maryland	6	–	6	Utah	2	–	2
Massachusetts	16	–	15	Vermont	2	–1	1
Michigan	13	+2	17	Virginia	10	–	9
Minnesota	10	–	9	Washington	5	+1	6
Mississippi	8	–1	7	West Virginia	6	–	6
Missouri	16	–2	13	Wisconsin	11	–	10
Montana	2	–	2	Wyoming	1	–	1

Notes

Preface

1. Betty B. Rosenbaum, "The Urban-Rural Conflict as Evidenced in the Reapportionment Situation," *Social Forces* 12 (March 1934): 421–26; Hubert Searcy, "Problems of Congressional Reapportionment," *Southwestern Social Science Quarterly* 16 (June 1935): 58–68; Frederick L. Paxson, *Post-War Years: Normalcy, 1918–1933* (Berkeley and Los Angeles, 1938), pp. 185–87; Margo J. Anderson, *The American Census: A Social History* (New Haven, 1988), pp. 140–56. For examples of political scientists, see the notes to Chapter 1. The only recent United States history textbook to mention reapportionment in the 1920s is George Brown Tindall, *America: A Narrative History* (New York, 1984), p. 996. Tindall learned of the issue from me.

2. David Burner, *The Politics of Provincialism: The Democratic Party in Transition, 1918–1932* (New York, 1967), p. 106; Andrew Sinclair, *Prohibition: The Era of Excess* (Boston, 1962), p. 91.

3. Inspection of a dozen manuscript collections of congressmen's papers, however, failed to yield any important information on the reapportionment controversy. These manuscript collections included the papers of Tom Connally, Frank Lester Greene, Charles L. McNary, Mills W. Ogden, Key Pittman, Henry T. Rainey, and Wallace Humphrey White, all in the Library of Congress; the papers of Furnifold Simmons and George Holden Tinkham, both at Duke University; and the papers of Robert Doughton, O. Max Gardner, and Claude Kitchin, all at the University of North Carolina. This sample suggested that congressmen probably conducted little correspondence pertaining to reapportionment. They and their constituents must have assumed they agreed on the issue.

4. A longer version of the chapter appeared as "Urban-Rural Conflict in the 1920s: A Historiographical Assessment," *Historian* 44 (November 1986): 26–48.

5. J. Morgan Kousser, "History QUASSHed: Quantitative Social Scientific History in Perspective," *American Behavioral Scientist* 23 (July–August 1980): 885.

Chapter 1: The Historiographical Importance of Urban-Rural Conflict in the 1920s

1. Henry F. May, "Shifting Perspectives on the 1920s," *Mississippi Valley Historical Review* 43 (December 1956): 405–27; Richard L. Lowitt, "Prosperity Decade, 1917–1928," in *Interpreting and Teaching American History*, ed. William E. Cartwright and Richard L. Watson, Jr. (Washington, D.C., 1961), pp. 231–63; Burl Noggle, "The Twenties: A New Historiographical Frontier," *Journal of American History* 53 (September 1966): 299–314; Noggle, "Configurations of the Twenties," in *The Reinterpretation of American History and Culture*, ed. Cartwright and Watson (Washington, D.C.: 1973), pp. 465–90; Gerald N. Grob and George A. Billias, "The 1920s: Decade of Decline or Destiny?" in *Interpretations of American History: Patterns and Perspectives*, vol. 2, *Since 1865*, ed. Grob and Billias, 4th ed. (New York, 1982), pp. 249–65.

2. Ferdinand Tonnies, *Community and Society (Gemeinschaft and Gesellschaft)*, trans. and ed. Charles P. Loomis (East Lansing, 1957), originally published in German in 1877 (see especially the Foreword by Pitirim Sorokin, pp. vii–viii); Ferdinand Tonnies, *Ferdinand Tonnies on Sociology: Pure, Applied, and Empirical*, ed. with intro. by Werner J. Cahnman and Rudolph Herberle (Chicago, 1971), esp. pp. vii–xxii; Robert A. Nisbet, *The Sociological Tradition* (New York, 1966), pp. 73–80; Edward Shils, "The Contemplation of Society in America," in *Paths of American Thought*, ed. Morton White and Arthur M. Schlesinger, Jr. (Boston, 1963), pp. 396–400; Linda Stoneall, *Country Life, City Life: Five Theories of Community* (New York, 1983), pp. 6–11.

3. Lowry Nelson, *Rural Sociology: Its Origin and Growth in the United States* (Minneapolis, 1969), p. 113 and passim.

4. John Dewey, "The American Intellectual Frontier," *New Republic* 30 (May 10, 1922): 303–5.

5. Lewis Mumford, "The City," p. 17; H. L. Mencken, "Politics," p. 24; Louis Raymond Reid, "The Small Town," pp. 287–90, all in *Civilization in the United States: An Inquiry by Thirty Americans*, ed. Harold E. Stearns (New York, 1922).

6. John Moffat Mecklin, *The Ku Klux Klan: A Study of the American Mind* (New York, 1924), pp. 95–125. Mecklin attributed much of the Klan's success to the impact of World War I: "The Klan has literally battened upon the irrational fear psychology that followed on the heels of the war" (p. 122).

7. Andre Seigfried, *America Comes of Age* (New York, 1927), pp. 3, 74, 76, 130–37.

8. H. Richard Niebuhr, *The Social Sources of Denominationalism* (New York, 1929), p. 184; Niebuhr, "Fundamentalism," in *Encyclopedia of the*

Social Sciences, ed. Edwin R. A. Seligman (New York, 1931), pp. 526–27.

9. Walter Lippmann, "The Causes of Political Indifference Today," *Atlantic Monthly* 139 (February 1927): 261–68; reprinted in Lippmann, *Men of Destiny* (New York, 1927), pp. 18–34.

10. Frederick Lewis Allen, *Only Yesterday: An Informal History of the Nineteen-Twenties* (New York, 1931), pp. 20–77, 186, 188, 195. For analyses of *Only Yesterday*, see Kenneth S. Lynn, "Only Yesterday," *American Scholar* 49 (Autumn 1980): 513–18, and William L. Burton, "'Yesterday' Revisited," *Illinois Quarterly* 36 (September 1973): 49–64.

11. Darwin Payne, *The Man of Only Yesterday: Frederick Lewis Allen* (New York, 1975), pp. 99, 289 n. 33.

12. William Preston Slosson, *The Great Crusade and After, 1914–1928*, vol. 12 of A History of American Life, ed. Arthur M. Schlesinger and Dixon Ryan Fox (New York, 1931), pp. 287, 297–303, 307–14, 319; Frederick L. Paxson, *Recent History of the United States, 1865 to the Present*, rev. and enlarged ed. (Boston, 1937), pp. 588–602; Samuel Eliot Morison and Henry Steele Commager, *The Growth of the American Republic* (New York, 1937), pp. 525, 543, 545; George E. Mowry, "The First World War and American Democracy," in *War as a Social Institution: The Historians' Perspective*, ed. Jesse D. Clarkson and Thomas C. Cochran (New York, 1941), pp. 176–79; Harold U. Faulkner, *American Political and Social History* (New York, 1947), pp. 654–57; Faulkner, *From Versailles to the New Deal: A Chronicle of the Harding-Coolidge Era*, vol. 51 of The Chronicles of America (New Haven, 1950), p. 127.

13. Arthur M. Schlesinger, Sr., "The City in American History," *Mississippi Valley Historical Review* 27 (June 1940): 43–66; Kenneth C. McKay, *The Progressive Movement of 1924* (New York, 1947), pp. 99–100; Paxson, *Post War Years*, pp. 165, 315; Harold J. Laski, *The American Democracy: A Commentary and an Interpretation* (New York, 1948), pp. 148–57, 287.

14. Samuel Lubell, *The Future of American Politics* (New York, 1952), pp. 38–39.

15. John Higham, *Strangers in the Land: Patterns of American Nativism, 1860–1925* (New Brunswick, N.J., 1955), pp. 264–330; Norman Furniss, *The Fundamentalist Controversy, 1918–1931* (New Haven, 1954), pp. 28–29.

16. Richard Hofstadter, *The Age of Reform: From Bryan to F.D.R.* (New York, 1955), pp. 282–302; Arthur M. Schlesinger, Jr., "Richard Hofstadter," in *Pastmasters*, ed. Marcus Cunliffe and Robin Winks (New York, 1969), pp. 278–315. Hofstadter's status anxiety interpretation of urban-rural conflicts failed to appreciate the agricultural depression that affected many rural areas and that should have prompted interest politics and not status politics, according to Hofstadter's own theory.

17. Schlesinger, "Richard Hofstadter," and essays cited in note 1. See

reviews of *The Age of Reform*, Edward C. Kirkland, *American Historical Review* 61 (May 1956): 255–56; John D. Hicks, "Politics in Pattern," *Saturday Review of Literature*, October 22, 1956, pp. 12–13; D. W. Brogan, "Fifty Years of Dreams, Protests, and Achievement," *New York Times Book Review*, October 16, 1955, p. 7.

18. Edmund A. Moore, *A Catholic Runs for President: The Campaign of 1928* (New York, 1956), p. 34 and passim; Arthur M. Schlesinger, Jr., *The Crisis of the Old Order, 1919–1933* (Boston, 1957), p. 98.

19. William E. Leuchtenburg, *Flood Control Politics: The Connecticut River Valley Problem, 1927–1950* (Cambridge, Mass., 1953), esp. chap. 1, "Sources of Conflict," pp. 1–15; William E. Leuchtenburg, *The Perils of Prosperity, 1914–1932* (Chicago, 1958); Don S. Kirschner, "Conflicts and Politics in the 1920s: Historiography and Prospects," *Mid-America* 48 (October 1968): 225.

20. Leuchtenburg, *Perils*, pp. 7, 204–24, esp. 204–5.

21. Ibid., pp. 208–9, 213, 217, 219, 223.

22. Ibid., pp. 137, 139, 230, 237.

23. Ibid., pp. 7, 9–10, 225–28.

24. Reviews of *The Perils of Prosperity*, Clarke A. Chambers, *Mississippi Valley Historical Review* 45 (December 1958): 522–23; James H. Shideler, *American Historical Review* 64 (October 1958): 202–3; Ransom E. Noble, *Annals of the American Academy of Political and Social Science* 322 (March 1959): 178; Robert Lasch, "History at Its Best: Events That Led up to the Great Depression," *St. Louis Post-Dispatch*, June 1, 1959, p. 4c; Harvey Wish, "Half-Remembered Yesterdays of a Restless Generation," *New York Times Book Review*, July 13, 1958, p. 3; John D. Hicks, *Journal of Economic History* 19 (March 1959): 135–36.

25. Lowitt, "Prosperity Decade," p. 232 n. 1; Noggle, "The Twenties," p. 314 n. 25; Noggle, "Configurations of the Twenties," p. 490 n. 97; Roderick Nash, *The Nervous Generation: American Thought, 1917–1930* (Chicago, 1970), p. 26; Grob and Billias, "The 1920s," pp. 249–65. Sales figures supplied by Stan Plona, Marketing Department, University of Chicago Press.

26. John M. Blum et al., *The National Experience* (New York, 1963), pp. 610–13; John A. Garraty, *The American Nation* (New York, 1966), pp. 698–704; David A. Shannon, *Twentieth Century America* (Chicago, 1963), pp. 275–93; Gerald D. Nash, *The Great Transition: A Short History of Twentieth-Century America* (Boston, 1971), pp. 159, 177–78; David W. Noble, David A. Horowitz, and Peter N. Carroll, *Twentieth Century Limited* (Boston, 1980), pp. 185–211; Robert A. Divine et al., *America, Past and Present* (Glenview, Ill., 1984), p. 731; George E. Mowry, ed., *The Twenties: Fords, Flappers, and Fanatics* (Englewood Cliffs, N.J., 1963), pp. 1, 89, 121, 136, 154; E. David Cronon, ed., *Twentieth Century America: Selected Readings* (Homewood, Ill.,

1965), pp. 341, 372; Loren Baritz, ed., *The Culture of the Twenties* (Indianapolis, 1970), pp. xxiv–xxxvii; Joan Hoff Wilson, ed., *The Twenties: The Critical Issues* (Boston, 1972), pp. xxi–xxii; George E. Mowry, *The Urban Nation, 1920–1960* (New York, 1965), pp. 2, 23, 27, 31–35; Donald R. McCoy, *Coming of Age: The United States during the 1920s and 1930s* (Baltimore, 1973), pp. 139–41. Innumerable other similar books also apply the urban-rural conflict idea to the 1920s.

27. Paul L. Murphy, "Sources and Nature of Intolerance in the 1920s," *Journal of American History* 51 (June 1964): 60–76; David M. Chalmers, *Hooded Americanism: The History of the Ku Klux Klan* (New York, 1965), p. 2 (emphasis added); Robert Moats Miller, "The Ku Klux Klan," in *Change and Continuity in Twentieth-Century America: The 1920s*, ed. John Braeman, Robert H. Bremner, and David Brody (Columbus, 1968), pp. 215–56, esp. p. 234; Charles C. Alexander, *The Ku Klux Klan in the Southwest* (Lexington, 1965), pp. 27–29; Sinclair, *Prohibition*, p. 5 (Hofstadter wrote a brief introduction to Sinclair's volume); Joseph R. Gusfield, *Symbolic Crusade: Status Politics and the American Temperance Crusade* (Urbana, 1963), pp. 124–25; Robert A. Hohner, "The Prohibitionists: Who Were They?" *South Atlantic Quarterly* 68 (Autumn 1969): 491–505.

28. Paul A. Carter, *The Decline and Revival of the Social Gospel* (Ithaca, 1956), pp. 35–37, 46–58, 265, and passim; Lawrence W. Levine, *Defender of the Faith: Williams Jennings Bryan, The Last Decade, 1919–1925* (New York, 1965), pp. 180–81 and passim.

29. Burner, *Politics of Provincialism*, pp. 78–79 and passim. Another thorough but brief explication of the urban-rural interpretation is James H. Shideler, "Flappers and Philosophers, and Farmers: Rural-Urban Tensions of the Twenties," *Agricultural History* 47 (October 1973): 283–99.

30. Kenneth T. Jackson, *The Ku Klux Klan in the City, 1915–1930* (New York, 1967), pp. 233–49; Robert Alan Goldberg, *Hooded Empire: The Ku Klux Klan in Colorado* (Urbana, 1981), p. 181; Larry R. Gerlach, *Blazing Crosses in Zion: The Ku Klux Klan in Utah* (Logan, 1982), p. 131. In the same year that his book appeared, Jackson joined Hofstadter and Leuchtenburg at Columbia University. Goldberg's mentor, John M. Cooper, had studied under Hofstadter at Columbia.

31. James H. Timberlake, *Prohibition and the Progressive Movement, 1900–1920* (Cambridge, Mass., 1963), pp. 1–3, 152; Norman H. Clark, *The Dry Years: Prohibition and Social Change in Washington* (Seattle, 1965), pp. 114–27; Joseph R. Gusfield, "Prohibition: The Impact of Political Utopianism," in *Change and Continuity in Twentieth-Century America*, pp. 257–308; Ernest R. Sandeen, *The Roots of Fundamentalism: British and American Millenialism, 1800–1930* (Chicago, 1970); George M. Marsden, *Fundamentalism and American Culture: The Shaping of Twentieth-Century Evangelicalism,*

1870–1925 (New York, 1980), p. 188; Paul A. Carter, "The Fundamentalist Defense of the Faith," in *Change and Continuity in Twentieth-Century America*, pp. 179–214; Gregory H. Singleton, "Fundamentalism and Urbanization: A Quantitative Critique of Impressionistic Interpretations," in *The New Urban History*, ed. Leo F. Schnore (Princeton, 1974), pp. 205–77; Virginia Gray, "Anti-Evolution Sentiment and Behavior: The Case of Arkansas," *Journal of American History* 57 (September 1970): 365. Carter's curious attitude toward the urban-rural theme can be followed in the above works and in his *Another Part of the Twenties* (New York, 1977), which criticized the "unthinking stereotyped" use of 1920 as a watershed year and doubted the theme's validity (see pp. 1–17, 184, 185, 187) and in his *The Twenties in America* (New York, 1968; 2d ed., 1975), which first accepted the urban-rural interpretation and then modified it in the later edition. See also William E. Ellis, "Evolution, Fundamentalism, and the Historians: An Historiographical Review," *Historian* 44 (November 1981): 15–35.

32. Allan J. Lichtman, *Prejudice and the Old Politics: The Presidential Election of 1928* (Chapel Hill, 1979), p. 231. Cf. Burner, *Politics of Provincialism*, pp. 179–216.

33. Mary Beth Norton et al., *A People and a Nation: A History of the United States* (Boston, 1982), vol. 2, *Since 1865*, pp. 668–97, esp. 670 and 684–88. The Preface indicates that Chudacoff had primary responsibility for chapter 24, "The New Era of the 1920s" (see p. xiv).

34. Stanley Coben, "The First Years of Modern America, 1918–1933," in *The Unfinished Century: America since 1900*, ed. William E. Leuchtenburg (Boston, 1973), pp. 255–353, esp. 260–68, 281–85, 289–92. See also Coben, "The Assault on Victorianism in the Twentieth Century," *American Quarterly* 27 (December 1975): 604–25. That entire issue of *American Quarterly* pertained to Victorianism in America.

35. Robert H. Wiebe, "Modernizing the Republic, 1920 to the Present," in Bernard Bailyn et al., *The Great Republic: A History of the American People* (Lexington, Mass., 1977), pp. 1053–1270, esp. 1056–61, 1126, 1129–33. See also Wiebe's *The Segmented Society: An Introduction to the Meaning of America* (New York, 1975).

36. Ellis Hawley, *The Great War and the Search for a Modern Order: A History of the American People and Their Institutions, 1917–1933* (New York, 1979), pp. 11, 14, 71–72, 182, and passim.

37. Warren Susman, *Culture and History: The Transformation of American Society in the Twentieth Century* (New York, 1984), p. xx and passim; Daniel Horowitz, *The Morality of Spending: Attitudes toward the Consumer Society in America, 1875–1940* (Baltimore, 1985); Daniel J. Singal, "Beyond Consensus: Richard Hofstadter and American Historiography," *American Historical Review* 89 (October 1984): 1001; Richard Franklin Bensel, *Section-*

alism and American Political Development, 1880–1980 (Madison, 1984), pp. 17–21. Leuchtenburg's *Perils of Prosperity* anticipated some of the producer-consumer interpretation by emphasizing the consumerism of the 1920s.

38. Robert K. Dykstra, "Town-Country Conflict: A Hidden Dimension in American Social History," *Agricultural History* 38 (October 1964): 195.

39. Frank Freidel and Alan Brinkley, *America in the Twentieth Century*, 5th ed. (New York, 1982), pp. 187–95; Goldberg, *Hooded Empire*; Don S. Kirschner, *City and Country: Rural Responses to Urbanization in the 1920s* (Westport, Conn., 1970). For another example of the persistence of the urban-rural theme, see Geoffrey Perrett, *America in the Twenties: A History* (New York, 1982), pp. 10–11 and passim.

Chapter 2: Reapportionment before 1920

1. Clinton Rossiter, *1787: The Grand Convention* (New York, 1966), pp. 169–71, 173–79, 183–85; Max Farrand, *The Framing of the Constitution of the United States* (New Haven, 1913), pp. 68–82 and 85–90. In *The Politics of Size: Representation in the United States, 1776–1850* (Ithaca, 1987), Rosemarie Zagarri devotes fewer than ten pages to the reapportionments of the House of Representatives after the Constitutional Convention; instead she focuses more on the Constitutional Convention, large state–small state conflicts, reapportionments of the state legislatures, movement of state capitals, and squabbles over electing congressmen by individual district or at large.

2. Rossiter, *1787*, pp. 185–96; Farrand, *Framing*, pp. 91–112; George B. Galloway, *History of the House of Representatives* (New York, 1961), pp. 1–4.

3. For the Constitution's provisions regarding reapportionment, see Article I, Sections 2 and 4.

4. Herman V. Ames, "The Proposed Amendments to the Constitution of the United States during the First Century of Its History," in *Annual Report of the American Historical Association for the Year 1896*, vol. 2 (Washington D.C., 1897), pp. 42–45, 320; Robert A. Rutland, *The Birth of the Bill of Rights* (Chapel Hill, 1955), pp. 202 and 233.

5. Gerald Carson, "The Great Enumeration," *American Heritage* 31 (December 1979): 6–17; Edmund J. James, "The First Apportionment of Federal Representatives in the United States," *Annals of the American Academy of Political and Social Science* 9 (January 1897): 1–41, esp. 9–10; Michael L. Balinski and H. Peyton Young, *Fair Representation: Meeting the Ideal of One Man, One Vote* (New Haven, 1982), pp. 11–13.

6. James, "First Apportionment," pp. 10–12; Balinski and Young, *Fair Representation*, pp. 13–15.

7. James, "First Apportionment," pp. 12, 31–41, and passim; Balinski and Young, *Fair Representation*, pp. 15–22.

8. James, "First Apportionment," pp. 12, 28, 31–32.

9. Lawrence F. Schmeckebier, *Congressional Apportionment* (Washington, D.C., 1941), pp. 111–13; Balinski and Young, *Fair Representation*, p. 23.

10. Balinski and Young, *Fair Representation*, pp. 23–25.

11. Ibid., pp. 25–34; Congressional Quarterly, *Congressional Quarterly's Guide to Congress*, 2d ed. (Washington, D.C., 1976), p. 562; Schmeckebier, *Congressional Apportionment*, pp. 112–13.

12. Schmeckebier, *Congressional Apportionment*, p. 113; Congressional Quarterly, *Congressional Quarterly's Guide to Congress*, pp. 562, 567; Balinski and Young, *Fair Representation*, pp. 34–35.

13. Ames, "Proposed Amendments," pp. 56–57; Schmeckebier, *Congressional Apportionment*, p. 113.

14. Balinski and Young, *Fair Representation*, p. 37; Schmeckebier, *Congressional Apportionment*, pp. 113–17; Congressional Quarterly, *Congressional Quarterly's Guide to Congress*, pp. 527–28.

15. See all sources cited in note 14.

16. Schmeckebier, *Congressional Apportionment*, p. 117; Frederick W. Moore, "Representation in the National Congress from the Seceding States, 1861–1865," *American Historical Review* 2 (January 1897): 278–93 and 2 (April 1897): 461–71.

17. Anderson, *American Census*, pp. 75–82.

18. Schmeckebier, *Congressional Apportionment*, pp. 117–18; Balinski and Young, *Fair Representation*, p. 37.

19. Balinski and Young, *Fair Representation*, pp. 38–40; Schmeckebier, *Congressional Apportionment*, pp. 118–19; Zechariah Chafee, Jr., "Congressional Reapportionment," *Harvard Law Review* 42 (June 1929): 1015–47.

20. See all sources cited in note 19.

21. Balinski and Young, *Fair Representation*, pp. 40–42; Schmeckebier, *Congressional Apportionment*, p. 119; Congressional Quarterly, *Congressional Quarterly's Guide to Congress*, p. 531.

22. Schmeckebier, *Congressional Apportionment*, pp. 119–20; Congressional Quarterly, *Congressional Quarterly's Guide to Congress*, pp. 528, 533; Balinski and Young, *Fair Representation*, pp. 46–47.

Chapter 3: The Controversy in the 1920s

1. *New York Times*, July 26, 1920, p. 7, and October 9, 1920, p. 14; *New Republic* 34 (October 20, 1920): 177; *Washington Post*, October 9, 1920, p. 4.

2. U.S. Department of Commerce, Bureau of the Census, *Fourteenth Census of the United States, 1920: Population* (Washington, D.C.: U.S. Government Printing Office, 1921), 1: 43 (hereafter cited as *Census, Population*,

1920); "The Increase in Urban Population," *American City* 23 (December 1920): 612; "City Growth and Rural Loss," *Literary Digest* 65 (May 29, 1920): 22; "Congress Must Be Reapportioned on Basis of 1920 Census Figures," *Brotherhood of Locomotive Firemen and Enginemen's Magazine* 69 (October 15, 1920): 19.

3. *New York Times*, December 4, 1920, p. 12, and December 18, 1920, p. 1; U.S. Congress, House, *Congressional Record*, 66th Cong., 3d sess., 1920, p. 10 (hereafter cited as *Cong. Rec.*); *Washington Post*, December 18, 1920, p. 1.

4. *Cong. Rec.*, 66th Cong., 3d sess., 1920, p. 11; *New York Times*, October 17, 1920, sec. 4, p. 9, and December 18, 1920, p. 1; *Nation* 34 (October 28, 1920): 230; *Washington Post*, December 18, 1920, p. 1.

5. *Cong. Rec.*, 66th Cong., 3d sess., 1920, pp. 10, 305, and 447; U.S. Congress, House, Committee on the Census, *Apportionment of Representatives, Hearings on HR 14498, 15021, 15158, and 15217,* 66th Cong., 3d sess., 1920, pp. 1–25 (hereafter cited as House, *Hearings*, 1920 or 1921).

6. House, *Hearings*, 1921, pp. 97–115, esp. 100, and 1920, pp. 28–85, esp. 35 and 45; *New York Times*, December 31, 1920, p. 2, and January 5, 1921, p. 4.

7. House, *Hearings*, 1920, pp. 35, 38, and 56; *Washington Post*, January 6, 1921, p. 6.

8. *New York Times*, January 7, 1921, p. 8; *Washington Post*, January 7, 1921, p. 6.

9. *New York Times*, January 9, 1921, p. 3; *Cong. Rec.*, 66th Cong., 3d sess., 1920, pp. 859–61; *Washington Post*, January 9, 1921, sec. 2, p. 4.

10. *Cong. Rec.*, 66th Cong., 3d sess., 1921, pp. 1434–35.

11. Ibid., pp. 1627–28, 4692 (extended remarks), 1630, and 1642. See ibid., pp. 1626–56 and 1677–94, for the entire debate; see also *New York Times*, January 19, 1921, p. 2, and January 20, 1921, p. 15; *Washington Post*, January 19, 1921, p. 3, and January 20, 1921, p. 1.

12. *Cong. Rec.*, 66th Cong., 3d sess., 1921, pp. 1648, 1629, 1630, and 1636.

13. Ibid., pp. 1627–28, 1647, 1648, 1640.

14. Ibid., pp. 1645–46, 1678, and 1682.

15. Ibid., pp. 1628, 1635, and 1650.

16. Ibid., pp. 1632, 1648, 1642, 1643, 1652, and 1630–31.

17. Ibid., pp. 1647, 1628–29, and 1630–31.

18. Ibid., pp. 1634–35, 1649, and 1652.

19. Ibid., pp. 1628, 1649, 1650, and 1653.

20. Ibid., pp. 1679–80, 1682, and 1693.

21. *New York Times*, January 24, 1921, p. 8; "Quality, Not Quantity, in the House," *Literary Digest* 68 (February 5, 1921): 14.

22. *New York Times*, January 24, 1921, p. 3, and February 3, 1921, p. 2; "The Siegel Reapportionment Bill," *Capitol Eye* 1 (January 1922): 3; "Report Upon the Apportionment of Representatives," *Journal of the American Statistical Association* 17 (December 1921): 1004.

23. Edward V. Huntington, letter to the editor, *New York Times*, January 16, 1921, sec. 7, p. 3; Huntington, "A New Method of Apportionment of Representatives," *Journal of the American Statistical Association* 17 (September 1921): 859–70.

24. *New York Times*, October 31, 1964, p. 29; *Who Was Who in America*, vol. 4, 1961–68 (Chicago: Marquis Who's Who, 1968), p. 1014; Balinski and Young, *Fair Representation*, pp. 46–47.

25. *Dictionary of American Biography*, supplement 5, 1951–55 (New York, 1977), pp. 338–39; Balinski and Young, *Fair Representation*, pp. 49–50.

26. Huntington, "New Method," p. 860; examples from "Report Upon the Apportionment of Representatives," pp. 1008–9, and from Chafee, "Congressional Reapportionment," pp. 1032–36.

27. "Report Upon the Apportionment of Representatives," pp. 1004, 1005, and 1010.

28. U.S. Congress, House, Committee on the Census, *Hearings before a Subcommittee of the Committee on the Census*, 67th Cong., 1st sess., 1921, pp. 9, 18, 60–61, 28, 64, 35, 29, and 39; "Congressional Reapportionment—the Arguments against Increasing Size of House," *Commercial and Financial Chronicle* 113 (October 15, 1921): 1620–22.

29. *Cong. Rec.*, 67th Cong., 1st sess., 1921, pp. 6312–13; *New York Times*, July 21, 1921, p. 4; *Washington Post*, July 16, 1921, p. 6, and July 21, 1921, p. 5.

30. *New York Times*, October 13, 1921, p. 17.

31. *Cong. Rec.*, 67th Cong., 1st sess., 1921, pp. 6308–9. See ibid., pp. 6308–47 and 6348–49, for the entire debate; see also *New York Times*, October 15, 1921, p. 15; *Washington Post*, October 15, 1921, p. 4.

32. *Cong. Rec.*, 67th Cong., 1st sess., 1921, pp. 6311–12; *New Republic* 36 (May 18, 1921): 322–23.

33. *Cong. Rec.*, 67th Cong., 1st sess., 1921, pp. 6315–16.

34. Ibid., pp. 6313, 6329, and 6314.

35. Ibid., pp. 6313, 6330, 6327, and 6331.

36. Ibid., pp. 6317, 6320, and 6327.

37. Ibid., pp. 6320–21 and 6328.

38. Ibid., p. 6339.

39. Ibid., pp. 6340, 6345, and 6348.

40. Robert K. Murray, *The Politics of Normalcy: Governmental Theory and Practice in the Harding-Coolidge Era* (New York, 1973), pp. 43–45.

41. Ibid., p. 46; Murray, *The Harding Era: Warren G. Harding and His Administration* (Minneapolis, 1969), pp. 127–28.

42. U.S. Congress, *Congressional Directory*, 68th Cong., 1st sess., May 1924, p. 190; *Cong. Rec.*, 67th Cong., 1st sess., 1921, pp. 475–77 and 490; *Cong. Rec.*, 67th Cong., 2d sess., 1922, p. 3326; *Cong. Rec.*, 68th Cong., 1st sess., 1923, pp. 35, 305, and 479; *New York Times*, February 10, 1922, p. 14, March 3, 1922, p. 6, May 15, 1922, p. 4, July 9, 1923, p. 4, December 5, 1923, p. 2, and March 9, 1924, p. 5.

43. *New York Times*, March 9, 1924, p. 5; *Cong. Rec.*, 68th Cong., 1st sess., 1924, pp. 4181–82 and 10552.

44. *Cong. Rec.*, 68th Cong., 2d sess., 1925, pp. 3588–89.

45. *New York Times*, January 11, 1923, p. 18.

46. Ibid., December 10, 1925, p. 10.

47. U.S. Congress, House, Committee on the Census, *Apportionment of Representatives in Congress amongst the Several States, Hearings on HR 111, 413, 398, and 3808*, 69th Cong., 1st sess., 1926, pp. 6, 12, and 11 (hereafter cited as House, Hearings, 1926).

48. Ibid., pp. 58, 43, 46, 44, and 30–32.

49. Ibid., pp. 26–27 and 37–38.

50. *Washington Post*, March 24, 1926, p. 4; *New York Times*, April 5, 1926, p. 14.

51. *Cong. Rec.*, 69th Cong., 1st sess., 1926, pp. 7141, 7138, and 7147–48; *New York Times*, April 9, 1926, p. 6; *Washington Post*, April 4, 1926, p. 5, and April 9, 1926, p. 4.

52. *New York Times*, April 12, 1926, p. 20; "Congressmen Dodge Reapportionment," *Literary Digest* 89 (April 24, 1926): 12.

53. *New Republic* 46 (May 12, 1926): 343, and June 30, 1926, p. 153.

54. Ray T. Tucker, "Our Delinquent Congress," *New Republic* 47 (May 26, 1926): 11–13.

55. Ibid.

56. Robert B. Smith, "What's the Constitution among Friends?" *Independent* 116 (May 18, 1926): 542.

57. *Nation* 123 (July 7, 1926): 1.

58. Frederick L. Paxson, "Our Representatives in Washington: How Their Number Sometimes Changes with the Growth of Population in the United States, and Sometimes Doesn't," *World Review* 2 (May 3, 1926): 161–62.

59. *New York Times*, September 10, 1926, p. 2, and December 22, 1926, p. 3.

60. U.S. Congress, House, Committee on the Census, *Apportionment of Representatives amongst the Several States, Hearing on HR 13471*, 69th

Cong., 2d sess., 1927, pp. 1, 9–12 (hereafter cited as House, Hearing, 1927); *New York Times*, January 11, 1927, p. 5.

61. House, *Hearing, 1927*, pp. 13, 15, 7, 46, and 108.

62. Ibid., pp. 68, 78, 88, 93.

63. Ibid., pp. 117, 125, and 128.

64. Ibid., pp. 68, 65–66, 67, and 138.

65. *New York Times*, January 28, 1927, p. 7, and February 6, 1927, p. 18.

66. *Cong. Rec.*, 69th Cong., 2d sess., 1927, pp. 5414, 5421, 5422, and 5427; *New York Times*, March 3, 1927, p. 2; *Washington Post*, March 3, 1927, p. 5.

67. *Cong. Rec.*, 70th Cong., 1st sess., 1927, pp. 18, 20, 21, 23, 92, 100, and 270; *New York Times*, December 5, 1927, p. 2.

68. U.S. Congress, House, Committee on the Census, *Apportionment of Representatives, Hearing on HR 130*, 70th Cong., 1st sess., 1928, pp. 2–5 and 25–31.

69. Ibid., pp. 4 and 30–31.

70. Ibid., pp. 89–94 and 48–89.

71. *New York Times*, March 3, 1928, p. 2; *Washington Post*, March 3, 1928, p. 4.

72. *New Republic* 54 (March 14, 1928): 109; "Serious Results Might Accrue," p. 339; "Congress Refuses to Reapportion," p. 339; and "In Case of a Three-Cornered Situation," p. 340, all in *Review of Reviews* 77 (April 1928).

73. *New York Times*, May 13, 1928, p. 5; *Washington Post*, May 13, 1928, p. 5; *Cong. Rec.*, 70th Cong., 1st sess., 1928, p. 5916.

74. *Cong. Rec.*, 70th Cong., 1st sess., 1928, pp. 9002, 9012–13, 9096, 9086, and 9003. See ibid., pp. 9000–32 and 9085–9106, for the entire debate; see also *New York Times*, May 18, 1928, p. 13, and May 19, 1928, p. 32; *Washington Post*, May 18, 1928, p. 8, and May 19, 1928, p. 5.

75. *Cong. Rec.*, 70th Cong., 1st sess., 1928, p. 9087.

76. Ibid., pp. 9005, 9024, 9003, 9001, and 9025.

77. Ibid., p. 9090.

78. Ibid., 9097 and 9101.

79. Ibid., p. 9106.

80. "Misrepresentative Government," *Saturday Evening Post* 201 (August 18, 1928): 22; William Starr Myers, "Unconstitutional President?" *North American Review* 226 (October 1928): 385–89.

81. *New York Times*, November 24, 1928, p. 9, and December 4, 1928, p. 3; *Washington Post*, December 4, 1928, p. 3.

82. C. David Tompkins, *Senator Arthur H. Vandenberg* (East Lansing, 1970), p. 47; *Cong. Rec.*, 70th Cong., 2d sess., 1928, p. 933; *Cong. Rec.*, 70th Cong., 2d sess., 1929, pp. 1033 and 1348–49.

83. *New York Times*, December 12, 1928, p. 28; December 15, 1928, p. 5;

and January 5, 1929, p. 9; "Undemocratic Democracy," *Nation* 127 (December 19, 1929): 675; *Washington Post*, January 5, 1929, p. 10.

84. For examples of the Huntington-Willcox feud see the following four articles by Edward V. Huntington, "Reapportionment Bill in Congress," *Science* 67 (May 18, 1928): 509–10; "The Reapportionment Situation in Congress," *Science* 68 (December 14, 1928): 579–82; "Reply to Professor Willcox," *Science* 69 (March 8, 1929): 272; and "The Report of the National Academy of Sciences on Reapportionment," *Science* 69 (May 3, 1929): 471–73; and three articles by Walter F. Willcox, "The Apportionment of Representatives," *Science* 67 (June 8, 1928): 581–82; "The Apportionment Situation in Congress," *Science* 69 (February 8, 1929): 163–65; and "Professor Huntington's Method in Controversy," *Science* 69 (March 29, 1929): 357–58; and see the *New York Times*, December 12, 1918, p. 28, and December 16, 1928, p. 19; *Cong. Rec.*, 70th Cong., 2d sess., 1928, pp. 704, 699, and 705.

85. *Cong. Rec.*, 70th Cong., 2d sess., 1928, pp. 703–5, and 699; *New York Times*, December 16, 1928, p. 19.

86. *New York Times*, January 9, 1929, p. 3, January 10, 1929, p. 2, and January 5, 1929, p. 8.

87. *Cong. Rec.*, 70th Cong., 2d sess., 1929, pp. 1488, 1496, 1500, 1503, and 1493. See ibid., pp. 1485–1517 and 1583–1605, for the entire debate. See also *New York Times*, January 5, 1929, p. 8, January 11, 1929, p. 4, and January 12, 1929, p. 1; *Washington Post*, January 11, 1929, p. 5, and January 12, 1929, p. 1.

88. *Cong. Rec.*, 70th Cong., 2d sess., 1929, pp. 1597, 1584, and 1591.

89. Ibid., p. 1497.

90. Ibid., p. 1604.

91. Ibid., pp. 1604–5.

92. "Congressmen Vote to Obey the Constitution on Reapportionment," *Literary Digest* 100 (January 26, 1929): 14; "The House Revises Itself," *Outlook and Independent* 151 (January 30, 1929): 177.

93. "The States and the Electors," *Review of Reviews* 79 (February 1929): 41; "Machinery of Presidential Elections," ibid., p. 42. See also "Congress Too Cumbersome," p. 40, "Neglect to Reapportion," pp. 40–41, and "Adjustments Are Always Difficult," pp. 41–42, all in ibid.

94. Tompkins, *Vandenberg*, pp. 47–48; *Cong. Rec.*, 70th Cong., 2d sess., 1929, pp. 1711, 2172–77, and 2179. See ibid., pp. 2171–78, 3436–38, 4341–49, and 4551–55, for the entire debate. See also *New York Times*, January 25, 1929, p. 4; *Washington Post*, January 25, 1929, p. 11.

95. Tompkins, *Vandenberg*, p. 48; *Cong. Rec.*, 70th Cong., 2d sess., 1929, pp. 3436, 4243, 4245, 4246, 4551, and 4552; *New York Times*, February 15, 1929, p. 26, and February 26, 1929, p. 10.

96. Tompkins, *Vandenberg*, p. 48; *New York Times*, April 17, 1929, p. 1;

Cong. Rec., 71st Cong., 1st sess., pp. 107–8; "House Reapportionment Likely," *Review of Reviews* 79 (June 1929): 30.

97. U.S. Congress, Senate, Committee on Commerce, *Fifteenth Decennial Census—Apportionment of Representatives in Congress, Hearing on S. 2*, 71st Cong., 1st Sess., 1929, pp. 51 and 25–44; *New York Times*, April 21, 1929, p. 16.

98. *New York Times*, May 16, 1929, p. 30, and May 25, 1929, p. 2; U.S. Congress, Senate, Cong. Rec., 71st Cong., 1st sess., 1929, pp. 1329–35, 1844–46, 1323–24, 1851, 1856, 1861, 2071, 2078, 2149, 2152, and 2158–59. See ibid., pp. 1321–36, 1840–66, 2065–82, 2148–53, and 2154–60, for the entire debate.

99. Cong. Rec., 71st Cong., 1st sess., 1929, pp. 1710–11, 1865, 1908, 1910, 1967, 1962, 1978, 2054–55, and 1975; *New York Times*, May 26, 1929, p. 20, and May 29, 1929, p. 24.

100. Cong. Rec., 71st Cong., 1st sess., 1929, pp. 1971, 1979–80, and 2065.

101. Ibid., pp. 1321–27, 1841–56, and 1858–60.

102. Ibid., pp. 1325, 1612, 1614, and 1843.

103. Ibid., p. 2159; *New York Times*, May 30, 1929, p. 4; William C. Murphy, Jr., "Voiceless Voter," *Commonweal* 10 (May 29, 1929): 92–94; "House Reapportionment Likely," *Review of Reviews* 79 (June 1929): 30; *Washington Post*, May 30, 1929, p. 1.

104. Chafee, "Congressional Reapportionment," pp. 1015–47, esp. 1016–17, 1020, and 1045.

105. *New York Times*, June 5, 1929, p. 1; *Washington Post*, June 5, 1929, p. 2; Cong. Rec., 71st Cong., 1st sess., 1929, pp. 2338–43, 2271, 2348, 2364, and 2361.

106. Cong. Rec., 71st Cong., 1st sess., 1929, pp. 2448–49; *New York Times*, June 6, 1929, p. 3; *Washington Post*, June 6, 1929, p. 1; *Law Notes*, July 1929, p. 62.

107. Cong. Rec., 71st Cong., 1st sess., 1929, pp. 2279–82, 2363, and 2443–48.

108. *New York Times*, June 6, 1929, p. 3; Cong. Rec., 71st Cong., 1st sess., 1929, pp. 2439, 2531, and 2608–9; *Washington Post*, June 8, 1929, p. 2.

109. Cong. Rec., 71st Cong., 1st sess., 1929, pp. 2611–14, and 2616.

110. Ibid., pp. 2671–73, 2662–63, and 2673–74; *New York Times*, June 19, 1929, p. 30; *Washington Post*, June 9, 1929, p. 1, June 14, 1929, p. 2, and June 17, 1929, p. 1.

111. "Row over Reapportionment," *Literary Digest* 101 (June 22, 1929): 10.

112. Oliver McKee, Jr., "Town and Country," *Commonweal* 10 (August 7, 1929): 354–56.

113. *New Republic* 59 (June 19, 1929): 110.

Chapter 4: Voting on Reapportionment: A Test of Urban-Rural Conflict

1. Charles W. Eagles, "Congressional Voting in the 1920s: A Test of Urban-Rural Conflict," *Journal of American History* 76 (September 1989): 528–34.

2. For discussions of various influences on congressional voting, see Aage R. Clausen, *How Congressmen Decide: A Policy Focus* (New York, 1973); Lewis A. Froman, *Congressmen and Their Constituents* (Chicago, 1963); George B. Galloway, *The Legislative Process in Congress* (New York, 1953); Donald R. Matthews and James A. Stimson, *Yeas and Nays: Normal Decision-Making in the U.S. House of Representatives* (New York, 1975); Julius Turner, *Party and Constituency: Pressures on Congress*, rev. ed. by Edward V. Schneier, Jr. (Baltimore, 1970).

3. See all sources cited in note 2.

4. *Census, Population, 1920*, p. 43.

5. Ibid., pp. 157, 160, 228–29; *Congressional Directory*, 67th Cong., 1st sess. (Washington, D.C., 1921), pp. 30, 43 (hereafter cited as *Directory*).

6. *Census, Population, 1920*, pp. 43, 78, 229–58; *Directory*, 67th Cong., 1st sess., p. 5.

7. *Census, Population, 1920*, pp. 62–64, 70, 155; *Directory*, 67th Cong., 1st sess., p. 26.

8. See, for example, *Directory*, 67th Cong., 4th sess. (Washington, D.C., 1922); Kenneth C. Martis, ed., *The Historical Atlas of United States Congressional Districts, 1789–1983* (New York, 1982).

9. Martis, ed., *Historical Atlas*, pp. 222, 238, 240, 249–50, 164–65, 268–69.

10. *Directory*, 67th Cong., 1st sess., pp. 49–50; 68th Cong., 1st sess. (Washington, D.C., 1924), p. 99; U.S. Department of Commerce, Bureau of the Census, *Fifteenth Census of the United States, Metropolitan Districts: Population and Area* (Washington, D.C., 1931), p. 164.

11. Ballard Campbell in his fine study applies the methods used here and suggests using the index of disagreement, which he describes as "the obversion of the index of likeness." For discussion of the index of likeness see Lee F. Anderson, Meredith W. Watts, Jr., and Allen R. Wilcox, *Legislative Roll-Call Analysis* (Evanston, 1966), pp. 36, 44–45; Charles M. Dollar and Richard J. Jensen, *Historian's Guide to Statistics: Quantitative Analysis and Historical Research* (New York, 1971), pp. 107–8; Duncan MacRae, Jr., *Issues and Parties in Legislative Voting: Methods of Statistical Analysis* (New York, 1970), pp. 177–82; and Ballard C. Campbell, *Representative Democracy: Public Policy and Midwestern Legislatures in the Late Nineteenth Century* (Cambridge, Mass., 1980), p. 209.

12. U.S. Congress, House, Cong. Rec., 66th Cong., 3d sess., 1921, p. 1693; 67th Cong., 1st sess., 1921, p. 6348; 69th Cong., 1st sess., 1926, p. 7148; 69th Cong., 2d sess., 1927, p. 5427; 70th Cong., 1st sess., 1928, pp. 9085 and 9106; 70th Cong., 2d sess., 1929, p. 1604; 71st Cong., 1st sess., 1929, p. 2458.

13. For two predictions of the expected results, see New York Times, December 19, 1920, and May 13, 1920.

Conclusion

1. Anderson, American Census, p. 157. For a brief overview of post-1930 events, see Congressional Quarterly, Congressional Quarterly's Guide to Congress, 2d ed. (Washington, D.C., 1976), pp. 570–73.

2. Anderson, American Census, p. 157; Robert B. McKay, Reapportionment: The Law and Politics of Equal Representation (New York, 1965), pp. 65–68, 89–98, and passim; Emanuel Celler, "Congressional Apportionment —Past, Present, and Future," Law and Contemporary Problems 17 (1952): 268–75; Wesberry v. Sanders, 376 U.S. 1 (1964). At about the same time as the Wesberry v. Sanders case, the U.S. Supreme Court was also requiring the reapportioning of state legislatures on the principle of "one man, one vote," but the decisions had no direct connection to the apportionment of the national Congress. See McKay, Reapportionment, pp. 59–145.

3. See also Eagles, "Congressional Voting in the 1920s," which shows that significant urban-rural conflict did occur in voting on Prohibition and immigration restriction legislation.

4. Evidence of ethnocultural divisions continuing into the twentieth century can be found in John M. Allswang, A House for All Peoples: Ethnic Politics in Chicago, 1890–1936 (Lexington, 1971); Lichtman, Politics and the Old Prejudice; and John L. Shover, "Ethnicity and Religion in Philadelphia Politics, 1924–1940," American Quarterly 25 (December 1975): 499–515. The studies that find ethnocultural conflict in the twentieth century focus on northern urban areas and do not deal with politics nationally; even Lichtman's study specifically excludes all of the South from its analysis. Paul Kleppner, on the other hand, in Continuity and Change in Electoral Politics, 1893–1928 (Westport, Conn., 1987), has concluded, "Overall, the 1900–1928 data no longer give evidence of an electorate divided along ethno-religious lines into opposing party camps" (p. 224). For a few examples of the discussion of the ethnocultural issue in nineteenth-century politics, see Richard J. Jensen, The Winning of the Midwest: Social and Political Conflict, 1888–1896 (Chicago, 1971); Samuel T. McSeveney, The Politics of Depression: Political Behavior in the Northeast, 1893–1896 (New York, 1972); Paul Kleppner, The Cross of Culture: A Social Analysis of Midwestern Politics,

1850–1900 (New York, 1970). Reviews of the ethnocultural explanation include Samuel T. McSeveney, "Ethnic Groups, Ethnic Conflicts, and Recent Quantitative Research in American Political History," *International Migration Review* 7 (Spring 1973): 14–33, and Richard L. McCormick, "Ethnocultural Interpretations of Nineteenth-Century American Voting Behavior," *Political Science Quarterly* 89 (June 1974): 351–77.

5. One very preliminary and brief attempt to assess rural attitudes toward cities can be found in Clifford Anderson, "Agrarian Attitudes toward the City, Business, and Labor in the 1920s and 1930s," *Mississippi Quarterly* 14 (Fall 1961): 183–89. Anderson relies largely on farm periodicals and testimony before congressional committees.

6. Thomas Bender, *Community and Social Change in America* (New Brunswick, N.J., 1978), p. 13 and passim.

7. For a discussion of urban and rural ideal types and of the difficulties in explaining the differences between them, see Hal S. Barron, *Those Who Stayed Behind: Rural Society in Nineteenth-Century New England* (New York, 1984), pp. 1–15.

8. For a critique of studying recent American history by the decades, see Burl Noggle, "Doing History by the Decade: A Pattern in American Historiography, 1930–1980," *History Teacher* 16 (May 1983): 389–416; unfortunately, Noggle, who has written about the 1920s, did not carry his criticism back that far but accepted the standard demarcation of that decade as appropriate for study. Some scholars have already pursued urban-rural themes in earlier and later periods; see, for example, Wayne E. Fuller, "The Rural Roots of the Progressive Leaders," *Agricultural History* 42 (January 1968): 1–13; Alan Brinkley, *Voices of Protest: Huey Long, Father Coughlin, and the Great Depression* (New York, 1982), pp. xi–xii, 143–68; Raymond Arsenault, *The Wild Ass of the Ozarks: Jeff Davis and the Social Bases of Southern Politics* (Philadelphia, 1984). See also Eagles, "Urban-Rural Conflict in the 1920s."

Bibliography

Primary Sources (generally before 1930)

NEWSPAPERS

New York Times, 1919–30
Washington Post, 1919–30

PUBLIC DOCUMENTS

U.S. Congress, *Congressional Directory*, 1919–30.
U.S. Congress, *Congressional Record*, 1919–30.
U.S. Congress, House, Committee on the Census. *Apportionment of Representatives amongst the Several States, Hearing on HR 13471.* 69th Cong., 2d sess., 1927.
———. *Apportionment of Representatives, Hearing on HR 14498, 15021, 15158, and 15217.* 66th Cong., 3d sess., 1920 and 1921.
———. *Apportionment of Representatives in Congress amongst the Several States, Hearings on HR 111, 413, 398, and 3808.* 69th Cong., 1st sess., 1926.
———. *Apportionment of Representatives, Hearing on HR 130.* 70th Cong., 1st sess., 1928.
———. *Hearings before a Subcommittee of the Committee on the Census.* 67th Cong., 1st sess., 1921.
U.S. Congress, Senate, Committee on Commerce. *Fifteenth Decennial Census–Apportionment of Representatives in Congress, Hearing on S.2.* 71st Cong., 1st sess., 1929.
U.S., Department of Commerce, Bureau of the Census. *Fifteenth Census of the United States, Metropolitan Districts: Population and Area.* Washington, D.C., 1931.
———. *Fourteenth Census of the United States, 1920: Population.* Washington, D.C.: U.S. Government Printing Office, 1921.
Wesberrry v. Sanders 376 U.S. 1 (1964).

BOOKS

Garis, Roy L. *Immigration Restriction.* New York: Macmillan, 1927.
Haynes, Fred E. *Social Politics in the United States.* Boston: Houghton Mifflin, 1924.
Krutch, Joseph Wood. *The Modern Temper.* New York: Harcourt, Brace, 1929.
Lippmann, Walter. *Men of Destiny.* New York: Macmillan, 1927.
Lynd, Robert, and Helen Lynd. *Middletown: A Study in Contemporary American Culture.* New York: Harcourt, Brace, 1929.
Malin, James C. *The United States after the World War.* Boston: Ginn, 1930.
Mecklin, John Moffat. *The Ku Klux Klan: A Study of the American Mind.* New York: Harcourt, Brace, 1924.
Merz, Charles. *The Dry Decade.* Garden City, N.Y.: Doubleday Doran, 1931.
Niebuhr, H. Richard. *The Social Sources of Denominationalism.* New York: Henry Holt, 1929.
Siegfried, Andre. *America Comes of Age.* New York: Harcourt, Brace, 1927.
Sorokin, Pitirim A., and Carle C. Zimmerman. *Principles of Rural-Urban Sociology.* New York: Holt, 1929.

ARTICLES

"Adjustments Are Always Difficult." *Review of Reviews* 79 (February 1929): 41–42.
"Alien Representation." *Outlook* 156 (December 17, 1930): 609–10.
Bowman, Harold M. "Congressional Redistricting and the Constitution." *Michigan Law Review* 31 (December 1932): 149–79.
"Carving Thirty-Two States into Congressional Pie." *Literary Digest* 107 (December 6, 1930): 11–12.
"Census Discoveries about Us." *Literary Digest* 70 (July 9, 1921): 8.
"The Census Will Be Taken in April." *Review of Reviews* 80 (July 1929): 34.
"Census Will Make Congress Less Rural." *Business Week,* May 7, 1930, p. 30.
Chafee, Zechariah, Jr. "Congressional Reapportionment." *Harvard Law Review* 42 (June 1929): 1015–47.
"City Growth and Rural Loss." *Literary Digest* 65 (May 29, 1920): 22.
"Congress Evades Reapportionment." *Literary Digest* 92 (February 19, 1927): 13.
"Congress Must Be Apportioned on the Basis of 1920 Census Figures." *Brotherhood of Locomotive Firemen and Enginemen's Magazine* 69 (October 15, 1920): 19.
"Congress Refuses to Reapportion." *Review of Reviews* 77 (April 1928): 339.
"Congress Too Cumbersome." *Review of Reviews* 79 (February 1929): 40.
"Congressional Reapportionment—the Arguments against Increasing Size of

House." *Commercial and Financial Chronicle* 113 (October 15, 1921): 1620-22.

"Congressional Reapportionment: Provisions of Pending Bill, with Pro and Con Discussion." *Congressional Digest* 8 (February 1929): 33-53.

"Congressmen Dodge Reapportionment." *Literary Digest* 89 (April 24, 1926): 12.

"Congressmen Vote to Obey the Constitution on Reapportionment." *Literary Digest* 100 (January 26, 1929): 14.

"Depriving State of Representation." *Law Notes* 39 (February 1927): 201.

Dewey, John. "The American Intellectual Frontier." *New Republic* 30 (May 10, 1922): 303-5.

"Doubtful Good of Our City Growth." *Literary Digest* 66 (September 18, 1920): 17-18.

"'The Farmers' Party' in Congress." *Literary Digest* 70 (July 2, 1921): 14.

"From 65 to 435." *Searchlight* 5 (October 1920): 5-7.

Hard, Willard. "Leadership in the House." *Review of Reviews* 74 (August 1926): 159-64.

"House Reapportionment Likely." *Review of Reviews* 79 (June 1929): 30.

"The House Revises Itself." *Outlook and Independent* 151 (January 30, 1929): 177-78.

Huntington, Edward V. "The Apportionment Situation in Congress." *Science* 68 (December 14, 1928): 579-82.

———. "The Mathematical Theory of the Apportionment of Representatives." *Proceedings of the National Academy of Sciences of the United States of America* 7 (April 1921): 123-27.

———. "A New Method of Apportionment of Representatives." *Journal of the American Statistical Association* 17 (September 1921): 859-70.

———. "Reapportionment Bill in Congress." *Science* 67 (May 18, 1928): 509-10.

———. "Reply to Professor Willcox." *Science* 69 (March 8, 1929): 272.

———. "The Report of the National Academy of Sciences on Reapportionment." *Science* 69 (May 3, 1929): 471-73.

"In Case of a Three-Cornered Situation." *Review of Reviews* 77 (April 1928): 340.

"The Increase in Urban Population." *American City* 23 (December 1920): 612.

Lake, Kirsopp. "The Real Divisions in Modern Christianity." *Atlantic Monthly* 135 (June 1925): 755-61.

Lippmann, Walter. "The Causes of Political Indifference Today." *Atlantic Monthly* 139 (February 1927): 261-68.

"Machinery of Presidential Elections." *Review of Reviews* 79 (February 1929): 42.

McKey, Oliver, Jr. "Town and Country." *Commonweal* 10 (August 7, 1929): 354–56.
Mencken, H. L. "Politics." In *Civilization in the United States: An Inquiry by Thirty Americans*, edited by Harold E. Stearns, pp. 21–34. New York: Harcourt, Brace, 1922.
"Misrepresentative Government." *Saturday Evening Post* 201 (August 18, 1928): 22.
Mumford, Lewis. "The City." In *Civilization in the United States: An Inquiry by Thirty Americans*, edited by Harold E. Stearns, pp. 3–20. New York: Harcourt, Brace, 1922.
Murphy, William C., Jr. "Voiceless Voter." *Commonweal* 10 (May 29, 1929): 92–94.
Myers, William Starr. "Unconstitutional President?" *North American Review* 226 (October 1928): 385–89.
Nation 123 (July 7, 1926): 1.
"Neglect to Reapportion." *Review of Reviews* 79 (February 1929): 40–41.
New Republic 34 (October 20, 1920): 177; 36 (May 18, 1921): 332–33; 46 (May 12, 1926): 343; 47 (June 30, 1926): 153; 54 (March 14, 1928): 109; 59 (June 19, 1929): 110.
Niebuhr, H. Richard. "Fundamentalism." In *Encyclopedia of the Social Sciences*, edited by Edwin R. A. Seligman, pp. 526–27. New York: Macmillan, 1931.
"Our Decreasing Increase." *Literary Digest* 66 (July 17, 1920): 17.
"Our Gain and Loss in Population." *Literary Digest* 71 (December 3, 1921): 11.
Owens, F. W. "On the Apportionment of Representatives." *Journal of the American Statistical Association* 17 (December 1921): 958–68.
Paxson, Frederick L. "Our Representatives in Washington: How Their Number Sometimes Changes with the Growth of Population in the United States, and Sometimes Doesn't." *World Review* 2 (May 3, 1926): 161–62, 171.
"Persons Excluded in Making National Apportionment." *Law Notes* 33 (April 1929): 26.
"Problem of Reapportionment of Representatives." *Congressional Digest* 7 (December 1928): 340–43.
"Quality, Not Quantity, in the House." *Literary Digest* 68 (February 5, 1921): 14.
"Reapportionment." *Outlook* 156 (December 3, 1930): 526.
"Reapportionment." *Congressional Digest* 9 (December 1930): 314–15.
"Reapportionment and the Census." *World's Work* 59 (May 1930): 21–22.
"The Reapportionment Bill." *Capitol Eye* 1 (January 1921): 3–7.

"Reapportionment in Fall Is Congressional Bugaboo." *Business Week*, August 13, 1930, p. 22.
"The Reapportionment Situation in Congress." *Science* 68 (December 14, 1928): 579–82.
Reid, Louis Raymond. "The Small Town." In *Civilization in the United States: An Inquiry by Thirty Americans*, edited by Harold E. Stearns, pp. 285–96. New York: Harcourt, Brace, 1922.
"Reorganization of Congress." *Literary Digest* 68 (February 26, 1921): 36.
"Report Upon the Apportionment of Representatives." *Journal of the American Statistical Association* 17 (December 1921): 1004–13.
"Row over Reapportionment." *Literary Digest* 101 (June 22, 1929): 10.
Seavey, Warren A. "Unequal Representation in Congress." *Western Reserve Law Notes* 24 (October 1920): 124–26.
"Serious Results Might Accrue." *Review of Reviews* 77 (April 1928): 339–40.
"The Siegel Reapportionment Bill." *Capitol Eye* 1 (January 1922): 3–7.
Smith, Robert B. "What's the Constitution among Friends?" *Independent* 116 (May 18, 1926): 542, 558.
Smith, T. V. "The Bases of Bryanism." *Scientific Monthly* 16 (1923): 505–13.
"The States and the Electors." *Review of Reviews* 79 (February 1929): 41.
"Triumph of Cain." *Independent* (April 2, 1921): 346.
Tucker, Ray T. "Our Delinquent Congress." *New Republic* 47 (May 26, 1926): 11–13.
"Undemocratic Democracy." *Nation* 127 (December 19, 1929): 675.
Walsh, Orville A. "Government by Yokel." *American Mercury* 3 (October 1924): 199–205.
"What Congress Ought to Do." *Nation* 112 (April 20, 1921): 583.
"What the Census Tells Us." *Current Opinion* 71 (August 1921): 148–50.
Willcox, Walter F. "Apportionment of Representatives." *American Economic Review* 6 (March 1916): 3–16.
———. "The Apportionment of Representatives." *Science* 67 (June 8, 1928): 581–82.
———. "The Apportionment Situation in Congress." *Science* 69 (February 8, 1929): 163–65.
———. "Professor Huntington's Method in Controversy." *Science* 69 (March 29, 1929): 357–58.

Secondary Sources (generally after 1930)

BOOKS

Adams, Samuel H. *Incredible Era: The Life and Times of Warren Gamaliel Harding*. Boston: Houghton Mifflin, 1939.

Alexander, Charles C. *The Ku Klux Klan in the Southwest*. Lexington: University of Kentucky Press, 1965.

Allen, Frederick Lewis. *Only Yesterday: An Informal History of the Nineteen-Twenties*. New York: Harper, 1931.

Allswang, John M. *A House for All Peoples: Ethnic Politics in Chicago, 1890–1936*. Lexington: University of Kentucky Press, 1971.

Anderson, Lee F., Meredith W., Watts, Jr., and Allen R. Wilcox. *Legislative Roll-Call Analysis*. Evanston: Northwestern University Press, 1966.

Anderson, Margo J. *The American Census: A Social History*. New Haven: Yale University Press, 1988.

Arsenault, Raymond. *The Wild Ass of the Ozarks: Jeff Davis and the Social Bases of Southern Politics*. Philadelphia: Temple University Press, 1984.

Asbury, Herbert. *The Great Illusion: An Informal History of Prohibition*. Garden City, N.Y.: Doubleday, 1950.

Baker, Gordon E. *Rural versus Urban Political Power: The Nature and Consequences of Unbalanced Representation*. New York: Random House, 1955.

Balinski, Michael L., and H. Peyton Young. *Fair Representation: Meeting the Ideal of One Man, One Vote*. New Haven: Yale University Press, 1982.

Baritz, Loren, ed. *The Culture of the Twenties*. Indianapolis: Bobbs-Merrill, 1970.

Barron, Hal S. *Those Who Stayed Behind: Rural Society in Nineteenth-Century New England*. New York: Cambridge University Press, 1984.

Bender, Thomas. *Community and Social Change in America*. New Brunswick, N.J.: Rutgers University Press, 1978.

Bennett, David H. *Demagogues in the Depression: American Radicals and the Union Party, 1932–1936*. New Brunswick, N.J.: Rutgers University Press, 1969.

Bensel, Richard Franklin. *Sectionalism and American Political Development, 1880–1980*. Madison: University of Wisconsin Press, 1984.

Berger, Michael L. *The Devil Wagon in God's Country: The Automobile and Social Change in Rural America, 1893–1929*. Hamden, Conn.: Archon, 1979.

Blum, John M., et al. *The National Experience*. New York: Harcourt, Brace and World, 1963.

Boyd, William J. D. *Changing Patterns of Apportionment*. New York: National Municipal League, 1965.
Brinkley, Alan. *Voices of Protest: Huey Long, Father Coughlin, and the Great Depression*. New York: Knopf, 1982.
Burner, David. *The Politics of Provincialism: The Democratic Party in Transition, 1918–1932*. New York: Knopf, 1967.
Campbell, Ballard C. *Representative Democracy: Public Policy and Midwestern Legislatures in the Late Nineteenth Century*. Cambridge, Mass.: Harvard University Press, 1980.
Carter, Paul A. *Another Part of the Twenties*. New York: Columbia University Press, 1977.
———. *The Decline and Revival of the Social Gospel*. Ithaca: Cornell University Press, 1956.
———. *The Twenties in America*. New York: Thomas Y. Crowell, 1968; 2d ed., 1975.
Chalmers, David M. *Hooded Americanism: The History of the Ku Klux Klan*. New York: Doubleday, 1965.
Clark, Norman H. *Deliver Us from Evil: An Interpretation of American Prohibition*. New York: Norton, 1976.
———. *The Dry Years: Prohibition and Social Change in Washington*. Seattle: University of Washington Press, 1965.
Clausen, Aage R. *How Congressmen Decide: A Policy Focus*. New York: St. Martin's, 1973.
Congressional Quarterly. *Congressional Quarterly's Guide to Congress*. 2d ed. Washington, D.C.: Congressional Quarterly, 1976.
———. *Congressional Quarterly's Guide to U.S. Elections*. Washington, D.C.: Congressional Quarterly, 1975.
———. *Representation and Apportionment*. Washington, D.C.: Congressional Quarterly, 1966.
Cronon, E. David, ed. *Twentieth Century America: Selected Readings*. Homewood, Ill.: Dorsey, 1965.
Cummings, Milton C., Jr. *Congressmen and the Electorate: Elections for the United States House and the President, 1920–1964*. New York: Free Press, 1966.
Divine, Robert A., et al. *America, Past and Present*. Glenview, Ill.: Scott Foresman, 1984.
Dixon, Robert G., Jr. *Democratic Representation: Reapportionment in Law and Politics*. New York: Oxford University Press, 1968.
Dollar, Charles M., and Richard J. Jensen. *Historian's Guide to Statistics: Quantitative Analysis and Historical Research*. New York: Holt, Rinehart, and Winston, 1971.

Dubofsky, Melvyn, et al. *The United States in the Twentieth Century.* Englewood Cliffs, N.J.: Prentice-Hall, 1978.
Erikson, Ann M. *Congressional Districting.* Columbus, Ohio: Legislative Service Commission, 1965.
Farrand, Max. *The Framing of the Constitution of the United States.* New Haven: Yale University Press, 1913.
Faulkner, Harold U. *American Political and Social History.* New York: F. S. Crofts, 1947.
———. *From Versailles to the New Deal: A Chronicle of the Harding-Coolidge Era.* Vol. 51 of The Chronicles of America series. New Haven: Yale University Press, 1950.
Freidel, Frank, and Alan Brinkley. *America in the Twentieth Century.* 5th ed. New York: Knopf, 1982.
Froman, Lewis A. *The Congressional Process: Strategies, Rules, and Procedures.* Boston: Little, Brown, 1967.
———. *Congressmen and Their Constituencies.* Chicago: Rand McNally, 1963.
Furniss, Norman. *The Fundamentalist Controversy, 1918–1931.* New Haven: Yale University Press, 1954.
Galloway, George B. *History of the House of Representatives.* New York: Crowell, 1961.
———. *The Legislative Process in Congress.* New York: Crowell, 1953.
Garraty, John A. *The American Nation.* New York: Harper & Row, 1966.
———, ed. *Dictionary of American Biography.* Supplement 5, 1951–55. New York: Charles Scribner's Sons, 1977.
Gerlach, Larry R. *Blazing Crosses in Zion: The Ku Klux Klan in Utah.* Logan: Utah State University Press, 1982.
Goldberg, Robert Alan. *Hooded Empire: The Ku Klux Klan in Colorado.* Urbana: University of Illinois Press, 1981.
Gusfield, Joseph R. *Symbolic Crusade: Status Politics and the American Temperance Crusade.* Urbana: University of Illinois Press, 1963.
Hacker, Andrew. *Congressional Districting: The Issue of Equal Representation.* Washington, D.C.: Brookings Institution, 1963.
Hamilton, Howard. *Legislative Apportionment: Key to Power.* New York: Harper & Row, 1964.
Hansen, Royce. *The Political Thicket: Reapportionment and Constitutional Democracy.* Englewood Cliffs, N.J.: Prentice-Hall, 1966.
Hawley, Ellis. *The Great War and the Search for a Modern Order: A History of the American People and Their Institutions, 1917–1933.* New York: St. Martin's, 1979.
Hicks, John D. *The Republican Ascendancy, 1921–1933.* New York: Harper, 1960.

Higham, John. *Strangers in the Land: Patterns of American Nativism, 1860–1925.* New Brunswick, N.J.: Rutgers University Press, 1955.
Hofstadter, Richard. *The Age of Reform: From Bryan to F.D.R.* New York: Knopf, 1955.
Holt, W. Stull. *The Bureau of the Census: Its History, Activities and Organization.* Washington, D.C.: Brookings Institution, 1929.
Horowitz, Daniel. *The Morality of Spending: Attitudes toward the Consumer Society in America, 1875–1940.* Baltimore: Johns Hopkins University Press, 1985.
Jackson, Kenneth T. *The Ku Klux Klan in the City, 1915–1930.* New York: Oxford University Press, 1967.
Jensen, Richard J. *The Winning of the Midwest: Social and Political Conflict, 1888–1896.* Chicago: University of Chicago Press, 1971.
Jewell, Malcolm E., ed. *The Politics of Reapportionment.* New York: Atherton Press, 1962.
Jewell, Malcolm E., and Samuel C. Patterson. *The Legislative Process in the United States.* New York: Random House, 1966.
Kirschner, Don S. *City and Country: Rural Responses to Urbanization in the 1920s.* Westport, Conn.: Greenwood, 1970.
Kleppner, Paul. *Continuity and Change in Electoral Politics, 1893–1928.* Westport, Conn.: Greenwood, 1987.
———. *The Cross of Culture: A Social Analysis of Midwestern Politics, 1850–1900.* New York: Free Press, 1970.
Laski, Harold J. *The American Democracy: A Commentary and an Interpretation.* New York: Viking, 1948.
Leuchtenburg, William E. *Flood Control Politics: The Connecticut River Valley Problem, 1927–1950.* Cambridge, Mass.: Harvard University Press, 1953.
———. *The Perils of Prosperity, 1914–1932.* Chicago: University of Chicago Press, 1958.
Levine, Lawrence W. *Defender of the Faith: William Jennings Bryan, The Last Decade, 1919–1925.* New York: Oxford University Press, 1965.
Lichtman, Allan J. *Prejudice and the Old Politics: The Presidential Election of 1928.* Chapel Hill: University of North Carolina Press, 1979.
Lubell, Samuel. *The Future of American Politics.* New York: Harper & Row, 1952.
MacRae, Duncan, Jr. *Issues and Parties in Legislative Voting: Methods of Statistical Analysis.* New York: Harper & Row, 1970.
Marsden, George M. *Fundamentalism and American Culture: The Shaping of Twentieth-Century Evangelicalism, 1870–1925.* New York: Oxford University Press, 1980.

Martis, Kenneth C., ed. *The Historical Atlas of United States Congressional Districts, 1789–1983.* New York: Free Press, 1982.
Matthews, Donald R., and James A. Stimson. *Yeas and Nays: Normal Decision-Making in the U.S. House of Representatives.* New York: Wiley, 1975.
McCoy, Donald R. *Coming of Age: The United States during the 1920s and 1930s.* Baltimore: Penguin, 1973.
McKay, Kenneth C. *The Progressive Movement of 1924.* New York: Columbia University Press, 1947.
McKay, Robert B. *Reapportionment: The Law and Politics of Equal Representation.* New York: Twentieth Century Fund, 1965.
McSeveney, Samuel T. *The Politics of Depression: Political Behavior in the Northeast, 1893–1896.* New York: Oxford University Press, 1972.
Moore, Edmund A. *A Catholic Runs for President: The Campaign of 1928.* New York: Ronald Press, 1956.
Morison, Samuel Eliot, and Henry Steele Commager. *The Growth of the American Republic.* New York: Oxford University Press, 1937.
Mowry, George E., ed. *The Twenties: Fords, Flappers, and Fanatics.* Englewood Cliffs, N.J.: Prentice-Hall, 1963.
———. *The Urban Nation, 1920–1960.* New York: Hill and Wang, 1965.
Murray, Robert K. *The Harding Era: Warren G. Harding and His Administration.* Minneapolis: University of Minnesota Press, 1969.
———. *The Politics of Normalcy: Governmental Theory and Practice in the Harding-Coolidge Era.* New York: Norton, 1973.
Nash, Gerald D. *The Great Transition: A Short History of Twentieth-Century America.* Boston: Allyn and Bacon, 1971.
Nash, Roderick. *The Nervous Generation: American Thought, 1917–1930.* Chicago; Rand McNally, 1970.
Nelson, Lowry. *Rural Sociology: Its Origin and Growth in the United States.* Minneapolis: University of Minnesota Press, 1969.
Nisbet, Robert A. *The Sociological Tradition.* New York: Basic Books, 1966.
Noble, David W., David A. Horowitz, and Peter N. Carroll. *Twentieth Century Limited.* Boston: Houghton Mifflin, 1980.
Noggle, Burl. *Into the Twenties: The United States from Armistice to Normalcy.* Urbana: University of Illinois Press, 1974.
Norton, Mary Beth, et al. *A People and a Nation: A History of the United States.* Boston: Houghton Mifflin, 1982.
Parsons, Stanley B. *The Populist Context: Rural versus Urban Power on a Great Plains Frontier.* Westport, Conn.: Greenwood, 1973.
Paxson, Frederick L. *Post War Years: Normalcy, 1918–1933.* Berkeley and Los Angeles: University of California Press, 1938.

Bibliography

———. *Recent History of the United States, 1865 to the Present*. Rev. and enlarged ed. Boston: Houghton Mifflin, 1937.
Payne, Darwin. *The Man of Only Yesterday: Frederick Lewis Allen*. New York: Harper & Row, 1975.
Perrett, Geoffrey. *America in the Twenties: A History*. New York: Simon and Schuster, 1982.
Rice, Arnold S. *The Ku Klux Klan in American Politics*. Washington, D.C.: Public Affairs Press, 1962.
Rossiter, Clinton. *1787: The Grand Convention*. New York: Macmillan, 1966.
Rutland, Robert A. *The Birth of the Bill of Rights*. Chapel Hill: University of North Carolina Press, 1955.
Sandeen, Ernest R. *The Roots of Fundamentalism: British and American Millenialism, 1800–1930*. Chicago: University of Chicago Press, 1970.
Schlesinger, Arthur M., Jr. *The Crisis of the Old Order, 1919–1933*. Boston: Houghton Mifflin, 1957.
Schmeckebier, Lawrence F. *Congressional Apportionment*. Washington, D.C.: Brookings Institution, 1941.
Shannon, David A. *Twentieth Century America*. Chicago: Rand McNally, 1963.
Shi, David. *The Simple Life: Plain Living and High Thinking in American Culture*. New York: Oxford University Press, 1985.
Sinclair, Andrew. *Prohibition: The Era of Excess*. Boston: Atlantic Monthly Press, 1962.
Sklar, Robert, ed. *The Plastic Age, 1917–1930*. New York: George Braziller, 1970.
Slosson, William Preston. *The Great Crusade and After, 1914–1928*. Vol. 12 of *A History of American Life*, edited by Arthur M. Schlesinger and Dixon Ryan Fox. New York: Macmillan, 1931.
Soule, George. *Prosperity Decade: From War to Depression, 1917–1929*. New York: Rinehart, 1947.
Stearns, Harold E., ed. *Civilization in the United States: An Inquiry by Thirty Americans*. New York: Harcourt, Brace, 1922.
Stoneall, Linda. *Country Life, City Life: Five Theories of Community*. New York: Praeger, 1983.
Susman, Warren. *Culture and History: The Transformation of American Society in the Twentieth Century*. New York: Pantheon, 1984.
Timberlake, James H. *Prohibition and the Progressive Movement, 1900–1920*. Cambridge, Mass.: Harvard University Press, 1963.
Tindall, George Brown. *America: A Narrative History*. New York: Norton, 1984.
Tompkins, C. David. *Senator Arthur H. Vandenberg*. East Lansing: Michigan State University Press, 1970.

Tonnies, Ferdinand. *Community and Society (Gemeinschaft and Gesellschaft)*. Translated and edited by Charles P. Loomis. East Lansing: Michigan State University Press, 1957. Originally published in German in 1877.

———. *Ferdinand Tonnies on Sociology: Pure, Applied, and Empirical*. Edited with an introduction by Werner J. Cahnman and Rudolph Herbele. Chicago: University of Chicago Press, 1971.

Turner, Julius. *Party and Constituency: Pressures on Congress*. Baltimore: Johns Hopkins University Press, 1951. Rev. ed. by Edward V. Schneier, Jr., 1970.

White, Morton, and Lucia White. *The Intellectual versus the City: From Thomas Jefferson to Frank Lloyd Wright*. Cambridge, Mass.: Harvard University Press, 1962.

Who Was Who in America. Chicago: Marquis Who's Who, 1968.

Wiebe, Robert H. *The Segmented Society: An Introduction to the Meaning of America*. New York: Oxford University Press, 1975.

Wilson, Joan Hoff, ed. *The Twenties: The Critical Issues*. Boston: Little, Brown, 1972.

Zagarri, Rosemarie. *The Politics of Size: Representation in the United States, 1776–1850*. Ithaca: Cornell University Press, 1987.

ARTICLES

Ames, Herbert V. "The Proposed Amendments to the Constitution of the United States during the First Century of Its History." In *Annual Report of the American Historical Association for the Year 1896*, Vol. 2. Washington, D.C.: U.S. Government Printing Office, 1897.

Anderson, Clifford. "Agrarian Attitudes toward the City, Business, and Labor in the 1920s and 1930s." *Mississippi Quarterly* 14 (Fall 1961): 183–89.

Baritz, Loren. "The Culture of the Twenties." In *The Development of an American Culture*, edited by Stanley Coben and Lorman Ratner, pp. 150–78. Englewood Cliffs, N.J.: Prentice-Hall, 1970.

Brady, David W. "A Reevaluation of Realignments in American Politics: Evidence from the House of Representatives." *American Political Science Quarterly* 79 (March 1985): 28–49.

Brogan, D. W. "Fifty Years of Dreams, Protests, and Achievement." Review of *The Age of Reform*, by Richard Hofstadter, *New York Times Book Review*, October 16, 1955, p. 7.

Burton, William L. "'Yesterday' Revisited." *Illinois Quarterly* 36 (September 1973): 49–64.

Carson, Gerald. "The Great Enumeration." *American Heritage* 31 (December 1979): 6–17.
Carter, Paul A. "The Fundamentalist Defense of the Faith." In *Change and Continuity in Twentieth Century America: The 1920s*, edited by John Braeman, Robert H. Bremner, and David Brody, pp. 179–214. Columbus: Ohio State University Press, 1968.
Celler, Emanuel. "Congressional Apportionment—Past, Present, and Future." *Law and Contemporary Problems* 17 (1952): 268–75.
Chambers, Clarke A. Review of *The Perils of Prosperity, 1914–1933*, by William E. Leuchtenburg. *Mississippi Valley Historical Review* 45 (December 1958): 522–23.
Coben, Stanley. "The Assault on Victorianism in the Twentieth Century." *American Quarterly* 27 (December 1975): 604–25.
———. "The First Fifty Years of Modern America, 1918–1933." In *The Unfinished Century: America since 1900*, edited by William E. Leuchtenburg, pp. 255–353. Boston: Little, Brown, 1973.
———. "A Study in Nativism: The American Red Scare of 1919–1920." *Political Science Quarterly* 79 (March 1964): 52–75.
Dewey, Richard. "The Rural-Urban Continuum: Real but Relatively Unimportant." *American Journal of Sociology* 66 (July 1960): 60–66.
Dykstra, Robert K. "Town-Country Conflict: A Hidden Dimension in American Social History." *Agricultural History* 38 (October 1964): 195–204.
Eagles, Charles W. "Congressional Voting in the 1920s: A Test of Urban-Rural Conflict." *Journal of American History* 76 (September 1989): 528–34.
———. "Urban-Rural Conflict in the 1920s: A Historiographical Assessment." *Historian* 49 (November 1986): 26–48.
Ellis, William E. "Evolution, Fundamentalism, and the Historians: An Historiographical Review." *Historian* 44 (November 1981): 15–35.
Friedman, Robert S. "The Urban-Rural Conflict Revisited." *Western Political Quarterly* 14 (June 1961): 481–95.
Fuller, Wayne E. "The Rural Roots of the Progressive Leaders." *Agricultural History* 42 (January 1968): 1–13.
Garson, Robert A. "Political Fundamentalism and Popular Democracy in the 1920's." *South Atlantic Quarterly* 76 (Spring 1977): 219–33.
Gilbert, Jess. "Rural Theory: The Grounding of Rural Sociology." *Rural Sociology* 47 (Winter 1982): 609–33.
Goldberg, Robert A. "Beneath Hood and Robe: A Socioeconomic Analysis of Ku Klux Klan Membership in Denver, Colorado, 1921–1925." *Western History Quarterly* 11 (April 1980): 181–98.
Gray, Virginia. "Anti-Evolution Sentiment and Behavior: The Case of Arkansas." *Journal of American History* 57 (September 1970): 352–66.

Grob, Gerald N., and George A. Billias. "The 1920s: Decade of Decline or Destiny?" In *Interpretations of American History: Patterns and Perspectives.* vol. 2, *Since 1865,* edited by Grob and Billias, pp. 249–65. 4th ed. New York: Free Press, 1982.
Gusfield, Joseph R. "Prohibition: The Impact of Political Utopianism." In *Change and Continuity in Twentieth Century America: The 1920s,* edited by John Braeman, Robert H. Bremner, and David Brody, pp. 257–308. Columbus: Ohio State University Press, 1968.
Hicks, John D. "Politics in Pattern," review of *The Age of Reform,* by Richard Hofstadter. *Saturday Review of Literature,* October 22, 1955, pp. 12–13.
———. Review of *The Perils of Prosperity, 1914–1933,* by William E. Leuchtenburg. *Journal of Economic History* 19 (March 1959): 135–36.
Hohner, Robert A. "The Prohibitionists: Who Were They?" *South Atlantic Quarterly* 68 (Autumn 1969): 491–505.
James, Edmund J. "The First Apportionment of Federal Representatives in the United States." *Annals of the American Academy of Political and Social Science* 9 (January 1897): 1–41.
Kirkland, Edward C. Review of *The Age of Reform,* by Richard Hofstadter. *American Historical Review* 61 (May 1956): 255–56.
Kirschner, Don S. "Conflicts and Politics in the 1920s: Historiography and Prospects." *Mid-America* 48 (October 1968): 219–33.
Kousser, J. Morgan. "History QUASSHed: Quantitative Scientific History in Perspective." *American Behavioral Scientist* 23 (July–August 1980): 885–904.
Lasch, Robert. "History at Its Best: Events That Led up to the Great Depression." Review of *The Perils of Prosperity, 1914–1933,* by William E. Leuchtenburg. *St. Louis Post-Dispatch,* June 1, 1959, p. 4c.
Lowe, George D., and Charles W. Peek. "Location and Lifestyle: The Comparative Explanatory Ability of Urbanism and Rurality." *Rural Sociology* 39 (Fall 1974): 392–420.
Lowitt, Richard L. "Prosperity Decade, 1917–1928." In *Interpreting and Teaching American History,* edited by William E. Cartwright and Richard L. Watson, Jr., pp. 231–63. Washington, D.C.: National Council for the Social Studies, 1961.
Lynn, Kenneth S. "Only Yesterday." *American Scholar* 49 (Autumn 1980): 513–18.
May, Henry F. "Shifting Perspectives on the 1920s." *Mississippi Valley Historical Review* 43 (December 1956): 405–27.
———. "The Twenties: Normalcy and Reaction." In *Problems in American History,* edited by Richard W. Leopold and Arthur S. Link, pp. 788–836. New York: Prentice-Hall, 1952.

McCormick, Richard L. "Ethnocultural Interpretations of Nineteenth-Century American Voting Behavior." *Political Science Quarterly* 89 (June 1974): 351–77.
McSeveney, Samuel T. "Ethnic Groups, Ethnic Conflicts, and Recent Quantitative Research in American Political History." *International Migration Review* 7 (Spring 1973): 14–33.
Miller, Robert Moats. "The Ku Klux Klan." In *Change and Continuity in Twentieth Century America: The 1920s*, edited by John Braeman, Robert H. Bremner, and David Brody, pp. 215–56. Columbus: Ohio State University Press, 1968.
Miller, William D. "Rural Values and Urban Progress: Memphis, 1900–1917." *Mississippi Quarterly* 21 (Fall 1968): 263–74.
Moore, Frederick W. "Representation in the National Congress from the Seceding States, 1861–1865." *American Historical Review* 2 (January 1897): 278–93 and 2 (April 1897): 461–71.
Mowry, George E. "The First World War and American Democracy." In *War as a Social Institution: The Historians' Perspective*, edited by Jesse D. Clarkson and Thomas C. Cochran, pp. 170–84. New York: Columbia University Press, 1941.
Murphy, Paul L. "Sources and Nature of Intolerance in the 1920s." *Journal of American History* 51 (June 1964): 60–76.
Noble, Ransom E. Review of *The Perils of Prosperity, 1914–1933*, by William E. Leuchtenburg. *Annals of the American Academy of Political and Social Science* 322 (March 1959): 178.
Noggle, Burl. "Configurations of the Twenties." In *The Reinterpretation of American History and Culture*, edited by William E. Cartwright and Richard L. Watson, Jr., pp. 465–90. Washington, D.C.: National Council for the Social Studies, 1973.
―――. "Doing History by the Decade: A Pattern in American Historiography, 1930–1980." *History Teacher* 16 (May 1983): 389–416.
―――. "The Twenties: A New Historiographical Frontier." *Journal of American History* 53 (September 1966): 299–314.
O'Brien, Patrick J. "A Reexamination of the Senate Farm Bloc, 1921–1933." *Agricultural History* 47 (July 1973): 248–63.
Polsby, Nelson W. "The Institutionalization of the U.S. House of Representatives." *American Political Science Review* 62 (March 1968): 144–68.
Polsby, Nelson W., Miriam Gallaher, and Barry Spencer Rundquist. "The Growth of the Seniority System in the U.S. House of Representatives." *American Political Science Review* 63 (September 1969): 787–807.
Rosenbaum, Betty B. "The Urban-Rural Conflict as Evidenced in the Reapportionment Situation." *Social Forces* 12 (March 1934): 421–26.

Schlesinger, Arthur M., Jr. "Richard Hofstadter." In *Pastmasters*, edited by Marcus Cunliffe and Robin Winks, pp. 278–315. New York: Harper & Row, 1969.

Schlesinger, Arthur M., Sr. "The City in American History." *Mississippi Valley Historical Review* 27 (June 1940): 43–66.

Schnore, Leo F. "The Rural-Urban Variable: An Urbanite's Perspective." *Rural Sociology* 31 (June 1966): 131–43.

Searcy, Hubert. "Problems of Congressional Reapportionment." *Southwestern Social Science Quarterly* 16 (June 1935): 58–68.

Shideler, James H. "Flappers and Philosophers, and Farmers: Rural-Urban Tensions of the Twenties." *Agricultural History* 47 (October 1973): 283–99.

——. Review of *The Perils of Prosperity, 1914–1933*, by William E. Leuchtenburg. *American Historical Review* 64 (October 1958): 202–3.

Shils, Edward. "The Contemplation of Society in America." In *Paths of American Thought*, edited by Morton White and Arthur M. Schlesinger, Jr., pp. 392–410. Boston: Houghton Mifflin, 1963.

Shover, John L. "Ethnicity and Religion in Philadelphia Politics, 1924–1940." *American Quarterly* 25 (December 1975): 499–515.

Sinclair, Barbara Deckard. "Party Realignment and the Transformation of the Political Agenda: The House of Representatives, 1925–1938." *American Political Science Review* 71 (September 1977): 941–53.

Singal, Daniel J. "Beyond Consensus: Richard Hofstadter and American Historiography." *American Historical Review* 89 (October 1984): 976–1004.

Singleton, Gregory H. "Fundamentalism and Urbanization: A Quantitative Critique of Impressionistic Interpretations." In *The New Urban History*, edited by Leo F. Schnore, pp. 205–77. Princeton: Princeton University Press, 1974.

Stewart, Charles T. "The Urban-Rural Dichotomy: Concepts and Uses." *American Journal of Sociology* 64 (September 1958): 152–58.

Thompson, James J., Jr. "Southern Baptist City and Country Churches in the Twenties." *Foundations* 17 (October–December 1974): 351–63.

Van Es, J. C., and J. E. Brown, Jr. "The Rural-Urban Variable Once More: Some Individual Level Observations." *Rural Sociology* 39 (Fall 1974): 373–91.

Wiebe, Robert H. "Modernizing the Republic, 1920 to the Present." In Bernard Bailyn et al., *The Great Republic: A History of the American People*, pp. 1053–1267. Lexington, Mass.: Heath, 1977.

Wish, Harvey. "Half-Remembered Yesterdays of a Restless Generation." Review of *The Perils of Prosperity, 1914–1933*, by William E. Leuchtenburg, *New York Times Book Review*, July 13, 1958, p. 3.

Index

Adams, John Quincy, 25–26
Adorno, Theodore, 8
Alabama paradox, 29–31
Alexander, Charles C., 14
Aliens, 54, 76, 79, 82–83, 117–18; included in enumerated population for reapportionment, xi, 34, 50–52, 61, 63; and urban-rural thesis, 3–11 passim; Hoch plan to exclude from census, 70–71, 80; Sackett proposal to exclude, 77–78. *See also* Nativism; Immigration restriction
Allen, Frederick Lewis, 5–6, 7–13
American Economic Association, 42, 43
American Mathematical Society, 43, 44
American Statistical Association, 42, 43, 45
Anti-Saloon League, 71
Articles of Confederation, 21
Aswell, James B., 37–38
Atlantic Monthly, 4–5

Baltimore American, 42
Baltimore Evening Sun, 83
Bankhead, William B., 66, 80
Barbour, Henry E., 54, 57; for House with 435 seats, 35, 63; opposes enlarged House, 39; proposes limit at 435, 42, 50–51; objects to committee inaction, 52–53; seeks discharge of bill, 56
Baritz, Loren, 14
Bee, Carlos, 35
Beedy, Carroll L., 49, 67
Bender, Thomas, 122
Bensel, Richard Franklin, 19
Bettleheim, Bruno, 8
Billias, George A., 1, 13
Bill of Rights, 23
Black, Eugene, 41, 48
Black, Hugo, 75–76
Blacks: denied the right to vote, 34, 40, 47–48, 51–52, 58, 63, 80, 117; testify before Census Committee, 35–36. *See also* Fourteenth Amendment
Blaine, James G., 77–78
Bland, Oscar E., 38–39
Blanton, Thomas L., 35, 48, 53, 63
Blease, Coleman L., 77
Blum, John M., 13–14
Boston Evening Transcript, 83
Boston Guardian, 35
Brigham, Elbert S., 61, 70
Brinkley, Alan, 19
Brinson, Samuel M., 40
Bryan, William Jennings, 2, 4, 8, 9, 12, 15
Burner, David, ix, 15, 93, 120
Burton, Theodore E., 45

Campbell, Ballard, 147 (n. 11)
Cannon, Joseph G., 33

Capper, Arthur, 77
Carraway, Thaddeus H., 77
Carroll, Peter N., 14
Carter, Paul, 15, 16, 17, 138 (n. 31)
Celler, Emanuel, 66, 72
Census: 1790–1910, 23–30
Census, Bureau of, 35, 43, 47, 60, 64, 68; criticized, 39; bill for automatic reapportionment by 64–65; defines urban and rural districts, 87; defines metropolitan district, 88
Census Committee, House, 33, 42, 49, 56, 116–17; hearings by, 32, 34–36, 45–46, 54–55, 59–62, 63–65; lack of hearings and action, 52–54; bills sent back to, 51, 67, 69–70, 73
Census Committee, Senate, 42, 45
Census of 1910, 74, 116
Census of 1920, ix–x, 21, 53, 73–75 passim, 116; reveals urban majority, 2; results of, 32; accuracy questioned, 38–39, 46, 49, 51, 55, 62, 65, 116; used in roll-call analysis, 87–90
Census of 1930, ix, xi, 21, 32, 55–67 passim, 76, 79; date for, 76, 81–82; workers for, 78–80
Census of 1940, 117
Chafee, Zechariah, 79
Chalmers, David, 14
Chambers, Clark, 12–13
Chapman, Virgil, 66
Chicago Daily News, 56
Chindbloom, Carl Richard, 81
Chudacoff, Howard P., 17–18
Civil War, 27–28
Clancy, Robert H., 67
Clark, James Beauchamp, 33, 39
Clark, Norman A., 16
Cleveland Plain Dealer, 73

Coben, Stanley, 18–19
Cole, Cyrenus, 48–49
Colored Council of Washington, 35
Commager, Henry Steele, 6
Commerce, Secretary of, 59–66 and 71–76 passim
Commerce Committee, Senate, 74; hearings held by, 76
Commonweal, 79
Congress, U.S.: 66th, 32–42; 67th, 45–51; 68th, 51–53; 69th, 54–62; 70th, 62–82
Constitution, U.S., xi, 47, 52, 55, 58, 67; establishes House, 21–23; and reapportionment, 22, 45, 50, 56–58, 65–79 passim, 108; calls for decennial census, 22–23; set original ratio for representation, 24. *See also* Three-fifths compromise; Fourteenth Amendment
Constitutional Convention, 21–22, 31, 50
Coolidge, Calvin, 54, 59
Cooper, John M., 137 (n. 30)
Cronon, E. David, 14
Curtis, Charles, 75

Dayton Journal, 42
Democrats (Democratic Party), 28, 51, 55; Burner's study of, ix, 120–21; and urban-rural interpretation, 7–15 passim; oppose bill in Census Committee, 62, 69; roll-call analysis of voting, 93–115; and reapportionment after 1940 census, 117
Denison, Edward Everett, 82
Depression, 5
Des Moines Tribune Capital, 73
Detroit Free Press, 56

Dewey, John, 2–3, 5, 7
Dickinson, Jesse, 72
Divine, Robert, 14
Durkheim, Emile, 2
Dykstra, Robert K., 19

Eighteenth Amendment, 10, 58, 71
Elections: of 1824, 65; 1872, 74; 1876, 74; 1912, 74; 1928, 68, 74
Electoral College, 28, 59, 67, 68, 74
Encyclopedia of the Social Sciences, 4
Evens, Hiram Wesley, 70

Fairfield, Louis W., 36–41 passim, 51
Faulkner, Harold U., 7
Faust, Charles L., 52
Fenn, Hart, 54, 59, 62, 63, 72–73, 81–82
Fess, Simeon D., 40
Fifteenth Amendment, 47
Fitzgerald, Roy G., 54
Fourteenth Amendment, 28, 34–36, 47, 71, 74, 80. See also Tinkham, George Holden
Fox, Dixon Ryan, 6
Freidel, Frank, 19
Fundamentalism, political, 11
Fundamentalism, religious, 85, 108, 121; and urban-rural interpretation, x, 1–18 passim. See also Scopes, John Thomas
Furniss, Norman, 8

Garraty, John, 14
Gemeinschaft, 2, 14, 122
George, Walter, 77
Gerlach, Larry, 16
Gesellschaft, 2, 14, 122
Gillett, Frederick H., 78
Glynn, James P., 40

Goldberg, Robert Alan, 16, 19, 137 (n. 30)
Goodykoontz, Wells, 47
Gray, Virginia, 16, 17
Greeley, Horace, 74
Greene, Frank L., 38
Gregory, William V., 82
Grob, Gerald N., 1, 13
Gusfield, Joseph, 15, 16

Hamilton, Alexander, 24, 25
Harding, Warren G., 52
Hardy, Rufus, 37
Harper's, 5
Harrison, Byron Patton, 75–76
Harvard Law Review, 79
Harvey, George H., 35
Hawes, Harry B., 77
Hawley, Ellis, 18–19
Heflin, James Thomas, 77
Hersey, Ira G., 38, 45, 66
Hicks, John D., 13
Higham, John, 8
Hill, Joseph A., 35, 43, 60, 64
Hoch, Homer, 70–71, 80
Hofstadter, Richard, 8–10, 15, 135 (n. 16), 137 (n. 30), 137 (n. 27)
Hohner, Robert A., 15
Hoover, Herbert, 17, 32, 75, 82
Horowitz, Daniel, 19
Horowitz, David, 14
House of Representatives: size of districts in, 22–31, 47–57 passim, 72, 118; nature of districts in, 26–30, 72–73, 80–81, 117–18; size of, 33–54 passim, 65, 96, 116–17; efficiency of, 33–47 passim; cost of, 36, 37, 40, 46, 53; districts used for roll-call analysis, 87–90
Hull, Cordell, 33
Humphreys, Benjamin G., 41

Huntington, William V., 46, 70, 76; advocates method of equal proportions, 43–45; testifies before Census Committee, 60–61; assists Zechariah Chafee, 79. *See also under* Reapportionment, methods of

Immigration restriction, 70, 81, 108, 118, 121; and urban-rural interpretation, x, 1–18 passim; roll-call analysis of voting on, 85. *See also* Aliens
Index of disagreement, 90
Interior, Secretary of, 27, 28, 63

Jackson, Andrew, 2
Jackson, Kenneth, 16
Jacobstein, Meyer, 55, 64, 66–67
Jefferson, Thomas, 24–25, 26
Jermane, W. W., 83
Johnson, Hiram, 76, 81
Johnson, James Weldon, 35
Johnson, Paul B., 38–39
Jones, Marvin, 40, 42

Kahn, Florence P., 64
Kirschner, Don S., 10, 19
Knox, Henry, 24
Kousser, J. Morgan, xii
Ku Klux Klan, 85, 108, 121; and urban-rural thesis, x, 1–19 passim; involved in preventing reapportionment, 58; and Hoch's proposal to exclude aliens, 70–71; opposes urban Catholic power, 83; and effects of World War I, 134 (n. 6)

LaFollette, Robert, 12
LaGuardia, Fiorello, 67, 70
Langley, John W., 49–50

Larsen, William W., 35–36, 48
Laski, Harold, 7–8
Leuchtenburg, William E., 10–13, 18, 137 (n. 30), 139 (n. 37)
Levine, Lawrence, 15
Lichtman, Allan J., 17, 148 (n. 4)
Lippmann, Walter, 2, 4–5, 7
Literary Digest, 42, 56
Little, Edward C., 38
Longworth, Nicholas, 56, 61–62, 65, 69, 75
Lowitt, Richard L., 1, 10, 13
Lowndes, William, 25
Lozier, Ralph F., 64, 71; attacks 1920 census, 55; opposed smaller House, 55; criticizes 435 limit for House, 60, 66; defends rural representation, 61; opposes delegating power to executive, 63
Lubell, Samuel, 8
Luce, Robert, 71

McAdoo, William Gibbs, 10
McCarthyism, 8–9
McCoy, Donald, 14
McKay, Kenneth C., 7
McKee, Oliver, Jr., 83
McKellar, Kenneth, 77
McLeod, Clarence J., 54, 63, 69; criticizes inaction on reapportionment, 53; asks for Coolidge's intervention, 59; leads support for Fenn bill, 71; on Conference Committee, 81; supports November 1 for census, 82
Madden, Martin B., 41
Madison, James, 22
Mannheim, Karl, 8
Mapes, Carl, 72
Marsden, George M., 16, 17

Martis, Kenneth C., 89
May, Henry F., 1
Mecklin, John Moffat, 3, 136 (n. 6)
Mencken, H. L., 2, 3, 5
Metropolitan districts: defined, 88
Michener, Earl C., 66
Miller, Robert Moats, 14
Milligan, Jacob L., 37
Modernism, 18–19, 121–23
Moore, Edmund A., 10
Morrison, Samuel Eliot, 6
Most-rural districts: defined, 88
Mowry, George E., 6–7, 14
Mumford, Lewis, 2, 3
Murphy, Paul L., 14
Murphy, William C., Jr., 79
Myers, William Starr, 68

Nash, Roderick, 13
Nation, 34, 58, 70
National Association for the Advancement of Colored People, 35, 58
National Equal Rights League, 35
National Republican, 34
Nativism, x, 1, 6, 8, 77. See also Aliens
New Deal, 9
New Jersey plan, 21–22
New Republic, 2, 33, 57, 65
New York Evening Post, 56–57
New York Telegram, 73
New York Times, x, 13, 33, 42, 44, 46, 53, 55, 56, 61, 65, 71, 80, 96
Niebuhr, H. Richard, 2, 4, 7, 8
Noble, David W., 14
Noggle, Burl, 1, 10, 13, 149 (n. 8)
North American Review, 68

Omaha World-Herald, 42
Outlook and Independent, 73

Paxson, Frederick L., ix, 6, 7, 58–59
The Perils of Prosperity, 1914–1932, 10–13, 139 (n. 37)
Philadelphia Public Ledger, 58, 72
Philadelphia Record, 73
Pittman, Key, 77
The Politics of Provincialism, 1914–32, ix–x, 15, 93, 120
Polk, James K., 26
Populism, 9–10
Progressivism, 9–10, 12
Prohibition, 81, 83, 118, 121; and urban-rural thesis, ix, x, 1–18, 71; and Hoch proposal, 71; and Fenn bill, 71; roll-call analysis of voting on, 85. See also Eighteenth Amendment

Raleigh News and Observer, 56
Ramseyer, William C., 65
Randolph, Edmund, 24
Rankin, John E., 47–48, 55, 60–67 passim, 71, 81–82
Reapportionment (1792–1911), 23–31
Reapportionment, bills for in 1920s: Siegel bill, 34–52; Barbour bill, 35, 63; Blanton bill, 35, 63; Fenn bill, 59–69 passim; McLeod bill, 63; Vandenberg bill, 69–75
Reapportionment, methods of, 54, 59–61, 67, 117; rejected fractions, 24–25; Vinton or Hamilton, 24–31; Adams, 25–26; major fractions (Webster or Willcox), 26–46 passim, 60–82 passim; Interior Department, 27, 28, 59, 63; equal proportions (Huntington), 43–46, 59–82; by President, 54–55, 76–78, 81–82; by Commerce Department

Reapportionment (continued) (Census Bureau), 59–75 passim; constitutional amendment, 70–71
Reconstruction, 28
Red Scare, 5
Reed, Daniel Alden, 80–81
Reid, Louis Raymond, 3
Republicans (Republican Party), 28, 51, 55, 69, 74; caucus supports larger House, 33–34, 46; and black vote, 36; support Fenn bill, 61–62; roll-call analysis of voting on, 93–115; deserve more study, 121
Review of Reviews, 65, 73–74, 79
Roll-call analysis, xi, 85–115
Roosevelt, Franklin Delano, 8
Rules Committee, House, 65
Rural: definitions of, 2, 87–88
Rural sociology, 2

Sackett, Frederic M., 77
St. Louis Post-Dispatch, 13, 73
Sandeen, Ernest R., 16–17
Saturday Evening Post, 67–68
Schafer, John C., 70
Schlesinger, Arthur M., Jr., 10
Schlesinger, Arthur M., Sr., 6, 7
Scopes, John Thomas, 5, 10, 11, 17
Seattle Times, 42, 83
Senate, U. S., 63, 69, 74–79, 81–82
Shannon, David, 14
Shideler, James H., 13, 137 (n. 29)
Siegel, Isaac, 32–47 passim
Siegfried, Andre, 3–4
Sinclair, Andrew, ix, 14–15
Singal, Daniel J., 19
Singleton, Gregory H., 16, 17
Sisson, Thomas U., 40
Slosson, William Preston, 6, 7, 13
Smith, Alfred E., 8, 10, 12, 17, 68

Smith, Robert B., 58
Snell, Bertrand H., 56, 61–62, 69
Social Gospel, 15
Sorokin, Pitrim, 2
Status anxiety and status politics, 9, 135 (n. 16)
Strong, James George, 61
Sullivan, Mark, 83
Susman, Warren, 19
Sutherland, Howard, 42
Swanson, Claude A., 76

Three-fifths compromise, 22, 28
Thurston, Lloyd, 61, 63
Tilden, Samuel J., 29
Tilson, John, 59, 61–62, 65, 69, 75, 80
Timberlake, James, 16
Tincher, Jasper N., 39
Tinkham, George Holden: calls for enforcement of Fourteenth Amendment, 34–37, 47–48, 52, 63, 71, 80. See also Blacks; Fourteenth Amendment
Tonnies, Ferdinand, 2, 14, 122
Towner, Horace M., 49
Trotter, Monroe, 35
Tucker, Ray T., 57–58

Urban: definitions of, 2, 87–88
Urban-rural interpretation, x–xii; historiography of, 1–20; roll-call test for, 85–115; assessment of, 116–24

Vaile, William, 50
Vandenberg, Arthur, 69, 74–81
Veterans, 37, 46
Victorianism, 18–19, 122–23
Vinton, Samuel F., 27
Virginia Plan, 21
Voigt, Edward R., 55

Wagner, Robert F., 78
Wallerstein, Immanuel, 19
Walsh, David I., 74, 77–78
Washington, George, 24–25
Watson, Charles E., 75
Weber, Max, 2
Webster, Daniel, 26
Wesberry v. Sanders, 118
White, Hays B., 61
White, Walter, 35
Wiebe, Robert H., 18, 19
Willcox, Walter F., 30, 43–46 passim, 60–61, 64, 70
Wilson, Joan Hoff, 14

Wish, Harvey, 13
Women's suffrage: effect on representation, 37, 40, 46, 117
Wood, William R., 39
World War I: postwar disillusionment, 5–7, 14, 134 (n. 6); disruptive effects of on population, 39, 49, 116

Xenophobia, 4, 10. *See also* Nativism

Zimmerman, Carle C., 2

www.ingramcontent.com/pod-product-compliance
Lightning Source LLC
Chambersburg PA
CBHW032026230426
43671CB00005B/211